*NORTH TO ALASKA
AND BACK*

# OTHER BOOKS OF BARRY BLACKSTONE

Though None Go With Me

Rendezvous In Paris

Though One Go With Me

Scotland Journey

The Region Beyond

Enlarge My Coast

From Dan to Beersheba and Beyond

The Uttermost Part

Homestead Homilies

Rover: A Boy's Best Friend

# NORTH TO ALASKA AND BACK

By Barry Blackstone

RESOURCE *Publications* • Eugene, Oregon

NORTH TO ALASKA AND BACK

Copyright © 2018 Barry Blackstone. All rights reserved. Except for brief quotations in critical publications or reviews, no part of this book may be reproduced in any manner without prior written permission from the publisher. Write: Permissions, Wipf and Stock Publishers, 199 W. 8th Ave., Suite 3, Eugene, OR 97401.

Resource Publications
An Imprint of Wipf and Stock Publishers
199 W. 8th Ave., Suite 3
Eugene, OR 97401

www.wipfandstock.com

PAPERBACK ISBN: 978-1-5326-4784-0
HARDCOVER ISBN: 978-1-5326-4785-7
EBOOK ISBN: 978-1-5326-4786-4

Manufactured in the U.S.A.

I dedicate this memorable trip to my two alaska travling compaions: my dear wife and lifelong partner coleen and to our first born soldier, son scott. Thanks for all the memories from our alaska adventure together.

# Contents

*Prelude: North To Alaska* | ix
*Acknowledgement* | xiii
*Introduction: Desiring A Trip To Alaska* | xv

1. A License to Fish | 1
2. The Alaska Pipeline | 4
3. North Pole, Alaska | 7
4. King Crab Verses Maine Lobster | 10
5. Fishing with Scott | 13
6. Into the Wilderness | 16
7. Tour Guide | 19
8. First Trip into Denali | 22
9. Rose's Café | 25
10. Looking for the Big Five | 28
11. Scott Spots the First Grizzly | 31
12. More Denali Wildlife | 34
13. Mount McKinley | 37
14. An Extraordinary Bear Encocunter | 40
15. Resting on the Banks of the Nenana | 43
16. Chum at Montana Creek | 46
17. Prince William Sound and High Hills | 49
18. Gallery Lodge and Crooked Creek | 52
19. A Moose River Pink | 55
20. Kenai Surprises | 58
21. Deadhead Rainbows | 61
22. Fried Spam and Grill Cheese Sandwiches | 64
23. Leaving the Kenai for King's Ranch | 67
24. Combat Fishing and the Bass Pro Shop | 70
25. King Ranch | 73

26. A Kansas Wheat Farmer and a German Cook | 76
27. Mother Moose and Her Baby | 80
28. Devotions at Kingdom Air Corps | 83
29. Four-Wheeling to the Matanuska River | 86
30. Flight over a Glacier | 89
31. The Splendor at the Summit | 92
32. Dwayne King-Bush Pilot, Extraordinar | 95
33. Overlooking Kingdom Air | 98
34. Fire on a Mountain | 101
35. A Night in Chickaloon | 104
36. Valdez Waterfalls | 108
37. Our First Valdez Eagle | 111
38. Valdez Pinks and Valdez Fishers | 114
39. Eagles in the Wind | 117
40. The Turning of the Tide | 120
41. Eight Days on the Road | 124
42. Gold Dredge #8 | 127
43. An Ornament of Gold | 130
44. The Wonder of Autumn | 133
45. A Beer Commercial Hymn | 136
46. On a Plane for California | 139
47. Beading for Grayling | 142
48. Making the Local Newspaper | 145
49. Shaking the Dust off his Feet | 148
50. A 90th Birthday and a 3rd Anniversary | 151
51. Starting Our Trip Home | 155
52. The Alaskan Highway and Afghanistan | 159
53. The Purple Heart | 163
54. Plan C | 167
55. Bison in British Columba | 170
56. Slim Jims, Twinkie's, and Cheetos | 173

*Conclusion: Kidney Stone Miracle* | 176
*Postlude: . . . . . . . And Back* | 179

*Prelude*

# North To Alaska

ALASKA. THE VERY NAME invokes images of grandeur, even if you have never been there. For over fifty years I had only heard of Alaska, read about Alaska, and enjoyed larger-than-life Alaskan tales. Also, for nearly fifty years in my preaching, I have used Alaska as an illustration of a place like Heaven, never having been there but still believing in a place called Alaska and the wonders of Alaska, just like a place called Heaven, and the wonders of Heaven (I Corinthians 2:9) "Eye hath not seen, nor ear heard, neither have entered into the heart of man, the things which God hath prepared for them that love him." This is certainly true of Heaven, I believe, and now I know of Alaska as well. I haven't been to Heaven yet, but I have been to Alaska. Everything I dreamed it would be, heard it would be, hoped it would be and more is true. Now I too have a few stories of my own to share after a two-week odyssey into the great land. Actually the word Alaska comes from an Aleut word, "al-ay-ek-sa" which is literally translated 'the great land' or 'mainland'. I certainly didn't cover the whole of Alaska. It is 586,400 square miles, twice the size of Texas and one-fifth as large as the rest of the United States of America. I covered just basically what I call The Alaska Circle: Fairbanks to Denali to Anchorage to Kenai to the Glenn Highway to Valdez to Delta Junction, and back to Fairbanks, with a few choice stopping-off spots among those distant places. It seems it takes four hours of hard driving to get to any one place in Alaska.

    The people I knew, who had visited Alaska before me, told me that Alaska was like no other place on earth. I had seen high mountains before Alaska, but not like the mountains of Alaska. I had seen great rivers before Alaska, but not like the rivers of Alaska. I had seen wide-open spaces before Alaska, but not like the wide-open spaces of Alaska. The Psalmist says that we ought to "praise the Lord from the earth. . .mountains, and all hills...beasts...and creeping things...His name is above the earth..." (Psalms 148:7-13) Being a Mainiac by birth, I thought a wildlife encounter or a natural beauty would never surprise me. Maine, I thought, had the best, but Alaska changed my opinion. I found it a sparsely populated land with hardly more than one way to get anywhere, but I also found it a spectacular, scenic land with once-in-a-lifetime views around every twist of the road, whether of glaciers, or lakes, or rivers, or oceans, or mountains, or caribou, or sheep, or moose, or bear. Three of the largest species of bear live in Alaska, and we saw two of them, up close and personal. This is not a place for you if you like people, but if you love the out-of-the-way, the isolated, the secluded, and open spaces you will love Alaska. Now I have more to praise God for, for I have witnessed first-hand more of His amazing handiwork in creation. When He made Alaska, He truly formed a diverse landscape, and He put some very special creatures in this dynamic land. Some of these are unique to Alaska alone, found nowhere in the United States or in any part of the rest of the world.

My first recollection of Alaska came through an old 1960s tune by Johnny Horton called "North to Alaska". Remember the lyrics? "Big Sam left Seattle in the year 1892, with George Pratt his partner, and his brother Bill too. They crossed the Yukon River and found bonanza gold, below that old white mountain just a little southeast of Nome. Sam crossed the majestic mountain to the valley far below. He talked to his team of huskies as they mushed on through the snow, with the northern lights running wild in the land of the midnight sun. Yes, Sam McCord was a mighty man in the year of 1901. George turns to Sam with gold in his hands. Said Sam your're looking at a lonely lonely man. I'd trade all the gold that is buried in this land, for one small band of gold on sweet Jenny's hand. Cause a man needs a woman to love him all the time. Remember, Sam a true love is so hard to find. I'd build for Jenny a honeymoon home below that old white mountain just a little southeast of Nome. Where the river is windin' big nuggets they're findin', north to Alaska, goin' north, the rush is on!" The ballad spoke of the famous Alaskan Gold Rush. Coleen and I went through Seattle to get to Alaska just as Sam McCord did. While we were in Alaska, we were able to pan for gold. But the big nuggets, Coleen and I were able to handle one that was worth $75,000 later on in our trip, were found in Alaska in the 19th and 20th centuries. The gold I found in Alaska will be found in the chapters before you, the golden memories that will stay with me the rest of my life in the memory vaults of my mind. Come with me as I relive the thrill of catching my first Arctic Grayling, Dolly Varden, Pink and Chum Salmon, and the biggest Rainbow Trout I have ever landed. See through my eyes the heights of Mount McKinley in all of its glory, and view the mighty Matanuska Glacier from a small plane. Boy, did we feel small! Witness wildlife like caribou, Dall sheep, brown bears and their cubs, sea otters, bison, deer, and moose as if you were watching a *National Geographic* special. Taste the unique flavors and savor of Alaska: baked salmon, king crab, and moose stew. Stand with me as I feel the rush of hundreds of salmon against my legs trying to make it home to spawn. You will need your nose to smell the beginning of autumn, your eyes to see the bigness that is Alaska, your hands to literally pick up fish out of a creek, your legs to walked the tundra and wade a glacial stream, and your feet to go those extra few feet to get the right angle for a once-in-a-lifetime photograph. So come with me *North to Alaska* as I journey with my wife of forty-one years, Coleen, and our soldier-boy, son Scott. Scott, our tour guide, had been in Alaska for nearly two years serving with the United States Army out of Fort Wainwright in Fairbanks before we arrived. Follow along and experience the variety and vistas of our 50th State. It will be a fast-paced trip as you will see, but the encounters will be extraordinary, the scenery will be breathtaking, and the memories will be worthy of a song!

Barry Blackstone

# Acknowledgement

I would not have gotten this book project finished if not for the editing and compiling by my dear sister Sylvia. I would like to thank her for the hours and days she spent reading and correcting the errors in the original script. Sharing in the sad departure of her nephew (the hero of this book, my son Scott, passed away at the age of 39 from lung and liver cancer, just eight month before the editing process was done), this was also a labor of love for her. Thanks again Sis!

*Introduction*

# Desiring A Trip To Alaska

I HAVE COME TO believe that my "...Father which is in heaven give(s) good things to them that ask Him." (Matthew 7:11) Sometimes our prayer requests aren't about needs or even wants; they are simply about desires. Such was the case when in the early 1980s I started to pray about visiting one of the places on this planet that has always drawn my interest. There are many spots in this world I have never desired to see: the Caribbean or Cuba, Spain or Siberia, Mongolia or Mexico, Tanzania or Thailand, to name a few, but for most of my life I have been interested in Australia, Israel, Scotland, India (four wonderful places I have already had a chance to explore), and Alaska. I have never been drawn to visit any state south of the Mason-Dixon line or southwest of the Mississippi River, but I have visited a few. You might say Alaska has been on my bucket list for a while, and through it has never been a priority, it has been a desire. But with Israel and India and Scotland and Australia, I only asked, and in God's good timing, He answered my prayers.

The events surrounding my Alaskan trip began, I believe, with the birth of my son Scott. As with many of the places I have visited, most seem to be connected with my children or family members. For example, I never thought I would visit Texas until Marnie moved there for her graduate work. To this day, I don't believe I would ever have visited Israel if it were not for my daughter and her connection to Dallas Theological Seminary; the same is true with Alaska. Many of my heart's desires had been pending at the Throne of Grace for years, if not for decades. As I look back, God's timing is often connected with the joy of sharing an experience with someone you love at a crossroad time in his or her life. Such was the case with Alaska. Scotland was wonderful, and it was even more memorable because my wife Coleen was able to share it with me on our 30th wedding anniversary. I wrote of this thrill in a book I called *Scotland Journey*. Israel was inspiring and what made it even more special was my daughter Marnie was able to do it with me because of the death of my Uncle Paul. To know why, you must read the book I wrote about our shared experiences titled *From Dan to Beersheba and Beyond*. I believe the Lord delayed my trip to Alaska, so I would be able to share it with Scott. Scott, Coleen, and I recorded the top five experiences of our shared trip. I will share them later in the book, but for me #1 on that list was to experience it with Scott!

Scott joined the United States Army in 2006 and, during his obligations to our country, he served in a variety of places including three overseas tours: Iraq, Afghanistan, and Kuwait. When he was stateside, he spent the bulk of his time at Fort Bragg in North Carolina, but, for his last duty-station, Fort Wainwright in Fairbanks, Alaska was home. When Scott got back from a nine-month tour of Kuwait, he called and asked if I would fly to Alaska and help him drive home to Maine. Scott was leaving the Regular Army for the Reserves, but before he could settle into his new life in Wilmington, North Carolina, he had to return to the state where he had enlisted. In the spring of 2014, I realized that the Good Lord was answering a decades-old petition. I had started praying in April of 1982 that I might see Alaska someday, so my wife and I started to make plans for our Alaskan Tour. Who better to show us the sights than our son who had pretty much driven all over southeast Alaska in his job as a HET (Heavy Equipment Transporter) driver for the US Army? Scott would get his honorable discharge from the Regular Army on August 13, 2014 and my wife and I would arrive in Fairbanks, Alaska by way of Bangor, Maine, Philadelphia, Pennsylvania, and Seattle, Washington on the fourteenth.

Over the next ten days, we would travel the main routes through southeastern Alaska. Our journey of 2,613 miles started in Fairbanks with a salmon bake including King Crab, another of my desires, and then on to Denali National Park and Preserve for some of the most amazing animal and nature sightings I have ever witnessed. From Denali we traveled south to the Kenai Peninsula and some marvelous rainbow trout fishing and more breathtaking scenery. After two days, we journeyed back through Anchorage and then up the Glenn Highway to visit our only friends in Alaska, Dwayne and Caroline King, missionaries with Kingdom Air Corp, a ministry that trains pilots to fly into the remotest areas of the world, including Siberia. After a spectacular air flight over one of the biggest glaciers in Alaska and a four-wheeler ride that brought us face to face with a moose, we moved on to Valdez for a chance to see one of the biggest salmon runs in the world. I had always dreamed of standing in a creek with more fish than water, and I did! On our away back to Fairbanks from Valdez, we saw cascading waterfalls, more glaciers, huge mountain ranges, and more Alaskan wildlife. The day after we completed the Alaskan Circle (check out a map), my wife and I panned for gold just north of Fairbanks and found some! At the end of the tenth day of our Alaskan adventure, Scott and I put Coleen on a plane for California where she would visit with our daughter, Marnie, and new son-in-law, Josue, who were married just two months before. Scott and I prepared for our long road trip (4,854 miles) back to Maine in just THREE AND A HALF DAYS! Why?

Postscript: Perhaps the greatest miracle of the trip was that within 30-hours of arriving back in Ellsworth, I had a bad kidney stone attack and required emergency surgery. It was an attack that could have happened anywhere along the 12,492 miles I had traveled over the previous seventeen days. When God grants you the desire of your heart, He takes care of the details including the timing of a kidney stone attack, one of three. I have come to believe the Holy Spirit directed us to hurry home.

We seem to have this popular misconception about our heavenly Father. I believe this is one of the reasons Jesus came to correct the misconceptions about our Father and His. As Jesus preached about prayer in His classic Sermon on the Mount, He shared about asking and seeking and knocking at the Throne of Grace (Hebrews 4:16), and then He made this argument: "For every one that asketh receiveth; and he that seeketh findeth; and to him that knocketh it shall be opened. Or what man is there of you, whom if his son ask bread (Would I say no to Scott about helping him drive back to Maine?), will he give him a stone? Or if he asks a fish (Did I say no to Marnie when she asked me to drive her to Texas?), will he give him a serpent? If ye then, being evil, know how to give good gifts unto your children, how much more shall your Father in heaven give good things to them that ask Him?" (Matthew 7:8-11) Granted, no father, including the Heavenly Father, would give to his children something they asked for that might harm or hurt them. But something to please them? Why not? Do I still have a few more desires on my bucket list? I do! Will they all be answered? I don't know. But this I do believe; my Father has granted so many of my desires up to now, and I believe that if He grants me many more years on this planet I will be saying with the Psalmist again as I did after my Alaskan Adventure: "Thou hast given him (me) his (my) heart's desire, and hast not witholden the request of his (my) lips." (Psalms 21:2) Amen!

# Chapter One

# A License To Fish

Needless to say, one of the primary reasons I have been drawn to Alaska over the years is the unbelievable fishing opportunities found in that state. I have been an avid fly fisherman since the early 1970s and a fisherman since boyhood. Over the years I have fished all over the state of Maine and the Canadian Provinces of Quebec and New Brunswick. My primary prey has been salmon and trout, but by the time I headed for Alaska on August 13, 2014, I had caught thirty-one species of fish. One of my desires was to add to that total, and I did! I had learned that Alaska had five species of salmon running wild up its rivers: Coho or silver salmon, Sockeye or red salmon, Chinook or king salmon, Chum or dog salmon, and Pink or humpy salmon. Two of my favorite fish caught on a fly are the Landlock Salmon and the Atlantic Salmon, two species of fish that have given me the best thrills while fishing. On my study wall, I have mounted a 46-inch, 37-pound Atlantic I caught on the Restigouche River in Quebec, Canada, the largest fish I have ever caught on a fly. I was looking forward to adding some of the Alaskan species of salmon to my 'fish-caught' list.

Don't get me wrong. I like to salmon fish, but since childhood I have been a die-hard trout fisherman. My father Wendell took me fishing early in life and introduced me to the species call trout, and in particular the Brook Trout. Just a few weeks before I headed for Alaska, Dad and I went fishing for probably our last time to a favorite trout stream in our hometown of Perham, Maine. While in Alaska, my father turned ninety. There is a story about that day you don't want to miss. We had fished together for nearly all of my sixty-three years. Dad's last fish (his health is declining rapidly) was a brook trout, so as I prepared for Alaska I noted the trout species I could catch there: Steelhead, a sea-run rainbow trout, Rainbow, a fresh-water trout, Coastal Cutthroat Trout, Lake Trout, and Dolly Varden, and Arctic

Char, fish like a trout. I was also interested in the Arctic Grayling because my son said they came to the fly willingly. Another reason I desired to fish Alaska was the sizes these fish get. Like any other fisherman, numbers are great, but most of us will fish all day, and yes, years to catch the big one! The record fish weight in Alaska are as follows: Arctic Char-27 pounds, Arctic Grayling-5 pounds, Chum Salmon-32 pounds, King Salmon-97 pounds, Lake trout-47 pounds, Pink Salmon-12 pounds, Rainbow Trout-42 pounds, Red Salmon-16 pounds, and Silver salmon-26 pounds. So you will not be surprised if I tell you that the first thing I did when I got to Alaska was to go to a local fishing establishment and buy a license to fish.

Coleen and I left our home on the coast of Maine on a Wednesday at noon. A dear friend of ours Debra Hangge, her husband is my closest fishing partner, took us to catch a plane out of Bangor. We drove through a light drizzle as we covered the first thirty-one miles of our longest adventure (both mileage-wise and time-wise) together as husband and wife. Our longest trip before Alaska had been a ten-day 30th wedding anniversary trip to England, Scotland, and Wales, and despite flying over the Atlantic Ocean to the British Isles, our Alaskan adventure would cover 4,200 more miles—8,290 miles versus 12,492 miles. Our first stop was at the Philadelphia International Airport, and then we were off to the Seattle/Tacoma Airport where we picked up an Alaskan Airlines flight, 3 ½ hours long, directly to Fairbanks. It was early Thursday morning (1:30 A.M.) before we landed on Alaskan soil for the first time. In the first half day of our journey, we had already covered 5,588 miles; Alaska might just as well have been another country. Our son picked us up at the airport and drove us over to the Best Western Motel for a quick nap before our Alaskan tour officially began later that morning.

By 7:30 A.M., I was up getting my traveling companions breakfast as our early plans only involved staying in Fairbanks that day. The next morning we would be off to Denali, so what to do on our first day? I was happy when Scott said, "Let's go over to the sporting goods store and pick up your license just in case we get a chance to fish today." After breakfast we did just that, and the lady at the counter was very accommodating as Scott bought me my first (and hopefully not my last) Alaskan fishing license, a belated Father's Day present. I got a 14-day permit that cost my dear son $80. It would last me until we headed for home. Little did I know before our first day in Alaska was over I would get to fish. That will be in another chapter and another fish story.

One of the best-recognized facts of Jesus calling His disciples is the reality that the majority of them were fishermen. I believe at least seven of the twelve fished for a profession (John 21:20). For me, my first Alaskan fishing trip brought together again two old fishing friends. Before Scott was two, I had taken him fishing, brook trout fishing, of course. For the next thirteen years, we fished numerous times including a couple of big fishing trips into Canada and fishing the mighty Atlantic salmon on the Penobscot River, in Maine. By the time Scott was fifteen, we had fished one hundred twenty-five days together, fishing in twenty-seven different fishing holes. By now you know I love to keep statistics! Scott had landed over three hundred fish, including fifteen different species of fish. But then, golf came into Scott's life. Over the next seventeen years, September 5, 1995 to July 1, 2012, Scott fished a little, but it wasn't until he came back from his Afghanistan tour that he fell in love with fly fishing all over again, and we began to fish together again. Over the last few years we have fished on a regular basis, and I was looking forward to fishing in Alaska with my old fishing partner. Peter wasn't wrong when he said, "I go a fishing!" (John 21:3) Jesus never rebuked Peter later on when they met on the shores of Galilee. I believe Jesus knew that Peter needed to go fishing to clear his head with all that had gone on over the previous few days. I came to believe on this trip with my Son that fishing was doing that with my Purple Heart recipient. Scott suffered three serious concussions while on tour. His last came after the HET in front of him was blown up in Afghanistan; an explosion so powerful my son had to be airlifted off the battlefield. Fishing helped. So a license to fish has become for my soldier-son a way to cope with the trauma he suffered on the battlefield: the loss of four good bubbies, the loss of some mental function, and the loss of his beloved wife. Fishing is a therapy that is being proven to be a genuine answer to some who have post-traumatic injuries from a time at war. Now it was time to fish together again, and both Scott and I had a license to fish in Alaska.

# Chapter Two

# The Alaskan Pipeline

One of our very first excursions into the wilds of Alaska was to the small town of Fox, just a few miles outside of Fairbanks. It only takes a few minutes from downtown Fairbanks, in any direction, to be in the wilderness that is most of Alaska. Our introduction to modern Alaska happened suddenly as Scott pointed out the first section of the Alaskan Pipeline we would experience in our travels. Before our Alaskan tour was finished, we would follow the pipeline from just north of Fairbanks to Valdez, a distance of three hundred sixty-four miles, not even half of its length!

Our introduction to the pipeline was a simple roadside park with a few pieces of artifacts and a couple of highway post boards explaining some of the aspects of one of the greatest engineering marvels of the modern world. I had seen plenty of pictures of the famous pipeline, but standing under a section of the raised line changes your concept of size and shape. The piece we walked around came out of the ground and ran for about half a mile before reentering the tundra just south of pumping station #7. There were two examples of how they kept the pipeline clean. There were huge inserts: an original one and a computer-controlled one. Beside the line as well was an explanation and some interesting facts about the pipeline: the eight-billion dollar project crosses three massive mountain ranges and over five hundred rivers and streams in its journey south to Valdez. Co and I got our picture taken together under a span of the Alaskan icon, the first of the trip. It was a typical tourist's photograph of Alaska, but it hasn't always been an icon of Alaska.

I learned that the real gold wasn't discovered until 1968. Up until the discovery of oil, Alaska was known for its forestry, gold mining, and fishery. Today one of the most watched reality shows on television is "The World's Deadliest Catch", a show about crab fishermen in the Bering Sea off Alaska. There had been oil discoveries in other parts of Alaska up to then, but nothing on the scale of Prudhoe Bay; at the time, the reserves would exceed the total of all known oil reserves in all of America. Because of environmental roadblocks and cultural opposition from the native people, the pipeline wasn't started until March 25, 1974 and not finished until May 31, 1977. By June 20, 1977, the oil was flowing and flows to this day and has the potential to run until 2075 or a hundred years. The pipeline runs for eight hundred miles from Prudhoe Bay to Valdez, underground and aboveground, over rivers and through mountain passes seemingly impossible! We traveled through one of those passes just north of Valdez, yet despite all the obstacles the line was finished. It was the largest privately funded construction project at the time, and, in our travels, we periodically passed by piece after piece of this amazing structure. Our journey only took us by the lower sections of the pipeline south of Fairbanks, it runs nearly five hundred miles north of that city, but we were able to witness the line snaking its way up the side of hills, down over mountains and through wide valleys, and over small streams. Just before I left Alaska, I got a few pictures of the pipeline bridging one of the mighty rivers of Alaska near Delta Junction. It looked so out of place in most places, yet its design seemed to fit all places!

    I did get to see the end of the line, where the pipeline dumps its cargo into the massive storage tanks at the main terminal in Valdez. One of my disappointments was I didn't get to see one of those huge supertankers being loaded. The first tanker to pick up Prudhoe Bay oil was the Arco Juneau on August 1, 1977. The only day I had to visit the Valdez Terminal there were no tankers in port. We did stop at Pumping Station #12, the last before Valdez, but once again nobody was around. Now a computer runs all the stations from a central place; the stations are only manned when there is a need. On our last day in Alaska together, Co and I would go to a gold mining dredge located near another section of the pipeline and hear a lecture about The Trans-Alaskan Pipeline System and discover that not all twelve pumping station are on line at the same time. Because of the distance and change of elevation, the oil must be first warmed and then forced through the system; why the need of the powerful pumping stations? The 48-inch pipe itself is a technological marvel with it stainless steel covering that shines like a lightning bolt when the sun hits it. This eight hundred mile connected pipe actually only sits on the iconic stanchions created to withstand the numerous earthquakes that shake Alaska almost daily. I have always wanted to experience an earthquake, and I was only three days out of Alaska when three hit Fairbanks, while at the same time, my wife was just north of the Napa Valley when the big 2014 quake hit. We both missed our chance to experience a shake, though my wife would say that was ok! The iron stanchions on which the pipeline sits were created to keep the permafrost frozen. This is why the pipeline doesn't buckle and twist with the coming of the annual summer thaw. The pipeline was created to roll with a quake and bend and not break. In its nearly forty-year history, it has performed exactly as its designers imagined.

After a short walk along the road that runs alongside the pipeline when it emerges from the tundra, I returned to Coleen and Scott as they waited my moment of exploration. I was actually looking for my first Alaskan wildlife. I am an explorer by nature and Alaska only added to my adventurous spirit. I had watched a number of documentaries on the building of the Alaskan Pipeline, and it was a joy to have witnessed the final product up close and personal. Whether a glimpse as we traveled back from Glenn Allen to Delta Junction or a chance to actually touch it outside of Fox, it reminded me of the mind of man that God was concerned about. "And the Lord said, Behold, the people is one, and they have all one language; and this they begin to do: and now nothing will be retrained from them, which they have imagined to do." (Genesis 11:6) I could not discover who was the first to have imagined a single pipeline from Prudhoe Bay to Valdez, but someone imagined it and many more planned it and even more built it. Today the Alaskan Pipeline is as much a part of the terrain of Alaska as its rivers and mountains and valleys. 'Manmade in the midst of God-made'. What has become a problem for mankind is the problem God cursed Babylon for. The idea that man would become so accustomed to doing things himself and in his way, he would soon forget about God, God's way, or the need of God. Was I impressed with The Trans-Alaskan Pipeline System? I certainly was. Did I stand in awe every time I saw it? I did. Could I even imagine how it was done? I couldn't. And then I thought, what man has made has only been there for less than forty years, while what God has created has been here for thousands of years. Eventually the Alaskan Pipeline will go the way of all manmade projects; rust or dust will get it in the end. That is why we can never, ever take our eyes off God. So as I looked at the pipeline, I looked over its impressive features and saw beyond the handiwork of God shadowing and overshadowing the handiwork of man!

## Chapter Three

## North Pole, Alaska

The Psalmist acknowledges in one of his psalms, "The north and the south thou hast created them. . ." (Psalms 89:12) I must admit that I am by my nature and upbringing a Northerner. I have rarely in my life headed south or desired to go south. I come from northern Maine, a northern state located in the northern hemisphere. Alaska was in the right direction when my son invited my wife and me to visit with him before his return south; my son, on the other hand, loves everything southern. As Coleen and I planned our stops in Alaska, the North Pole was one of Coleen first requests because of her passionate love of Christmas. Little did we know before our trip, but soon discovered on our first day in Alaska, that the North Pole was located just twenty miles or so outside Fairbanks. So after our first encounter with the Trans-Alaskan Pipeline, we headed east to go to the North Pole. Actually there were three reasons we took the time to find the North Pole: the famous Christmas town of Alaska, the family of my younger sister's husband, and two favorite Alaskan fishing holes of Scott's.

After a short drive from Fox, Alaska we drove into North Pole, Alaska and instantly were transported into Christmas, without the snow. That would come later! Candy canes lined the street, businesses and shops advertised the popular holiday, and sure enough, there was Santa Claus, all twenty-five feet of him, the biggest I had ever seen. He stood in front of his workshop where anything and everything Christmas could be bought. Before we headed into the shop we decided to visit the reindeer yard first. Sure enough, in a fenced-in area beside the shop, were the famous reindeer. I learned there that reindeer are only domesticated caribou. We had a good visit with the caretaker of the reindeer, a lady with a degree from the University of Alaska in caring for reindeer. Only in Alaska! She was knowledgeable and very quick to rebuke me when I tried to touch one of Rudolph's antlers.

According to her, this was a very sensitive time of the year for the deer. We wandered about and found Santa Claus had enough reindeer to pull his sleigh for the up and coming season. We saw Dasher, Dancer, Prancer, Vixen, Comet, Cupid, Donner, Blitzen, and, of course, Rudolph. However, there was no glowing nose!

After seeing the sleigh pullers and the sleigh, we were off to see Santa, the legendary bringer of Christmas gifts. He was off duty when we arrived, but would be back by two o'clock. The workshop was decorated in all the icons of a worldly Christmas, with all its fables, the universal character that is used to distract children from the real giver of Christmas presents. I was living again the nightmare of "The Night Before Christmas." But the true icon (Christ) of Christmas was missing: not a mention, not a picture, not a symbol of any kind. You have probably figured out by now I am not a fan of the modern Christmas, or anything to do with Christmas in the 21st century, even if it was located in the North sometimes. But, as all good tourists do in that part of Alaska, we went in and added our presence to the pretense and gave our money to the merchandizing of the memory of a baby born in Bethlehem to a story of a man in a red suit with a white beard. It was your typical Christmas shop. We have a number of them in Ellsworth for the tourists that travel north to Maine to see our coastline and eat our lobster. We wandered around for a while, and Coleen sent off postcards with the North Pole postal stamp to her mother and a few friends. Co bought a few Christmas presents, but within a short time we were off to another address. I was thankful our North Pole stay would be more than Santa Claus. We never did get to see the big guy, just his image in the statute in front of his shop. His chair was empty! I have been amazed that the words in an 1897 *New York Sun* article to a little girl named Virginia O'Hanlon are believed today by more children than the words of Luke in his Gospel. It has come down to which you believe: "Yes, Virginia, there is a Santa Claus. He exists as certainly as love and generosity and devotion exist. Not to believe in Santa Claus? You might as well not believe in fairies!" Which I don't! Or, "And it came to pass in those days. . . ..and she brought forth her firstborn son, and wrapped him in swaddling clothes, and laid him in a manger. . ." (Luke 2; 1-7)

I have mentioned already that besides our son Scott, the only people we knew in Alaska were the Kings, the missionaries with Kingdom Air Corp. Actually, we knew of another family in Alaska, family actually, but strangers. In 1986, my younger sister Lori married a man with two children. Her husband Darrell had a son Chad who had moved to Alaska nearly two decades before with his wife Tammy. In Alaska, they had two children, Konnor and Saydee, and lived in North Pole, Alaska. Even though I had only meet them once, I was determined that if I was that far from home and in their new hometown I would at least try to find them, even if just for my brother-in-law and sister's sake. So after we left Santa's Village, we started to look for the address my mother had given me before we headed for Alaska. It took us a bit of maneuvering, a couple of side lanes here and a dirt road there, but after about fifteen minutes, we landed in the dooryard of the Alaskan Bouchards. Chad, who worked for one of the biggest gold mines near Fox, was still at work. Tammy had a daycare in their home, and Konnor and Saydee were napping. We were only able to visit with Tammy for a few minutes, but it was nice to locate them and know when my mother speaks of them and their lives, I can relate and remember where they live, at the NORTH Pole! Konner and Sadie ride motorcycles, but not just for fun. Although they are still quite young, they are some of the top motorcross riders in their age group in Alaska.

I left North Pole for Fort Wainwright, where Scott was stationed, with a much better taste in my mouth. Family over fable any day for me. I would rather visit a Chad than a Claus. Even if at times we have to slip into fantasy, it is nice when we can always come back to reality. I am convinced that Heaven can be found somewhere in the north (Psalms 48:2), and if you find yourself at the North Pole just look up rather than look around and know you are closer to heaven than those stuck in the imaginations of their minds. I have always been a non-fiction kind of guy, even in the North Country!

## Chapter Four

## King Crab Versus Maine Lobster

One of the top ten things I wanted to do in Alaska was experience the savor and flavor of an Alaskan king crab. For years I had watched the reality show, "The World's Deadliest Catch", a television show about crab fishermen in the Bering Sea off Alaska. I had heard from countless people that the Alaskan Crab was as good as, if not better than the Maine Lobster, one of my favorite food groups. I wanted to make my own judgment on such a claim. We were still in our first full day in Fairbanks, Alaska and on our way back from North Pole village Scott announced to his mother and me he was taking us out for supper to the Alaskan Salmon Bake, an all-you-can-eat outdoor restaurant, and a Fairbanks landmark. Scott's two best friends in Alaska, Hailey and Brandon, were going to join us for a taste of Alaska and a special party.

We drove barely a mile from our motel when Scott parked his Tahoe in a huge lot by a small hill. Hailey and Brandon were waiting for us. There were few cars in the lot, but we had come early because Scott and I had an evening fishing trip on our minds. We entered the Alaska Salmon Bake through a prospector's tunnel. The Salmon Bake restaurant was also a museum of the gold mining heritage that is Fairbanks, the center for all gold mining in Alaska. In the tunnel were numerous artifacts of the gold mining history of the region, and when we came out on the other side of the hill, there before us was the gold mining machinery of a past period including a water jet still pumping water into a lagoon. A steam powered shovel, a caterpillar tractor, and a small dredge filled the ground around the open-air feeding establishment. At $32.50 a head, the price was expensive, but it was all you could eat king crab, baked salmon, deep-fried cod, and prime rib plus all the sides you can imagine in such a place. I headed straight for the king crab station to see if it stood up to my Maine lobster.

My first plate of food, I would eventually have four, was loaded with prime rib; I had to have my meat, another favorite food group, just in case I didn't like the crab. I also took a little cod, not a favorite fish of mine, and some of the baked salmon, not bad, but my taste buds were watering for that first taste of crab. Much like our Maine lobster, you have to do a bit of work for your first taste, but any good flavor is worth the wait, somewhat like the work it takes to prepare deep-fried partridge strips. The four of us found a picnic table under a lovely grove to eat our meal. It was a pleasant August afternoon, warm and sunny, which only added to the atmosphere of my first king crab supper. I might just as well say it right here, my first and my last! I don't believe I have ever had so much anticipation to taste a certain food than I had for the king crab. I had boldly approached the lady serving the crab with a smile on my face, anticipation in my mind and expectation in my mouth. I was expecting it to be at least equal to Maine lobster. I had also taken plenty of melted butter to dip my crab in, my most favorite way of eating lobster, drenched in butter. In my opinion, any other way of eating lobster is a sacrilege.

I was the first to have made the rounds through the various stations of food. I had skipped the salad bar, bread bar, and dessert bar. I was there to eat the fish of Alaska, and I wasn't going to fill my stomach on other foods I could get at home. I was also the first to get to our table, and I was the first to crack into my first crab leg and find the delicate meat inside. It looked like lobster to my eye. It felt like lobster to my fingers. It even had that fishy smell to my nose. But it didn't taste like lobster, mainly because it wasn't lobster, but could I taste something better than lobster? I am not a very good food critic because I rarely try anything new, just ask my wife who is a wonderful cook and loves to experiment. I eat only certain things, and I must admit I have a taste for Maine foods: meat and potatoes, gravy and fresh homemade bread, honey and potato doughnuts, and Maine seafood. I found the king crab tastelessly plain. How anybody can call that rich food and pay what they do for it baffles me! If it hadn't been dipped in butter it would have had no flavor at all. And I gave it a good tasting, a good test. I went back four times. I ate a couple of dozen crab legs, and I couldn't find a good taste in the lot. Don't get me wrong. It wasn't bad, but it wasn't Maine lobster either. Maybe that was my problem. I had set the bar too high for the Alaskan king crab, and it had been found wanting. I put it up against the best seafood in the world, and it could only have been a disappointment. My mouth was watering for lobster, and I got crab.

My verdict on Alaska king crab are the four words that were fingered on Belshazzar's place wall in Babylon by God Himself: "Mene, Mene, Tekel, Upharsin." (Daniel 5:25) I did get Scott's money's worth out of the meal because the prime rib was wonderful, and I certainly got my fill of king crab, but as Daniel told Belshazzar: Mene-the crab had been numbered and finished, Tekel-the crab has been weighted (and eaten) and had been found wanting, and Upharsin-the crab has been divided and Maine lobster is the clear winning and the king of all seafood! (Daniel 5:26-28) The kingdom of great seafood is found in Maine, not Alaska! The best part of the evening was the simple celebration we had celebrating Scott's honorable discharge from the United States Army. Hailey had brought a cake and the supper and dessert was the sweet taste of Scott surviving eight-years of service to his country, including three tours of duty involving two wars. I might have been disappointed with the king crab, but I will never be disappointed with my son's service to this land. Sometimes the best taste in your mouth isn't food!

## Chapter Five

## Fishing With Scott

After our quick tour of the Alaskan pipeline, the Christmas village of North Pole, and a Fairbank's fish bake, we returned to our motel so that Coleen might have a rest from her exhausting two days of travel. She didn't want to go evening fishing, but I did! For the first time in our Alaskan adventure, Scott and I suited up, waders and boots and fishing vests with fly rods in hand, for a few hours of arctic grayling and rainbow trout fishing. I had come to Alaska to see wilderness scenery, animal sightings, and my soldier-boy Scott, but I had also traveled to Alaska to experience its world famous fishery. This was the first time I had a chance to cast a fly after any of its fish.

We drove east from Fairbanks until we came to a marked side-road leading who knows where? Just a few hundred yards up that road was a small stream. Scott had caught arctic grayling there before, and the first fish I wanted to catch was the arctic grayling on a fly. Native to Alaska the Thymallus Articus, its scientific name, is identified best by its exceptionally large doral fin. Simply called grayling or sailfin, this fish was known for its aggressiveness towards flies, and I had come to Alaska to basically fly fish. I would be disappointed most of the time but not on my first evening in Alaska. Scott set me up in a spot just up from where the creek ran under the road through a culvert. I had done my homework; I was looking for a small fish, largest about 23 inches and weighing 5 pounds but most ranges between 7 and 14 inches. The grayling is a fish with a forked tail, a small mouth, and large scales. It wasn't long before I was getting rises to my floating fly, but only taps. I quickly realized that the fish in Chena Stream, my name for it as I have always named unknown fishing holes, were very small. With a small mouth fish, the need was for a small fly. I also switched to a wet fly called a red tag, a good fly for me in Maine. Scott was fishing below the culvert with

Brandon and Hailey who had showed up after the salmon bake; they too were fishing below the culvert. I had the best hole to myself and with the change in flies; I began to catch arctic graying on just about every cast. They averaged about 6 inches with the biggest at about 11 inches. They hit the fly well and gave a pretty good fight. Scott eventually joined me, and over the next hour, I landed 25 and Scott landed 14. Even though the size was small the numbers were great. If this was my first hour fishing in Alaska, I thought the best was yet to come.

The evening sun, though later than in Maine, was beginning to go down. We had started fishing around seven, and we would have until about ten to fish. After an hour, we headed up the road for a small pond that contained rainbow trout. I had come to Alaska to fish the rainbow trout, Oncorhynchus Mykiss, better known simply as "bow". I had first been introduced to the rainbow trout in 1985, and, for the next seven years, had enjoyed catching this ultra-aggressive trout. They say, and I believe, that the rainbow grows twice as fast, jumps twice as often, and fights twice as hard as any other trout in the world. My problem had been that I moved away from the only place I had found rainbow, a small pond in Northern Maine. So for thirteen years, I hadn't tested my wits against this aggressive adversary. In Alaska, the fish is found everywhere, and my first evening in only my second rainbow trout pond was not disappointing. Once again they were not as large as the ones found in Smith Pond, but the rainbow of North Pole Pond were both aggressive and numerous. Once Scott and I figured out where they were and what they were taking, the last hour of sunlight was memorable.

Hailey and Brandon joined us for about an hour at North Pole Pond, but the fishing was slow in that hour. We raised a few and Scott caught one, but the trout seemed to be sleeping. Shortly after our companions left, Scott moved to the far side of the pond. Within minutes I could hear Scott yelling, "I've found them!" I walked over to see what all the excitement was about and, sure enough, a large school of rainbows were feeding in a small cove. There was only room enough for one to fish because of the overhanging trees. It wasn't long before every cast was landing a rainbow. The flies of choice were the orange muddler, hornburgs, and the green emerger. What I remembered about my early experiences with the rainbow was true: a hard hit followed by a series of full-length jumps and a tough drag to shore. Over the next hour, Scott and I took turns landing the battling fish that averaged about 11 inches with the biggest measuring in at 13 inches. I eventually landed 20 and Scott 11. Not bad in our first three hours fishing in Alaska: seventy fish, one a new species for me, and the other an old friend.

About ten, with a bit of sunlight left, Scott and I headed back to the motel. I was tired as was Scott after our first world wind day in Alaska. We had nearly two weeks to go so we thought we might get a bit of rest for the many miles we would travel in the next few days. We talked of fishing together again as we traveled the twenty or so miles back into Fairbanks. Scott and I had been fishing partners since he was nearly two. I still remember the first day I took him to a small creek in the town of Westfield, Maine, to hopefully catch his first trout. He didn't, but the die was cast for the next fourteen years of our lives together. We would annually go fishing numerous times, and over those years, we experienced some great times together. Our fishing days seemingly ended when Scott discovered golf and drifted away. The joy I felt that first night in Alaska was the joy of Scott guiding me instead of me guiding Scott! Peter had said, "I go a fishing!" (John 21:3) That night at Chena Creek and North Pole Pond was "We went fishing!"

## Chapter Six

## Into The Wilderness

Our second day in Alaska was a traveling day. Our itinerary was to travel from Fairbanks to Denali (124 miles) in preparation for a full day in Denali National Park. We left Fairbanks around ten in a soft rain. Scott filled up his Tahoe with $79 worth of gas at $4.17 a gallon just before we got on to the George Park Highway. All that oil doesn't translate into cheap gas in Alaska! Within a few miles, we were in the wilderness. I don't know what I was expecting, but Jesus' great question about John the Baptist came to mind, "What went ye out into the wilderness to see?" (Matthew 11:7)

I have always enjoyed a wilderness journey: open spaces, rolling hills covered in woods, and all that. For some of us, the greatest glories of this planet are not found in towns or cities, even in a country city like Fairbanks. It is the high ridges and templed hills, deep valleys and wide rivers that draw people like me. The wilderness south of Fairbanks was to my liking. It is the utter stillness and quiet grandeur of unspoiled terrain; empty of people that has the greatest appeal for me. As I watched through the side window and the front window of Scott's car the unfolding wilderness, I could feel my heart slow and my mind relax as we traveled through unpolluted wilderness: a new vigor and fresh vitality came into my being. Far removed from the encroaching clamor of industry or human establishments, this wilderness highway was an oasis of tranquility. Now, on the other hand, our tour guide Scott likes his tunes when he travels, so I did have to block out the modern music coming from the front of the car. Scott had told his mother and me, if there was a place we wanted to stop then he would stop. We were in no hurry to bypass anything we wanted to see. Not far into the journey, we made our first stop in our wilderness wandering through Alaska.

On the brow of a high hill, we stopped at a scenic turnout. There before us was a secluded valley the size of Maine, or so it seemed. You could not see the end of it at either end. It just seemed to go on and on. Guarding its flanks were two virgin mountain ranges. I call them virgin because there seemed to be no sign of human activity anywhere. They seemed untouched by mortal man: no towering windmills like we now see on some of Maine's hills, or radio towers, not a single cell phone tower to obstruct the view. Stillness pervaded the side of the hill: no screaming chain saws, no bulldozers roaring, no planes or helicopters, no all-terrain vehicles to break the quietness. It was a picture perfect place of pristine stillness I have experienced in only a few places in my lifetime, but never in a place so expansive and huge! Today one has to travel a long way to find such a place that hasn't been ravished by the hands of modern man. Even in Maine, the wilderness areas have been logged over, cut through, and rare is the place where a logging road or a power line doesn't obstruct. But from where I was standing nothing but pure wilderness could be seen and heard. Heard, you might ask? How do you hear wilderness? It is the sound of nothing. It is the noise of silence. What a sound! The melodious tones of that sound rippled off the hills to my right and my left as sweet and clear as any I have heard in my lifetime.

If there was one thing I learned in my Alaskan odyssey, it was that such places still do exist, and my eyes were grazing upon one of those places that cloudy day south of Fairbanks. As more and more citizens of this planet engulf such places, it is important for the sanity of mankind to still have places like this to experience. We are being overwhelmed by the increasing metropolitan and industrialized urban centers to the sacrifice of wilderness. For too long the word wilderness has been seen as a dirty word, a place to be exploited and developed, yet we are taught by Christ Himself that it is important to go occasionally into the wilderness (Matthew 4:1). Some of the great men of the Bible were led into the wilderness for a period of time to learn what can only be learned in a wilderness setting. Such was my personal experience as we made our trek to Healy, Alaska, where we would spend our second night. So you won't think the entire 124 miles was like our first stop, we did pass through a couple of small villages like Nenana, but each hamlet was small enough that if you blinked you would miss it. I was also impressed with the Tanana River. It was much larger than the Chena River, which flowed through Fairbanks, but not the biggest we would see. The further we went into the wilderness between Fairbanks and Denali, the more I knew I would at least enjoy the terrain of Alaska.

About halfway to our destination for the day, I began to thank the Good Lord above for the privilege of being on this trip. I recognized again that not everybody gets to witness a wilderness as we were. Most people on this planet are imprisoned in another kind of wilderness: a manmade wilderness of concrete canyons, cliff-dwellers on manmade mountains called skyscrapers, valleys covered in asphalt, a treeless, waterless terrain of brick and glass. Most never have the opportunity to escape the city to the country as my wife and I have so often. Stillness and solitude and seclusion are what make this world tolerable, and a trip to a wilderness is just what the doctor orders for the rat race of the twenty-first century. Don't get me wrong. Can you find God in a city? Certainly, but I have come to believe He is better contacted with in the wilderness. For me the wilderness is like my God, or at least like the unchanging attribute of God. I know the trees of the wilderness grow and die, and even the mountains weather away, and the same water doesn't stay in the rivers, but in the hundred or so years people have been traveling the road from Fairbanks to Healy what truly has changed in the scenery? The sights they saw are what Scott, Coleen and I saw during that mid-day ride to Healy. The clouds come and go, the flowers come and go in season, the birds come and go, so many changes passing away, perishing, yet the wilderness terrain remains, or at least it does in Alaska.

Twice along the trail we had to stop for road construction, man's hand on the back of the wilderness. Each time as we waited I would step outside the car to breathe in that wilderness smell. A cooling breeze was blowing that day which moved the stunted tress lining the highway, but this only added to the haunting sound of the wilderness as the woodwind of the wilderness played a happy tune. The music of the wind is another element of the wilderness that soothes the soul and strengthens the spirit of a man who is looking for the tranquility of nature. What did I go into the wilderness to see? I went to shake the hand of God (Deuteronomy 8:17), to hear the voice of God (I Kings 19:12), and to see the face of God (Genesis 32:30) in an untouched corner of His creation.

# Chapter Seven

# Tour Guide

Just before one o'clock on our second day in Alaska, we found our sleeping place for the night, North Haven Lodge in Healy. We settled into a cozy room, but our minds were set on exploring the area around the entrance to Denali National Park, just a few miles away. Our tour guide Scott had made most of the pre-arrangements of where and how we would explore this amazing corner of Alaska. Besides being the tour guide, Scott was also our driver and our valet on this trip. Scott is the hero of this book, so I think it would be nice for you to know a little bit about his background.

He was born Scott Alexander Blackstone on November 7, 1977 in Concord, New Hampshire. Interestingly, I wrote this chapter on Scott's thirty-seventh birthday. Coleen and I were in our fourth year ministering at the Pembroke Bible Fellowship Church, an assembly we had started in 1973. Scott was three weeks late, according to those who set such times, but weighed in at just over seven pounds. Coleen delivered him naturally, and I was there to assist the midwife. Scott took all day—5:00 A.M. to 1:00 A.M. the next day to arrive. When Scott finally decided to enter the world, he came so fast the doctor didn't arrived until after he was out. Being our first child, Coleen and I were also surprised with the fact we were told by all the advancements of medicine that he was a girl, so when he stuck his head out, our first words were, "It's Scott!" Coleen and I had already picked out the names of our first two children. If it was a girl she would be called Marnie, a name found in a fictional book Coleen had read as a child, and if a boy, Scott, the name I wanted to call my second brother, but my parents settled on Michael Scott instead. All the indications throughout the pregnancy leaned towards a girl, so we planned accordingly. The good news is we did have one boy's outfit just in case, and now you know we needed it. I had the privilege to give Scott his first bath and in that first bath we heard his first cry. Scott didn't come into the world kicking or screaming as his sister did. With his big blue eyes wide open and with a calm and laid-back demeanor, Scott became a part of our family and our lives: a wonderful gift from God, a marvelous answer to prayer, eight years Coleen and I had waited, and a life-changing addition to our ministry.

Over the next eighteen years Scott moved with us from place to place. Scott wasn't even a year old when we made our first move back home to Maine. His first years were in Aroostook County in Northern Maine where I pastored Calvary Baptist Church in Westfield. Here he learned to fish and play ball. He started school, and it was here he gave his heart to the God of his fathers. Living close to grandparents, Scott was able to experience family roots, and it was also here Scott got his sister, Marnie. One of the joys of our lives has been the bond, friendship, and closeness of our two children. To say Scott and Marnie are two peas in pod would be an understatement. To this day they remain as close as ever, despite the miles that divides them. By the time we moved to an island off the coast of Maine, Eastport (Moose Island), Scott had developed his athletic skill in baseball, basketball, and soccer, and would show them off during his five years in the Eastport School system. By the time he was twelve, he was the starting pitcher on his Little League championship baseball team, the Eastport Expos. The team was undefeated, 12-0, and Scott won six of the games including a no-hitter and a shutout. He had 75 strikeouts in just 34 innings. He wasn't just a pitcher, but the clean-up batter in the line-up where he batted .652. When he wasn't pitching, he played shortstop and never made an error. After Little League, he started for the varsity junior high soccer team in the sixth grade. Over the next two years, his team had back-to-back undefeated seasons winning the league championship both years. Scott was an exceptional defensive player and also played goalie. But it would be in high school that Scott would excel to the highest level in his athletic accomplishments.

Scott was the starting guard on the varsity team in his freshman year. Scott played for a small Christian school, Temple Christian Academy, but they played the area public schools. A natural shooter, Scott scores 24 point in one contest and ended his first year with 160 points. His sophomore year saw him score 33 in one game while helping his team to the State Tournament and ending the year with 392 points for his high school career. By the time he reached his junior year, Scott was the primary shooter on the team and on an amazing night in January 1995, he scored 42 points, and ended the year with 759 points for his career. In the State of Maine, one of the most recognized accomplishments in high school basketball is the 1000-points plateau. Entering his senior year, Scott needed less than 250 points to join the few that reach the mark of 1000 points. In his first year Scott averaged ten points a game. In his second year, twelve points a game, and in his third year, twenty points a game. He would end his senior year with a scoring average of 28 points, including his best night ever when he scored an amazing 48 points. Scott ended his high school career by scoring 1198 points. I can verify these figures because I was at every game and recorded every point, and many of them on film. He certainly exceeding every expectation I ever had for him when I taught him to shoot and pitch and kick.

After high school Scott had a variety of jobs until at the age of twenty-nine he joined the United States Army. He did his boot camp training at Fort Knox, Kentucky. He did his heavy transportation training at Fort Leonard Wood, Missouri. His third duty station was at Fort Benning, Georgia before he was off to Fort Bragg, his home for the bulk of his career. Out of Fort Bragg, his units would make three overseas deployments. Between July 24, 2007 and October 19, 2008, he made twenty-five combat supply missions into all corners of Iraq driving over 25,000 miles through enemy territory. Between October 22, 2010 and October 22, 2011, he completed thirteen combat supply missions out of Camp Leatherneck, Afghanistan. His last mission earned him the Purple Heart, and between July 6, 2013 and April 1, 2014 he was at Camp Airfjohn, Kuwait helping to pull equipment out of the Afghanistan War. Over his eight years in the army, Scott won eleven medals and awards including the Combat Action Badge, the Iraqi and Afghanistan Campaign Medals, War on Terrorism Medal, Military Achievement Medal, Good Conduct Medal, Army Commendation Medal, and the one he is most proud of, the Drivers Badge. In six years, traveling over 300,000 miles, Scott was accident free. Who better to entrust our lives with for a grand tour of Alaska?

I found this verse in the Bible as I pondered our tour guide, "But it was thou, a man mine equal, my guide, and mine acquaintance." (Psalms 55:13) Coleen and I have had other guides on other trips during a vacation to here or there, but I think my wife would shout a hearty 'Amen' to me stating that the best guide of them all was our own son Scott. It was a joy; perhaps, the only time in our lives when we followed where Scott led and let him lead us around Alaska. As we left the North Haven Lodge for our first trip into Denali, we felt a wonderful peace to be experiencing this adventure with our son guiding the way!

## Chapter Eight

## First Trip Into Denali

Our first trek around Alaska took us from Fairbanks to Denali. On our way we passed through the villages of Ester, Nenana, Clear, Anderson, and Healy. The hamlet of Denali is your typical tourist town much like the small villages on the coast of Maine that attract thousands of out-of-staters every year. Motels and hotels and lodges and cabins for the visitors coming to the national park make up the bulk of the town. Then there are the shops and restaurants and novelty stores with anything and everything Alaska in the heart of town. I wondered where the locals actually lived; we discovered they live out-of-town. Our drive from Healy to Denali included a few stops because of road construction, but the scenery certainly made up for the delays. To enter the village of Denali you have to wind your way through a deep gorge (Nenana River Canyon) created by the fast flowing Nenana River. We stopped for a few minutes at a scenic turnout to view the river and the hamlet and take in the hills surrounding the town. The sky was threatening rain, and the wind was raw, but the landscape was warm and inviting. I walked down to the highway bridge that spanned the Nenana River. On the way, I came across my first unique road sign: a tall cedar pole with four branches. Each branch had a town and the miles to that town carved on it pointing in the direction to that town: North Pole-138, Fairbanks-124, Anchorage-238, and Homer-464.

The entrance to the park was near Riley Creek at mile marker 237 on Alaskan Highway #3. We drove into the Denali Visitors Center and walked through the Murie Science Center, which highlighted some of the animals we could see in the park as well as its history. All three of us wanted to see the scenery and the wildlife in person, so we quickly decided to drive further into the park itself. We discovered, however, that we could only go fifteen miles into the Savage River, and beyond that, we would have to take a tour bus. We decided to check out what we could see on our own before making a decision on a tour. We had brought along some food in a cooler and before we headed into Denali, Coleen made us a sandwich. With our stomachs full and in full anticipation of seeing a brown bear around every corner, we traveled up through Broad Pass until we came to the alpine region of the park. As with the terrain around Fairbanks, I was immediately touched by the hills on both sides of the alpine meadow we traveled through. An internal admiration for the Lord's handiwork began to rise in my soul as we drove the asphalt-covered miles to the Savage River. There was only one road and beyond the river was a dirt path at best. We saw no wildlife at all despite out constant searching for the anticipated sightings. We stopped a couple of times to get a picture or two, but no picture could take in the majesty of the terrain. The hills were more than giant heaps of rock and rubble and ridges as the sun came out halfway to the river to highlight the magnificent realm we were traveling through.

As we continued to explore the park, I began to sing in my heart an old church hymn I had learned as a child. The author, Maltbie Babcock, probably never visited Denali, but her words echoed off the vista before me:

> This is my Father's world, and to my listening ear.
> All nature sings, and round me rings the music of the spheres.
> This is my Father's world; I rest me in the thought.
> Of rocks and trees, of skies and seas-His hand the wonders wrought.
> This is my Father's world, the birds their carols raise;
> The morning light, the lily white declares their Maker's praise.
> This is my Father's world. He shines in all that's fair.
> In the rustling grass I hear Him pass; He speaks to me everywhere!

At that moment my everywhere was Denali, and I heard Him clearly as we slowly worked our way toward the Savage River. One of the thrills of our trip to Alaska was to see God's hand so unmistakably in the terrain of Denali, more beautiful and breathtaking than the limitations of my vocabulary can describe!

We stopped at the Savage River for a walkabout before heading back to the Visitor's Center. The wind was still raw, but with a fleece we all were comfortable. We took some pictures and walked a streamside trail still looking for wildlife. The only animal we saw on the whole trek was a blue jay with a broken wing. As Coleen and Scott rested on a log, I decided that this would be my only opportunity to fish in Denali, so I got my high-boots on and put my fly rod together and headed down to the water's edge. I hadn't been in Alaska long enough to know that rivers like the Savage were glacier rivers, full of silt and dirt with few fish. The water was a gray color, and it wasn't long before I realized I was wasting my time, but I could at least say I fished a river in Denali Park. We left around four in the afternoon and retraced our journey still looking for wildlife but finding none. At this point, it was our opinion that to see wildlife would be difficult if not impossible. We were leaning against a trip farther into the park, that is until we meet a lady in the gift shop of the Visitors Center who couldn't wait to tell somebody about her trip that day deep into the tundra. She must have overheard us discussing our options for the next day when she asked if we wanted to see the pictures she took on her tour earlier that morning and into the afternoon. There, before our eyes, were pictures of caribou walking down the road in from of her bus, brown bear feeding on the alpine slopes beside the park road, and Dall sheep grazing on the hills. Her picture show changed our minds, and we went immediately to the ticket counter to book our seats on one of the tours for the next day. Because a friend from church, Ryan McVeley, a park administrator at Acadia National Park, had given me a universal pass into all national parks, the trip for the three of us was only $103, saving us thirty dollars. We had booked a bus tour of 66 miles to a place called Eielson, an eight-hour tour that would be well worth a hundred bucks!

We made our way back to the North Haven Lodge with Paul's words to the Church at Philippi on our hearts: "According to my earnest expectation and my hope. . .." (Philippians 1:20) We had great expectations and anticipating hopes for the next day; little did we know that what we would experience would outdo any expectations we had and any hopes we had for seeing wildlife. All I can say now is to share with you another statement by the Apostle Paul to the Church at Ephesus: "Now unto Him that is able to do exceedingly abundantly above all that we ask or think. . .." (Ephesians 3:20) Scott was a great guide, but behind him was someone that could call within our view the greatest sights of Denali National Park, but, like our wait, you must wait to hear all the marvelous details of our amazing trek deep into the hinterland of Denali.

## Chapter Nine

## Rose's Café

We were back in Healy by late afternoon. So what do you do in an isolated Alaskan community with an evening to kill? In a brochure about Denali National Park, I learned that Healy was the place where most of those that work in or around Denali Park live. There are campgrounds for campers; there are tourist attractions headquartered in Healy, like ATV tours, bicycle tours and rentals, rafting tours down the Nenana River, as well as kayak tours and rentals all found in Healy. The town itself was off Route #3 on the Healy Spur Road, and, to our surprise, Healy even had a golf course. I thought that might draw son to an evening (remember the sun was not setting daily until after ten) on the links, but to my amazement, Scott said, "Let find somewhere to fish!"

On our map we found a small lake not far from the motel. As Coleen settled us into the small efficiency apartment at the North Haven Lodge, Scott and I went exploring. We were hoping to find a small stream or creek to wade that flowed into the lake with some spawning salmon in them, but all we could find was a small lake, and in particular Otter Lake, but no streams. We arrived at its shores just as a man and woman were coming off the lake. The wind had picked up and the only way to fish the lake properly would be from a boat or canoe, of which we had neither. We stopped long enough to ask how the fishing was on Otter Lake and found out it had been slow for the couple from Maine. Yes, you read that right, from Maine. It was a young husband and wife vacationing in Alaska who were avid fly fishers. I was provoked to ask where they were from when I noticed the man was wearing a Red Sox hat. One of the amazing aspects of our trip to Alaska was just how many Mainiacs we met there. I will share other encounters in future Alaskan stories. Our investigation of the side roads and dirt lanes of Healy proved fruitless for any fishable fishing holes, so by seven we were back wondering where we would have supper. To save money, our plans were to only eat out once a day. On the way into town, we had noticed a small restaurant, called Rose's Café, within walking distance of our room. We decided to experience the local cuisine and get to know the local culture of this small town.

The five-minute walk through a side trail from the motel to the café was highlighted by an abandoned tractor-trailer with the letters spelling out Welcome to Rose's Café in bold red paint. Next to the lettering was a drawing of a huge red rose, rustic but nicely done. On the top of the trailer was a long arrow, pointing travelers from the main highway to Denali that passed by the restaurant towards the café. As we walked up to the establishment, the only vehicles in the driveway were five ATVs; that should have told us something about the locals. Coleen first took notice of the mode of transportation because she loves to four-wheel, and one of her desires for Alaska was to ride an ATV. Eventually, she would! We climbed a series of steps and entered through a side door into a lobby where all the brochures of the local businesses lined the walls before we entered the large dining room. It was your typical mom and pop country restaurant with a counter on the back wall and a series of small tables scattered around the room. Rose was the waitress, the cashier, and helped with the cooking. It appeared that only three people worked there, and they seemed to be all of Eskimo decent. It was plain and down to earth with a homey atmosphere: random pictures and some off-color sayings on the wall. The dozen or so people already there all looked up when we came into the room; they returned to eating after they recognized us as tourists and no threat. The menu was home-style, and I ordered the special of the day, the beef dinner. Coleen had breakfast and Scott ordered a club sandwich. The meal was tasty and flavorful; the atmosphere was friendly. A half dozen people came in while we were eating and each of them said hello or nodded. And the bill was $45! Before we left, we watched the people on the ATVs that had preceded us into the café leave, and as they roared off on their four-wheelers, we noticed they all were carrying side arms, big guns. It made us think twice about our walk through the woods back to the lodge.

As we walked back from Rose's Café, I noticed the different light shows going on just north of Nenana River Canyon. One of the amazing vistas one can see in a mountainous region is the variety of lights dancing among the peaks of a mountain range. On that particular evening, it was the setting sun reflecting off the clouds, the hills, and the land; it had cleared a bit from the afternoon showers. I have always loved reflective light whether sunlight, moonlight, or starlight. I was transfixed that evening with the light patterns developing as the sun slipped behind the hills of Denali. We never got to see the Northern Lights, too early, but the rest of the lights of Alaska were memorable, including the lights over Healy. Just before we turned onto the roadway leading into the North Haven Lodge about a quarter of a mile off the main highway, I looked southward at the powerful panoramic view unfolding in the sky. Even the proudest of men must be humbled by the size and shape of such a view. I felt so small, insignificant! It makes one walk softly in the shadow of such grandeur and ponder the question of the Psalmist: "What is man, that thou art mindful of him?" (Psalms 8:4) Truly the light was fading fast, and, at best, the show was just an interlude, a single moment in time that causes one to reflect on just how great God is and how tiny man is. The terrain of Alaska seemed to do that to me.

As we made our way into the warmth of our room, I looked once more into the gathering darkness and the mountainous area we were calling home on that night in Alaska. Even in the glow of the artificial light coming from the lodge were shadows of trees and rocks but still no animals. Even the fading lights of August 15, 2014, lifted my spirit, stimulated my soul, and set my heart to singing.

> O Lord, my God! When I in awesome wonder
> Consider all the worlds Thy hands have made.
> I see the stars (I saw my first Alaskan stars over Healy); I hear the rolling thunder, Thy power throughout the universe displayed.
> When though the woods and forest glades I wander and hear the birds
> Sing sweetly in the trees; when I look down from lofty mountain grandeur
> And hear the brook and feel the gentle breeze.
> Then sings my soul, my Saviour God, to Thee; how great Thou art
> How great Thou art! Then sings my soul, my Saviour God, to Thee;
> How great Thou are, how great Thou art!

We had only been in Alaska for hardly forty-eight hours, and I had already been drawn into the Glory of my Lord. What would the morrow hold?

# Chapter Ten

# Looking For The Big Five

I was up at 7:30 A.M. on August 16, 2014, anticipating our day-trip into Denali. I had watched the *National Geographic* specials on America's noteworthy national parks and was excited to see the scenery and wildlife for myself, especially the big five: grizzly bear, Dall sheep, caribou, moose, and the wolf of Denali. As had been my custom on the trip, I got my traveling companions breakfast, paid for the room ($180) and by 9:00 A.M. we had packed Scott's Tahoe and were heading for the Wilderness Access Center of Denali National Park. Here we would pick up our bus for an eight-hour ride deep inside the park. Later, we would spend the night in a wonderful chalet on the Nenana River.

As we waited for our ten o'clock departure, I had a chance to talk with our bus driver Craig about our chances of seeing the big five. Craig, however, seemed to want to talk more about our odds of seeing Mount McKinley clearly. I was discouraged by his prediction, only a 30% chance, but I was soon refocused back on the big five to which he claimed it ought to be the big four. It was then he told me that sheep, caribou, and grizzly were our only real hope and that moose and black bear and wolves would be rare. Informative all day, Craig went on to explain that we would be more apt to see a grizzly bear or brown bear than a black bear. I was not concerned about seeing a black bear, even though I would see three before my Alaska adventure was over, because we have plenty of black bears in Maine, and I had seen my share. Craig was expecting us to see plenty of grizzly bears despite the fact that only between 300 and 350 live in the region we were traveling through. Weighing up to 600 pounds, we were expected to see them just about anywhere grazing as they prepared for the long, harsh Alaskan winter around the corner. He told me that we would watch carefully for them once we got twenty miles or so into the park, especially on the alpine ridges, open tundra, and along the gravel bars of the streams and brooks we would pass. They would be feasting on the berries, roots, bulbs, and tubers that were native to the park, but they were not above eating a ground squirrel, caribou, moose, or sheep if they had a chance. Their hibernation season was between October and April, and snow could be expected in the park any day now. We needed to keep our eyes open for a variety of browns and blonds, and sometimes a combination of both. These huge creatures would standout against the colors of an Alaskan autumn.

Through the day Craig would also explain about the other big animals of Denali, including the Dall sheep. When the idea for a park in the region surfaced in 1906, one of the first to venture into the area was Charles Sheldon. His purpose for coming to the region was to study the Dall sheep. These sheep were being hunted for food by the miners. Because of his concern for the survival of the unique sheep, Sheldon proposed the concept of a 'preserve' to save them from extinction. To this day, only 2,500 sheep live in the vastness of Denali surviving on the low-growing alpine plants year around. Unlike the grizzly, God created the Dall to survive out in the open through the harshest Alaskan winter. Our best bet for seeing a group of these white animals was beyond the Savage River in the canyons and ridges along the Toklat, Polychrome and Igloo. And then there were the caribou. About 2,000 caribou roamed the park, but unlike the bigger herds in Alaska and Canada, this collection of caribou rarely get together, but they are seen in smaller groups scattered throughout Denali. We were expected to find them in the open tundra and along the ridge tops where they can find lichens, their favorite food. Their greatest battle is with the insects that hound them and harass them for most of the summer, but we didn't need to worry for summer was far spend, and the day we rode into Denali was more autumn-like compared to the grand-old-days of summer. One interesting aspect about the species Adam called caribou (Genesis 2:20) is the fact that both the male and the female caribou grow antlers!

Scott's great expectation for our trip into Denali was to see a big bull moose, and according to Craig, over 2000 roam the region but rare had been the sighting of one recently. Maine has many moose, and of all the big animals of Maine I have probably seen more moose than any other creature. But, I have not seen the size of the moose that inhabit Alaska; some grow to nearly a ton in weight. Unlike the caribou, only the Bull Moose has antlers, and it was our hope to get a picture of a huge rack. My knowledge of moose taught me that they love standing water in ponds where they can eat water vegetation, of which we saw very little in the part of the park we were in. Winter was still a few weeks away when they would eat the leafless twigs and branches of low hanging trees to survive until the ponds thaw. And then there were the wolves of Denali. According to Craig, only between 60 and 100 inhabit Denali, but only visible in recent days in two places: between the park entrance and the Savage River and along the road to Wonder Lake. We had traveled the Savage River Road the day before and saw nothing, but we would be retracing that park road on the first part of our Denali tour. Just maybe this would be our day to see a wolf in the wild, one of God's most amazing dogs. I had seen Australia's dingo in 1972, and I was hoping to see Alaska's wolf in 2014.

At ten to ten, we climbed into a green park bus with Eielson on the front, our final destination. As I settled into my seat, I began to think of the Biblical explanation for the creation of Denali's big five. Throughout the day there would be evolutionary overtones to the information given us. Tragic is the deception of the Devil in the heresy of evolution. Despite this aspect of our tour, as with the *National Geographic* specials, I had a wonderful time viewing one of God's greatest creative masterpieces including some of the big five: "And God said, Let the earth bring forth the living creatures (caribou) after his kind, cattle, and creeping thing, and beast (grizzly bear) of the earth after his kind: and it was so. And God made the beast of the earth after his kind, and cattle after their kind, and every creeping thing (Dall sheep) that creepeth upon the earth after his kind: and God saw that it was good." (Genesis 1:24-25) Having carefully observed wildlife all of my life, I have come to one undeniable conclusion: if animals just happened as the evolutionist proclaims, then how could there be such a variety without a master designer? Each species unique in itself, for if from one beginning where did the 'after his kind' develop? No, we wouldn't see the big five, but in God's wise providence we would see five!

## Chapter Eleven

## Scott Spots The First Grizzly

The trip from the Wilderness Access Center to the Savage River was as uneventful as it had been the day before: beautiful scenery but no wildlife. As we crossed the bridge over the Savage River, we entered a new world, a world of grizzly bears.

Just beyond the Savage River Bridge was a park ranger's station, and we stopped for a few minutes while the resident ranger welcomed us officially into Denali National Park. It was there I learned that I had been completely legal to fish the Savage River the day before with my Alaskan license. My companions had questioned me on the issue, but the ranger made it clear that fishing was permitted even if there were very few fish this far up the stream! It was here we also learned we had entered a six million acre preserve, about the size of the State of Massachusetts! From the Savage River we travelled along Primrose Ridge with 5,095-foot Mount Margaret standing tall behind it. Twenty-three miles in, we crossed the Sanctuary River, which was much like the Savage with its gray-colored water and its gravel banks and riverbed. Nearly an hour and a half into our wandering tour, the gravel road meandered in and around small hills and flat tundra areas. We made our first planned stop at the Teklanika River Rest Area. We had covered nearly half the distance to our destination and still no animal sightings; we were beginning to wonder if we had made a mistake in giving a full day in Alaska to this adventure. Our bathroom stop lasted for about fifteen minutes, and while others took advantage of the pit stop, I went exploring for animals. Scott had traveled this far into the park the year before and had spotted moose in the river channel, but all I found was a meandering river broken up in small streams flowing through its width with that same gray-colored glacial water filling its veins. It was a huge river in its size and dimensions, but at that time of the year the water levels were very low. Again the scenery was awe-inspiring and breathtaking, but the animals of Denali seemed to be non-existent. However, everything changed in our Denali excursion once we crossed the Teklanika River.

From rolling hills, we soon entered a series of small canyons with high alpine slopes on the north side of the road. We were passing by the foothills of what is called the Wyoming Hills. We would pass Igloo Mountain (4,000 feet) and Sable Mountain (6,000 feet) before crossing Igloo Creek, 34-miles into the park. It was along that route that our first major grizzly sighting would take place, and son Scott would be the first to shout-out, "Three o'clock!" He wasn't mentioning the time but the direction on the clock where the grizzly bear could be seen. Scott's military training in spotting objects at a distance and the direction by which they could be seem would come in handy on this animal safari into the rugged wilderness of Denali. I think Scott spotted more Alaskan wildlife than anybody else on the bus, and there were nearly forty of us on this Denali trip. Just after passing a sharp corner in the roadway, to our right was a long sloping meadow running high up into a ridgeline that appeared a couple thousand feet in height. The bus was quiet with all tourists gazing intently out their windows for a glimpse of a sudden movement or a light color (sheep-white, caribou-gray, and grizzly-blonde). The whole world seemed still, serene, silent. A thin layer of clouds, like you get on a day of showers, blotted out the sun, but there was enough light to see well up the slope. Scott's sharp eyes caught the light blonde shape of a bear against the darker colors of the fall foliage. Within seconds, Scott had spotted two more bears grazing just above the first. Craig, our driver, had instructed us before we left the center to make the clock-direction reference when spotting something, and he would stop the bus so everybody could see what had been spotted. Scott's shout brought the bus to a smooth stop beside the road, and then it took the rest of us awhile to spot the bears. The distance was great, at least a half of a mile. They seemed small against the backdrop of the massive hillside. A fully-grown brown bear, its light-tan coat glistening, was slowly grazing up the slope closest to us. A second bear, a bit smaller, was doing the same thing fifty feet up the slope from the first and there just above the second bear was a third bear equally as small as the second. Twins? Craig felt they were a mother bear and two grown cubs, as it is not unusual for cubs to stay with their mother for a few years. One of the laws of Craig's bus was when an animal sighting happened everybody was to remain dead silent so as not to scare the creature. I had a hard time observing that law! There was no danger of that with these bears because of the distance, but we tried to observe the rule to practice for future sightings. What a rare and special treat I thought, not realizing that this was just the beginning of a series of sightings that would continue over the next few hours. So often my encounters with bears were fleeting, but our first three showed no sign of fear. Was it the distance or were they getting used to the buses stopping by their pasture? I think we could have watched them for hours if we had stayed, but after a score of pictures taken with Scott's telephoto lens, we moved on and within twenty-minutes Scott yelled out again, but this time, "One o'clock!"

Sure enough, a bit closer than the first three, were three more grizzly bears grazing up a hilly ridge. The terrain in that section of the park had great swaths of granite along its spine. The blonde-colored bears stood out even more than the other three, but like the first bears, these grizzlies were grazing in the foliage-covered areas. Berries seemed to be their intend and, once again, they paid no attention to the bus full of amazed tourists snapping pictures like they were the Prince of Wales, Lady Kate and baby George. Scott's camera pulled them closer than the natural eye could with their size. Impressive! Craig thought the weight would be 300 pounds for the mother and 200 pounds for each of the kids. I had the urge to get out and get closer, but that was another law on Craig's bus, no getting off! Again we could have watched the trio for hours, but we had many miles to travel, and at fifteen miles-per-hour, the travel was slow. I took one more look at the feeding bears as the bus got back on the road for Eielson, but I couldn't get the picture of the three bears out of my head. Even on the day of the writing of this chapter, I can still see the harmony and coordination of that family as they fed together on that alpine slope foraging for the final fruit of summer. It is a first-class lesson of peaceful co-existence and complete mutual trust. It was also the first time I understood the Biblical phrase "a ranging bear" (Proverbs 28:15). In the context of the verse, is speaks about 'a wicked ruler' and the first comparison is "a roaring lion"; now that is an easy one, but what of 'a ranging bear'? Ranging means, "going to and fro", here and there, and on two hillsides in Denali I witnessed the ranging bear, or the feeding bear, a bear that moves from spot to spot feasting on berries. None of the six bears seemed to stay very long in one place, but they were in constant motion moving from one berry bush to another. One of the overlooked characteristics of the last days is defined in Daniel 12:4 as ". . .many shall run to and fro. . ." like a ranging bear! We certainly live in a day were lots of people move from place to place, just like the grazing range of your average Denali grizzly. It is always amazing to me where the Good Lord decides to teach me a scriptural lesson or gives me a Biblical understanding.

## Chapter Twelve

## More Denali Wildlife

In my trip journal, I began to make notes of the times and the sightings of the wildlife we encountered in our Denali day-trip. It was at 11:40 A.M. (remember we left at 10), when Scott spotted the first trio of brown bears, and it was at high noon he spotted the second set of three grizzlies grazing. These two amazing sightings took place in Sable Pass on the only road into Denali, called the Park Road. Over the next half an hour, we climbed steadily until we arrived at our second planned stop located on the top of Polychrome Pass (3695 feet), 46-miles into our trip. From the top of the pass, we could look north to Polychrome Mountain (5,790 feet) and south to Pendleton Mountain (7,840 feet) and the deep wide tundra valley that stretched out for miles between these two mountain ranges. It was one of the biggest vistas I have ever experienced in my life. In the range of hills to the south, we could also see numerous glaciers in between the hills and mountains. It was here we took our only family picture of the trip. Why? The photograph shows the Blackstone family all bundled up and huddled up against the howling winds blowing down through the valley below, a 1000-foot drop. It was still an overcast day with the temperature in the 50s, but the wind chill had to be in the 40s, and threatening rain. We stayed about fifteen minutes to take pictures and stretch our legs. Scott and I climbed a nearby hill for a better view, but nowhere could the view be improved!

Over the 45-minutes we traveled between Polychrome Pass and the Toklat River, we saw our first caribou, a group of four at 12:40 A.M., wandering in the valley below. They were very hard to spot at first and not close enough to take a good photograph even with Scott's telephoto lens. Our third pit shop on the tour was at the Visitor's Center at Toklat River, 53-miles in. We only stopped a few minutes for a bathroom break, no facilities at Polychrome Pass, but not time enough to visit the center. We would do that on the way back. We were soon back on the road, and after Toklat, the animal sightings came in rapid succession as we traveled through a section of the Park Road called Highway Pass. These are the animal encounters I recorded in my journal through this section of the trip:

1. 1:20 P.M. Craig spots a group of eight Dall sheep grazing in a narrow valley between two high peaks. They are easy to spot, if not small spots really, with their bright-white coats. Despite the distance, maybe a mile, great to see!

2. 1:30 P.M. We spot a lone grizzly bear grazing about 300 yards from the bus!

3. 1:35 P.M. We spot two caribou beside the road barely twenty yards away in the tall bushes. Scott is able to get a series of up close pictures of one of the caribou as it walked in and out of the small trees. It is also at this time we see our first ptarmigan. We would eventually see four of these grouse-like birds, a lot like our partridge in Maine, and a rodent-like creature Craig called an arctic squirrel. With these two small creatures and the big three, caribou, grizzly, and Dall sheep, we would see five, though not the big five.

4. 1:40 P.M. We spot four more caribou near the road.

5. 1:45 P.M. We spot a lone caribou working his way along a creek bed.

6. 2:00 P.M. We had a double play. On the south side of the bus, a group of seven caribou appear grazing in a small meadow. That was the largest number we saw together all day. But our attention was soon shifted when someone shouted, "Big bear at three o'clock!" Sure enough, within a hundred yards of the bus, was a massive male grizzly lumbering along a ridge of low bush berries. What made this bear different from the other grizzlies we had seen is the fact it was totally brown, a dark brown at that. Craig thought maybe 500 pounds? We watched the monster walk and feed for about five minutes. I must admit I didn't want to get out or get any closer. Scott got some amazing photographs of the Big Brown Bear!

7. 2:05 P.M. We spot another two caribou, the last animals we would see until we headed back after viewing Mount McKinley.

During the two and a half hours since we had our first sighting, we saw eight grizzly bears, twenty caribou, and eight Dall sheep. If the trip stopped then and there I would have been content, but, as with all things in the Lord's will, the best was yet to come!

When I experience things like I did that day in Denali, especially in the category of thinking I surely have experienced the best of the best when in reality the best is yet to come, I think of these words first penned by Isaiah and then quoted by Paul, "...Eye hath not seen, nor ear heard, neither have entered into the heart of man, the things which God hath prepared for them that love Him." (Isaiah 64:4 and I Corinthians 2:9) I don't know what I imagined Denali would be like or what animals we would or would not see. My imagination was very small; my visions were tiny in comparison to what we eventually saw and heard those first four hours of our eight-hour trip into the backcountry of Denali. My life has been like that numerous times when I consider my little faith and tiny trust in the Almighty. "Is there anything too hard for the Lord? (Genesis 18:14) Certainly not! Then why do we seem content with a mountaintop experience thinking nothing could be better when in reality a best is just around the corner? I will never forget the lesson the Lord taught me between the first half of our trip into Denali and the return trip out of Denali. That is why, despite the wondrous things I have seen and heard up to this point in my life, I now expect the things which God hath prepared for me in the future to out-shine and out-do and out-amaze anything I have yet experienced! And why shouldn't I? I believe this because I am one of them that love Him, and I was traveling with others who felt the same. We will always be amazed with what God does for us, but we should never be surprised!

# Chapter Thirteen

# Mount McKinley

Our final miles to the Eielson rest area and observation plateau in Denali Park were simply amazing because of the growing presence of Mount McKinley in the far distance. We slipped past Stony Dome (4,700 feet) as we slowly made our way through Thorofare Pass. The road had turned into a series of dead-man curves and switchbacks, but each time we came back around and our bus was heading northwest, we saw McKinley again. The prophecy that only 30% of park visitors get to see the mountain in all of its glory was turning in our favor with each twist and turn of the road. The clouds were beginning to clear after a few showers along the 66-mile trip to Eielson, and the mountain was coming alive with shades of white and reflected light. Our heavenly Father was clearing the weather so we would be able to fully experience the grandeur of America's highest hill!

A little after two o'clock on August 16, 2014, our tour bus pulled into the parking lot at Eielson. About a half dozen other park buses were there, but the crowd seemed small compared to the massive wilderness surrounding us. Mount McKinley was still thirty-eight miles away, yet it seemed to be right in front of us. Despite the occasional cloudbank, the mountain and mountains of the McKinley Range were clearly before our eyes. A huge map of our view on the overlook told me everything I wanted to know about what lay before my eyes. The first peak to clear the clouds was the North Peak of Mount McKinley standing at 19,470 feet. Then a few minutes later, the clouds cleared revealing the South Peak of Mount McKinley towering over the North Peak at 20,320 feet. They said it was really rare to see both peaks on a given day, so we were blessed! We even got to see Harper Glacier, the glacier between the two massive summits. Other mountain highlights shown to us were Browne Tower (14,600 feet) and Karsten's Ridge. Then there was Mount Carper at 12,550 over a mile below the tallest peaks of

McKinley. We saw Taylor Spur (15,070 feet) and what they called Wickersham Wall and Pioneer Ridge, the most used mountaineering path up to the summit of the North Peak. Below the ridge was another huge glacier, Muldrow Glacier. There was also in front of us, perhaps the closest, a place they called Peter's Dome (10,600 feet). The mountains were covered in ivory, white snow from top to bottom. Even though we couldn't see the base because of the hills between us, those hills were clear of snow so the white against the brown of Alaska only made the view and vista that much more impressive, vivacious even. Interestingly, however, in the world of mountains and mountain heights, Mount McKinley only ranks 50th on the world's tallest mountains list, but for me it is the most amazing mountain I had seen in my lifetime to that point?

As I pondered the sight of a snow-laden McKinley, a profound peace settled in my soul. It was quiet at Eielson and the solitude was infectious. The Psalmist once wrote, "The mountains shall bring peace to the people. . . (Psalms 72:3). That day, under the shadow of McKinley, I felt at peace, a natural peace to be sure, but a spiritual peace as well. The fleeing clouds brought bright interludes of brilliance lasting only a few minutes at a time, but they were enough to stir my soul and thrill my spirit. The sun was at its zenith, so the reflected light came from above and not below; briefly, the topmost peaks were aflame, fire and ice. The combined beauty of white and light gave a warm tone to the mountain, not the rugged and dangerous hill it can be. Many have lost their lives trying to tame McKinley. Despite the hot rays of the sunlight striking the mountain, there was no melting going on; the mountain was just too high for that. It was as if someone had painted a picture on the landscape: unchanging, unmovable, and unaffected by mortal man. All we could do was look on the splendor of the sights, transfixed by a vision that will probably never be repeated in our lifetime. Unless I get to travel to the Punjab, where some of the Himalaya Mountains can be seen, and one of the places still on my bucket list, I will never see a higher mountain this side of eternity. So Mount McKinley was certainly a magical moment in my mountaineering experience. Many years ago, I compiled a series of observation and insights centering on my mountaintop experiences. It was called *Western Ridges* or *The Western Hills and the Holy Word* and based on the classic mountain verse written by the psalmist, "I will lift up mine eyes unto the hills, from whence cometh my help." (Psalms 121:10) I have more experiences now.

I was impressed the first time I visited Sugarloaf Mountain in the western hills of Maine in the fall of 2005. A couple attending our church at the time, Ken and Mary Mitchell, lent us a few days in their time-share near the mountain. The snow hadn't come yet, but Coleen and I are not skiers, so the visit was purely a get-away, out-of-town kind of adventure. In our early-married days, we lived in New Hampshire and toured the White Mountains of northern New Hampshire including the granddaddy of them all Mount Washington, but at only 6,288 feet it is a stepchild at best to McKinley. Even our Mount Katahdin in Maine barely reaches a mile into the atmosphere. It was my first trip to India in the winter of 2006 that exposed me to some higher hills, but the mountains of Kerala rarely reach 10,000 feet, half the size of Mount McKinley and without snow! To say I have had a fascination with mountains would be a wrong statement, but since Washington and Sugarloaf and Katahdin and the Ghats Mountains of India I have fallen in love with mountains. Like the oceans, I will not hesitate to go to the mountains any chance I get. My daughter lives in California now, and I can't wait to visit for two reasons: the Pacific Ocean, which I have seen twice, and the Sierra Hills in the Rocky Mountains. I have only seen them once and that was from 30,000 feet. McKinley only reignited my desire to return to the mountains.

I was born in the hills of Aroostook County in Northern Maine, but my desire is to climb higher and set my sights on higher ground just like I did the day we viewed Mount McKinley from afar. Johnson Oatman, Jr. said it best in his classic church hymn.

> I'm pressing on the upward way, new heights I'm gaining every day;
> Still praying as I'm onward bound, Lord, plant my feet on higher ground.
> My heart has no desire to stay where doubts arise and fears dismay;
> Though some may dwell where these abound,
> My prayer, my aim, is higher ground.
> I want to live above the world, though Satan's darts at me are hurled;
> For faith has caught the joyful sound, the song of saints on higher ground.
> I want to scale the utmost height and catch a gleam of glory bright;
> But still I'll pray till heaven I've found, Lord, lead me on to higher ground.
> Lord, lift me up and let me stand by faith on heaven's tableland;
> A higher plane than I have found, Lord, plant my feet on higher ground.

It is my belief that McKinley is not my last great and high mountain because John was taken to one in the new heaven and the new earth (Revelation 21:1) to see the new Jerusalem, and one day I not only want to see that mountain but to climb it as well (Revelation 21:10), and when I do, I can't imagine I will think of any mountain so grand as the day I viewed Mount McKinley in Alaska.

Chapter Fourteen

## An Extraordinary Bear Encounter

We left the shadow of Mount McKinley just before three o'clock on the afternoon of August 16, 2014. It was hard to begin our backtracking because the mountain was still showing off in the brightness of a mid-afternoon sun. Our bus driver had set the time for our return to the bus, and I noticed after all the pictures and the viewing of the mountain I still had about fifteen minutes to spare. Scott and Coleen decided to go into the gift shop and get out of the raw wind for their final few minutes at McKinley, but I decided to take a small path that ran below the observation station to a cliff overlooking a large stream that ran through Thorofare Pass. I also wanted to see Mount McKinley from another angle before I left this amazing place.

My pace was quick as I maneuvered my way through the narrow trail to the cliff below. I only encountered a few people with the same idea, but I didn't stop to visit. Within five minutes I was at the place I had noticed from far up on the ridgeline. It was windy in the open tundra, and the wind felt like the blast you get from a winter chill. I knew the mountain was thirty-eight miles away, but I felt I could feel the glacier snow even at that distance. I got my pocket New Testament out of my back pocket and began to read: "Nor yet that he should offer himself often, as the high priest entereth into the holy place every year with blood of others. . .and their sins and iniquities will I remember no more." (Hebrews 9:25 to Hebrews 10:17) I have been carrying a pocket New Testament in my back pocket since high school. The one I read overlooking Mount McKinley was #36 in the series. I keep them until I read through them then I retire them. By the time I finish reading one, it is pretty torn and tattered. It may have been the most inspiring place I have ever read the Word of God. On my way back to the bus, I thanked the Lord that I had gotten a chance to see such a sight: for me, 'a glimpse of glory bright'!

Our trip back to the park entrance was filled with mixed emotions. Almost immediately we started to see wildlife, but it was hard not to look back on the mountain as well. I believe we spotted, for a second time, the massive brown bear we had seen coming into Eielson. He was still grazing about a hundred yards on a ridgeline just off the road. We also saw the caribou again as we weaved our way over and around the series of small hills south of Eielson. Our last view of the mountain was at the 3,900-foot hill, the highest on the sixty-six mile trek, near Highway Pass, and almost immediately our attention was refocused from a distant mountain to a huge grizzly bear having a bath! It was my dear wife that made the announcement this time, "Bear! Three O'clock!" Coleen was the first to spot the bear in a creek bed to the right of the bus. It was some distance away, but we could see clearly the bear wading in a deep hole in the creek. The bus stopped and, with Scott's telephoto lens, the bear came to life even more. For the next five minutes, we watched the splishing and the splashing as the grizzly put on a show. After a good cleaning, the bear started walking up the shore shaking the water from its fur like a dog does, until it finally was lost from sight by some bushes. We thought it couldn't get any better than that, but we soon would be surprised again by the photogenic brown bears of Denali Park.

Over the next hour we retraced our journey back through the Toklat River valley were we saw more caribou, five to be exact, and just beyond the Toklat we saw two Dall sheep resting in a narrow gorge right beside the road, our closest encounter with the Denali sheep. Our pit stop at the visitor's center at Toklat River was nice. We had been on the road for six hours and still had a couple of hours to go. The gift shop was fine, although expensive. They did have some native furs of brown bears, (so soft) and antlers from sheep and moose. I took pictures of Coleen with each of the items to remember the live ones we saw. Our fifteen-minute break also gave us a chance to get a picture with our bus driver in front of his green, park bus. It was there we learned from Craig that this was his 705th trip into the park over his nine-year career. He was a wealth of information, and we could tell from his passion for the park that he was an environmentalist. A single man with a drive to travel, he told us his plans for the winter were to go and work in a park in South America, but that he would be back to Denali in the spring. And like any good guide, Craig had left the best for last! In the last two hours we would see a few more grizzlies, but the best of the best happened as we returned to Polychrome at mile marker #46. Remember this was the place we had made our second stop on our trip in the park; we would stop again but this time it wasn't to walk around.

Scott spotted it first, a mother grizzly strolling over the rise of a small hill to the left of the bus. The bus was making its way around a series of sharp corners with a thousand foot drop to our right and a fifty-foot rise to our left. Craig brought the bus to a stop as the mother bear waddled her way along the ridge, and, to our total delight, there right behind her came a small cub and right behind that cub a sister or a brother. Her silver coat was in direct contrast to the dark, brown coats of the cubs. The mother and cubs seemed unaffected by the bus standing in their way from crossing the park road. The cameras snapped and flashed as the mother grizzly literally walked the length of the bus along the ridgeline barely thirty feet away from the side of the bus. Her two children following in her footprints frolicked along as if they were totally alone, out on an adventure with Mum. Eventually the mother bear got far enough in front of the bus for her own satisfaction and came down off the hill and crossed directly in front of the bus. Spellbinding! It wasn't long thereafter that the cubs were also on the road. A stunned silence filled the bus as we all seemed to be in shock that we were witnessing such an extraordinary encounter with a family of brown bears. The mother grizzly seemed to be in no hurry, as she made sure her cubs crossed the dirt road without incident, and then she was off to feed on a series of berry bushes to the right of the bus. The whole episode took perhaps ten minutes and in the whole time hundreds of pictures were taken. Over the next ten minutes we lived within eyesight of those three bears as they meandered beside and in front of us. The obvious gentleness of the three bears towards each other was fully on display. The last we saw of the bear and her cubs was a fleeting flash of silver in the bushes and a double glimpse of brown in the shrubs as they began again to forage for fruit on the opposite side of the road. It was a marvelous and touching finale to our time spent together in Denali Park. Needless to say, that encounter was talked about for the rest of the trip back to the Visitor's center. What a rare (according to Craig) and wonderful treat the extraordinary encounter had been! So often man's encounters with wildlife are fleeting at best, but on Polychrome Ridge, we were able to interact with three brown bear for nearly twenty minutes. All toll we saw one ptarmigan, four arctic squirrels, ten Dall sheep, twenty-five caribou, and fourteen grizzly bears on our trip into Denali, but the best of the best was watching a family of three brown bears out on an afternoon stroll around a tour bus!

## Chapter Fifteen

## Resting On The Banks Of The Nenana

We left our second Alaskan resting place in Healy at 9:00 A.M., and we didn't get back from our Denali adventure until nearly 7:00 P.M. It was a tiring day, but a blessed one. We were still talking about all the wildlife and the mountains we saw as we exited the park and headed back to the settlement that had sprung up because of the profound interest in Denali National Park. We had reservation to sleep at the McKinley Chalet Resort on the banks of the Nenana River that night.

Once we found T chalet, (each chalet was given a letter of the alphabet and yes all 26 letters were covered with each chalet having 12+ rooms for a total of 478 places to stay), we settled into our rooms: a small living room area with a pullout bed where Scott slept, a good size bathroom, and a bedroom in the back whose windows opened up so you could hear the rush of the river. Each of the chalets was built on the banks of the impressive Nenana. Following a corner of the wide, glacier river, the chalets were placed in a semi-circle so that each chalet was within yards of the swift flowing stream. I knew immediately I would love this place because I had always enjoyed sleeping on the shore of any sea or body of water. As a boy I had slept on the banks of Beaver Brook, a favorite trout stream in Aroostook County, where I first experienced the solitude and serenity of resting by a river. Then it was the pleasant sounds of the Miramichi River in New Brunswick, Canada, and the tranquil flow of the mighty Restigouche River in Quebec, Canada that I had continued my love affair with sleeping next to flowing waters through the places my father-in-law, Stacy Meister, had taken me fishing. Then there was the Anchorage on Big Lake in Downeast Maine where my wife and family spent numerous nights listening to the lapping of waves against the granite shore. I still recall the nights my children and I camped out on the banks of Smith Pond and the sound of the wind blowing over water, another favorite fishing place. I wouldn't be fishing the Nenana, but I would be resting on the banks of the Nenana.

Shortly after we settled in, Coleen and I decided to explore the little hamlet while Scott took a nap. We promised him we would return with a pizza, so off we went to do a bit of Christmas shopping and scrapbook shopping and postcard shopping. The opposite side of the road from the resort was lined with small stores for about half a mile. We walked the boardwalk stopping at the shops we found interesting. Checking on the first pizza shop we found for prices and product, we soon discovered that the toppings for pizza in Alaska were different than the lower 48 with plenty of caribou and bear and moose to fill all the pizza you wanted. My wife decided we would check elsewhere! After picking up a few items, we finally found a traditional pizza joint just down the road from the McKinley Resort: Lynx's Pizza, and no, we didn't have to have lynx on it. We bought a 16-inch pizza for $28! Returning to the chalet we enjoyed the Alaskan pizza with Scott. It wasn't bad, but not the best. As we ate, we reminisced about our trip so far: three days in which our expectation had been sorely underestimated. Alaska had already given us more than we anticipated, and then there was the joy of hearing the water flowing outside our window.

When God created water (Genesis 1:6), He made a marvelous liquid that not only sustains life, but has within it movement, a therapeutic element. Granted, its power can shape and sculpt as it did in the Nenana River valley, even at places cutting through solid rock. The water content of the moisture in the air makes our terrestrial ball unique in our galaxy. But for me it is the sounds of water: splashing streams over a rocky base, ocean waves on a sandy shore, and roaring rivers outside your window that gives the greatest blessings from water. The high peaks we saw in Denali and around Denali are the first factors in this music of the river as they divert the moisture-laden clouds upward until those clouds empty themselves of their life giving droplets of $H_2O$. Sometimes and often times in Alaska those droplets fall as snow, kept in reserve until the warmth of the Sun returns and those individual snowflakes melt by the trillions to feed the Nenana, and other rivers like her. While we were traveling through the Nenana Valley, we watched the cloud-shrouded slopes and a number of times we felt the wetness of a light shower. Add to that the centuries of snow build up that created countless glaciers in the area, and with the melting of those glaciers the volume of water is increased, and that water results in the grayish hue to the Nenana and other glacial rivers like it. My joy of the Nenana wasn't in where the water came from, but the melody that was created as it splashed by T chalet of the McKinley Chalet Resort.

Amid all the variety of mountain and hill landscapes in Denali, water is the most pleasant in both sight and sound. Both are inescapable in Denali; whether the countless small streams we saw or the mighty Savage and Toklat Rivers we crossed over. We saw no sparking reflections on the Nenana when we were there because the clouds interfered, but I did heard the tumbling laughter of liquid over stone that has become all too familiar to my ear. Behind T chalet the river was growling as the river rushed over huge boulders on its way to a narrow gorge that lies between Healy and Denali where the river roars through a series of rapids. Many years ago the psalmist painted a picture of such a place with words. I share them now in remembrance of the night I went to sleep listening to the inspiring chorus of the Nenana River in Alaska:

> Thou coveredst it with the deep as with a garment: the waters stood above the mountains. At Thy rebuke they fled; at the voice of Thy thunder they hasted away. They go up by the mountains; they go down by the valleys unto the place (Nenana, Alaska), which Thou hast founded for them. Thou hast set a bound that they may not pass over; that they turn not again to cover the earth. He sendeth the springs into the valleys (a beautiful description of Denali), which run among the hills. They give drink to every beast (grizzly, caribou, sheep) of the field: the wild asses quench their thirst. By them shall the fowls of the heaven have their habitation, which sing among the branches. He watereth the hills from His chambers: the earth is satisfied with the fruit of thy works." (Psalms 104:6-13)

This is what we both saw and heard and experienced in a variety of places in Alaska, and especially the night we rested on the banks of the Nenana.

## Chapter Sixteen

# Chum At Montana Creek

My first Sunday in Alaska started with a special church service on the shore of the Nenana River. Granted, only one person attended this worship service that day, but I will remember it for a very long time.

I was once again the first one up and out the door. With no breakfast to get, I headed directly for the river. Within a short time, we would be on the road again heading south to the Kenai Peninsula. Before that happened, I wanted a few minutes alone with the designer of Denali. So I found a deadhead that had washed up on a gravel bar just behind T chalet for a pew. The clouds were still hanging low over the hills north of town. It was in the 50s, damp but not too cold. I took in the mist and light fog and the panorama of exquisite grandeur in a 180-degree turning of my head. The river flowed before me in a series of gentle ripples caused by the rocky terrain in that section of the riverbed. A small island was to my left, but with the low water, only the far side was waterlogged. The side I was resting on was void of a flow, but I could see clearly that at the right time of the year, my Alaskan sanctuary would also be under the glacier water. I got out my New Testament from my back pocket and began to read, "By faith Enoch was translated that he should not see death. . .By faith the harlot Rahab perished not with them that believed not, when she had received the spies with peace." (Hebrews 11:5-31) As I read and prayed, I thought of the wonderful joy that comes with worshipping the Almighty God in His creation. The original cathedral was a garden (Eden) and numerous chapels since that first sanctuary have been wilderness churches. Buildings not made by hands, but gathering places under stands of trees and rocky amphitheaters in desolate places. As I meditated and pondered my faith, a group of float tubes quickly passed in front of me, tourists enjoying the thrill of a morning ride through fifth-class waters. It surprised me just how fast they passed measured in the speed of the Nenana, and then they were gone, and I was back praising God and thanking him for a chance to experience this side of Denali, privately and alone in the great Alaskan wilderness. It was then a light rain fell, and I began to sing, "There shall be showers of blessings (Ezekiel 34:26), this is the promise of love. There shall be seasons refreshing, sent from the Saviour above." What a season I was enjoying in Denali.

I got up from my driftwood pew about a half an hour after finding my seat, but the sermon wasn't over. The hills before me, at the far bank of the Nenana, were covered in stunted trees, small bushes, and shrubs. Hoping to see some wildlife, I took one last look down the river and then up the river before returning to the nature trail that followed the contour of the river on the chalet side. Slowly I returned to find my companions still asleep, so I walked through the resort by the sleeping chalets from T up to D and then back to T again. Nobody seemed to be stirring as I strolled another half an hour. The shower passed with few raindrops; I didn't even get wet. By the time I returned to our chalet the second time, Scott was up looking for me and Coleen was getting ready for another day with her favorite two men. I told of my riverside adventures and showed them the few photos I had taken. These photos included my first ever selfie.

We left Denali at 9:00 A.M. and, within a few minutes, spotted our first moose of the trip. At ten we caught our first glimpses of the South Peak of McKinley as we traveled Route Three known as the Park's Highway towards Wasilla. The clouds were thick, but periodically we could make out McKinley through the overcast. In a matter of minutes, the atmospheric veils of low hanging clouds and the gray shrouds of sky would dissipate for a few seconds, and we would see the glory of the southern peak. Strongly, the light from the mid-morning sun intensified and the mountain could be seen through the side window of Scott's car. Then in a burst of heavenly glory, the splendor of the slope held a golden radiance for just a few seconds. To my boundless delight, the whole summit stood sparkling in a veil of white. Scott was hoping we would get a better view of the southern slopes of McKinley at a turnout he had visited on his travels to Anchorage, but by the time we arrived at eleven, the mountain was completely covered in fog and clouds, a disappointment for us. But it was not as disappointing because we had seen the full glory of McKinley the day before from Eielson. Shortly after leaving the observation place, it really started raining, but the rain would only last until we crossed Montana Creek. At first we were going to press on, but Coleen talked us into stopping for a few hours. It did not take much persuasion on her part! Our plans for the day were just to make our next rest stop, Galley Lodge on the Kenai Peninsula. This stop might have been the best non-planned stop on our entire Alaskan trip!

Scott and I quickly donned our fishing waders and rain jackets and put together our fly rods. Scott had stopped at Montana Creek before with no success. According to the sign by the campground on the creek, the silvers (coho salmon) were running, and I was determined to catch one. It took us nearly ten minutes to walk a muddy trail to a railroad track, and then another ten minutes to walk the tracks to the creek. It was smaller than I imagined, barely twenty feet across in places. You could see clearly that it could grow to four times that size when the water was high, but not in August 2014. I immediately began to see dead salmon everywhere. This was my first experience of seeing dead salmon like this. I had fished the Atlantic salmon for over two decades, but unlike Pacific salmon, Atlantic salmon don't die but return year after year. Pacific salmon make only one run, one spawn and then they die! The water was clear enough so we could see if there was salmon in the creek or not. No salmon, or so we thought. As we fished towards the outlet, I ran into a man from Ashland, Maine, about twenty miles from my boyhood home. This was our second Maine encounter. A lot of Mainiacs love to travel to Alaska it seems.

As I talked to my new friend from Maine, Scott had worked his way down the creek. It took me fifteen minutes to eventually catch up with him. Turning a sharp corner in the creek, I noticed my fishing partner on the opposite side of the creek with a bent rod; Scott was into a fish. By the time I maneuvered across the now 70-foot creek, Scott had landed a foot long sucker. But we could see that we had found the fishing hole of Montana Creek because the far bank was lined with spin fishermen and women. We had arrived where Montana Creek flows into the Susitna River, a very wide and fast flowing Alaskan waterway. Despite fly-fishing, Scott and I over the next hour would catch more salmon than anybody. Scott's first catch, after I arrived, landed him our first chum (dog salmon) of the trip. After about a five-minute fight, Scott landed the ten-pound, 28-inch salmon. The fly of choice by the chum of Montana Creek seemed to be a two-ought (size), pink-eyed, weighted fly. We simply threw down stream and jigged the fly through the deep hole. I did watch a lady from across the creek land a silver salmon, the only one we saw, but we watched plenty of chums being landed. We had promised Coleen that we would only leave her for a couple of hours so at 2 o'clock we headed back to the car. I eventually hooked five and landed one with Scott hooking three and landing all three. All the chum salmon we caught were about the same size: 26-28 inches, 8-10 pounds. Mediations, mountains, and Montana Creek made for a marvelous day in Alaska!

CHAPTER SEVENTEEN

# PRINCE WILLIAM SOUND AND HIGH HILL

COLEEN HAD JUST GOTTEN up from a nap when Scott and I returned from our Montana Creek fishing expedition. Within ten minutes we were on the road again and, by three in the afternoon of August 17, 2014, we were driving through Wasilla of Sarah Palin fame. As we left Wasilla it stopped raining, but the trip through Palin's town was slow; more cars than the highway would handle, so I can say I spent half an hour in Wasilla, but I never left the car. It took us another hour to make Anchorage, which was 358 miles from Fairbanks, but once again we simply drove through. By now you must know that I am a country boy and that I don't spend any more time than I need to in a city. Anchorage to me was a small city at best, but still a city. I am glad we pressed on because the views after Anchorage and Wasilla were what I had come to Alaska to see.

It was nearly five when we saw our first sights of the Gulf of Alaska. I thought the wilderness outside Fairbanks was big, and the grandeur of Denali will never be fully described in words by me, but Prince William Sound is huge, massive and the hills that hug its shoreline are nothing short of spectacular. Our trip around the northern most inlet of Prince William Sound and other such moments, have always left an indelible imprint on my mind. I think I will never again drive such a highway with steep cliffs on one side and deep, broad water on the other. It is beyond the capability of man to make something as big as the country I saw over the many hours it took for us to transverse that one turn. It was an intense, overwhelming awe-inspiring trip for me. I couldn't take my eyes off the vastness of the space of this small corner of the great Sound. The presence of divine artistry was everywhere, from the distant shore to the steep rugged cliffs on the highway side of the bay. This is the example of something that only the Almighty, in His amazing resourcefulness and infinite ability, could create, frame, and form with the power of a word: "Though faith we understand that the worlds (including Prince William Sound) were framed by the word of God, so that things which are seen were not made of things which do appear." (Hebrews 11:3) When the Sound first appeared to me, I thought as if I was the first to see it. It is times like this in my life when I am grateful to my God for the opportunity to witness such pageantry, such panoramic vistas that defy the imagination. I had known about Prince William Sound for a long time, even before the Exxon Valdez disaster, yet it wasn't until the afternoon I spent traveling only just a faction of it shores that I fully recognized the Hand of God on it and why the environmentalists were so upset with the oil spill.

It has been my good fortune to witness some wondrous places on God's crown jewel of the universe. Denali was amazing. My trips to the mountains of eastern Kerala have always had a special place in my heart. As a Mainiac, I still feel we have some of the best scenery in the world from our western hills to our rugged coastline to Aroostook County, but what I have seen and what I saw during that coastline drive put Prince William Sound and its surrounding hills in a completely different category based on sheer size. Even our cameras were not capable of recording the depth and breadth and height and width of the scenery surrounding us. That is why our memory is the only avenue we have to remember such events, such sights, and sites. Our memory has the incredible ability to store such happenings in the mental vaults of our minds. On days like this as I recall this journey around Cook's Inlet of Prince William Sound, I am both able to remember and reminisce. Another man might steal your silver and your gold, and another your precious possession, but who can take away your memories? It is not only the interplay of light, water, rain, and land, which our memories replay; there is also that subtle realization that you are sharing these moments with two other people. I can't remember us talking much during that section of our trip. I think the three of us were all caught up in the grandeur of the vista before us.

It took us five hours to travel from Montana Creek to the Gallery Lodge on the Kasilof River. Five hours of mostly high hills and deep bays. At such moments, a traveler stands humbled by the awe of his surroundings. Small is the word that comes to mind when you enter such a world, and you start singing in your heart: "This is my Father's world. . .. of rocks and trees, of skies and seas-His hand the wonders wrought." It is a world in which the soul and the spirit of man can find refreshment, rejuvenation, and restoration. I have called the mountains around Prince William Sound hills throughout this chapter, but only because of their size next to the sea. All the mountains I had seen up to this point in Alaska had been compared to the landscape they were near. It was our travels around Prince William Sound that gave me another comparison: landscape versus seascape. The massive sound, the huge inlet, the bigness of the Gulf of Alaska made the mountains smaller. With all of this as a background, we must go to such places with a humble heart, a submissive spirit, and a thankful mind that God is great. For despite the constant changing nature of man, of society, and yes, even the Church, places like Prince William Sound speaks to us of the solidity of our Sovereign, the endurance of Emmanuel, and the longevity of the Lord.

CHAPTER EIGHTEEEN

## GALLERY LODGE AND CROOKED CREEK

As we meandered our way down the Kenai Peninsula, we were confronted with more high hills, which were really massive mountains. We had left the Sound behind when we turned off Route 3, which would have taken us to Seward to the one road heading directly down the peninsula on Route 1 that eventually ended at a place called Homer, 464 miles from Denali. We had traveled Route 3 all the way from Fairbanks for over 400 miles. The miles consisted of a narrow, tree-lined highway. It was the most densely forested area we had seen in our travels to date. With the ocean on both sides of the peninsula, the annual moisture must be more than other parts of Alaska creating a perfect environment for more trees to flourish. The more we drove the more like Maine it became. Our final destination for the day was a lodge on the Kasilof River, a place Scott had found while determining our resting places for the trip. He had found it online, and I must admit we thought we were going to a rustic, primitive cabin on a wilderness river far from civilization and civilians. How wrong we were!

After a ten-hour day on the road, we eventually found the off-road lodge on a dirt lane just outside the village of Kasilof. Two very friendly dogs with no masters in sight greeted us. Scott called the number he had been given and discovered the owner was at Bible study: a good sign! The lady said she would be back within fifteen minutes and that we were to make ourselves at home. As we wandered around, we discovered our rustic, primitive cabin in the wild was really a modern lodge consisting of a main house were the owners lived and a second two-story building where their guests stayed. The two large structures sat on a high cliff overlooking a very high-water Kasilof River. The cedar board siding on the building gave the building a wilderness appearance, but everything about Gallery Lodge was up-to-date and far from roughing-it. The best aspect of the lodge was the view. The 100-foot drop to the river below only added to the vista of tall, thin furs lining the river from all angles. You could make out a few homes on the opposite side of the river, but not enough to take away the wilderness feeling. Hedges of trees on the lodge side hid the neighbors so you did feel like you had the place to yourself. I knew immediately I was going to love our two-night stay at Gallery Lodge, but were we the only guests? Did we have the place to ourselves?

True to her promise, the lady of the lodge did return within fifteen minutes. She was pleasant and informative as she told of the history of Gallery Lodge. The Lodge was the former home of a Kasilof river guide. Her husband was a military kid raised in Alaska. Even after his family moved out of Alaska, he returned again and again as an adult to fish the Kasilof River with the former owner of the property as his guide. There came a time when the guide wanted to sell and the lady's husband, a pilot of heavy transport planes, bought the property. At first they were going to only use it as their home, but a few years before our arrival they decided to turn it into a lodge and the second building was built. The lady was an artist, and her artwork could be seen throughout the lodge. She actually had her studio in a room on the second floor of the lodge overlooking the Kasilof, the inspiration for most of her art she said.

By eight we had settled into our room on the first floor, had a little supper, and Scott and I were asking if there was a place to fish close by. The Kasilof was off limits to us because of its thick wooded shoreline; we would need a boat. Our appointment for fishing the Kenai River with a guide wasn't until the next day, so where to fish? There were still a couple of hours of sunlight left in our day, and after our experience on Montana Creek, we were looking for another creek to fish. Our host showed us a map and a place called Crooked Creek only about a ten-minute drive from the lodge. Coleen was fine with a shower, a good book, and the view. Quickly gathering our fishing equipment, Scott and I were soon back in the Tahoe looking for Crooked Creek and a run of pink, humpy salmon making their way up the stream.

Sure enough, within five miles of the lodge, we discovered the tributary of the Kasilof River. As we would discover on the Kenai, the peninsula had received plenty of rain over the preceding weeks and the waterways were all high, including Crooked Creek. Eventually, we found a place to fish just behind a State Recreation Area. When we arrived, there were a dozen anglers up and down the shore, but as we discovered on the Kasilof, the banks were thick with trees; the spots to fly fish were few and far between. Scott had lure fishing equipment, but had left it back to Fairbanks thinking that fly rods would be enough. On a normal trip they might have been, but with high water it was difficult. Everybody else was using heavy spinning gear with even heavier lures. I had taken a reel with a sinking line and some large salmon flies I had used on the Miramichi River in Canada during spring fishing when the water is also high and swift. I found an opening in the tree line up stream, and Scott went below me to a bend in the river where a group of fishermen were casing their bait.

Over the next two hours, Scott and I threw everything but the kitchen sink at the humpies in Crooked Creek. The salmon haunted us and teased us with a constant series of rises and swirls right in front of us. The men we were fishing with had much better success, especially a man using a big, bright, fluorescent, orange spoon. He caught three huge pinks while we were there and had already caught two before we arrived. Scott took a couple of pictures of me holding his catch little knowing that the next day on the Kenai I would land humpies as big. Eventually I joined Scott on the corner. Just before dark Scott hooked into one of the elusive pinks. He fought the beast for about ten minutes before the fish spit the hook. We never did see how large it was because the glacier feed creek was a dark gray color. We stayed until everybody left and until darkness engulfed Crooked Creek. We had no trophies to brag about, but we did have another evening of fishing memories to add to the list we had started up at the North Pole stream and pond, the places we fished in our first evening in Alaska.

Within the hour after our returning from Crooked Creek, I was in bed. It had been another wonderful day seeing the sights and fishing the streams of Alaska with my dear wife and beloved son. Just before I dropped off to sleep with visions of fishing the world-famous Kenai River the next morning, I took time to thank the Good Lord for His wonderful blessings. Many years ago I came across a philosophy of Paul written down in a letter to the Christians of Thessalonica: "In everything give thanks: for this is the will of God in Christ Jesus concerning you." (I Thessalonians 5:18) Whether catching fish like we did at Montana Creek, or not catching fish like we did at Crooked Creek, our God is to be praised. *Everything* includes successful days and not so successful days. The Psalmist told us: "This is the day which the Lord hath made; we will rejoice and be glad in it." (Psalms 118:24) The Psalmist and Paul were speaking of the same precept. On our fifth day in Alaska, I was rejoicing and filled with gladness that our day had been so blessed. Fish or no fish, seeing McKinley or not seeing McKinley, rustic lodge or modern lodge. All a blessing.

## Chapter Nineteen

## A Moose River Pink

August 18, 2014 was the only designated fishing day of our entire Alaskan itinerary, despite the fact we had made plans to fish as often as we could, until the Kenai River.

Scott and I had fished only when the opportunity presented itself, like at the two fishing holes in North Pole, my few minutes at the Savage River, and then at Montana Creek and Crooked Creek. But this day had been planned since an early spring fishing trip to the Kenai shortly after Scott had returned from his third overseas deployment: a gift to himself for having survived another military adventure in the unpredictable and dangerous world of the Middle East. Scott had called me immediately after finishing his first day on the Kenai River with an idea to book a day for us in August. After he told me of the huge rainbows he caught, I told him to pick the date and we would make our Alaskan plans around the day. Our entire trip from Fairbanks to the Kenai Peninsula had been organized around this fishing adventure. Our guide Jeremy Anderson had been hired and the payment paid (over $200 a piece), so as we left Galley Lodge for mile marker 110 on Route One in Sterling, Alaska I was excited for the privilege of casting my fly into one of the best known salmon and trout rivers in the whole, wide world. I was also anticipating landing my biggest rainbow trout, and my expectation for a memorable fishing day had no bounds; it was time!

It took 45-minutes to travel back up the peninsula from Kasilof to Sterling and the Izaak Walton Campground, the designated meeting place with our guide. There was a boat-landing site in Sterling where the Moose River and the Kenai River join. Our starting time was eight, but we had arrived at 7:15 A.M. So what do you do while you wait for your Kenai fishing guide? Answer: you go fishing! The minute we pulled into the parking lot we could see the salmon jumping in the twenty-yard-wide Moose River. Pink humpy salmon were everywhere, and I was determined to catch one even before we started our planned eight-hour trip on the Lower Kenai. This massive waterway is divided into two major sections: the Lower Kenai runs from Skilak Lake to Cook's Inlet of Prince William's Sound, while the Upper Kenai runs from Kenai Lake to Skilak Lake, the best known part of the river and the equally famous Russian River. The most famous place on the Kenai River is where the Russian River and the Kenai River meet. This is where some of the biggest King Salmon are caught. The record is 97-pounds 4-ounces! Our travels up the Kenai would take us ten miles past the Naptowne Rapids to a section of the river called the Kenai Keys. But first—a pink salmon!

As I worked my way down a steep bank to the junction of the Moose and Kenai, I spotted my first eagle of our Alaska trip, a good omen. I also saw the almost constant rises of the salmon working their way out of the Kenai and into the Moose. They had come into the Kenai watershed at the outlet to the Cook Inlet, but they were Moose River salmon not Kenai River salmon. I had watched Atlantic salmon do the same thing on the Miramichi River in Canada and the Penobscot River in Maine, and I knew what I needed to do. Finding a nice place to stand on the riverbank, I started casting a four-ought Mickey Finn into the slow-flowing waters of the river. My father-in-law Stacy Meister, who died in 1997, had made the fly in the 1990s and would have been so proud to think it would catch a salmon in Alaska. I was actually standing under the highway bridge that spanned the river along Route One. The weak current allowed my heavy fly to sink deep into the water. I knew, like most salmon returning to spawn, hunger was not their motivation for striking a fly; it was the irritation factor I was going for as I cast again and again and stripped my fly through the waters of the Moose hoping to entice a pink to strike. I knew I would have about half an hour at best before Jeremy would arrive with his boat and the other 'sports', what guides call the people they guide, fishing with Scott and me that morning. Slowly and deliberately I worked my way down the shore of the river covering every section of the waterway. The distance across the river was short enough so I could cast the width of the stream. With each cast I came close to the salmon of Moose River, but no hookups. I was just about ready to give up and head back to the landing when I felt a slight hug on my line.

Sure enough I was into my first Moose River pink and my very first Alaskan humpy. I shouted to Scott who had given up fishing a few minutes before and was keeping an eye on Jeremy's arrival. Soon he was by my side as I played the six-pound, 26-inch fish to the bank. Unlike the pinks I would catch in Valdez in a few days, these pinks were full of fight. They had just returned from the ocean and had not as yet exhausted themselves again the flow of the river. It was a lot of fun wrestling my first pink salmon to shore. I had now caught a chum and a pink salmon. My hope was for "silver" later that day. Scott and I had just enough time to take a few pictures with my latest Alaskan conquest when we saw Jeremy launching his boat into the Kenai just below us. My fishing on the Moose was over, but I wasn't disappointed because I was after bigger game. I wasn't upset to leave the Moose River because I knew that "the grass was greener" on the Kenai!

The lesson of the Moose River is one that I have experienced many times, both in my fishing life and in my spiritual life. Paul said it best in a verse he sent to the Christians in Ephesus: "Redeeming the time." (Ephesians 5:16) Most people waste more time than they realize. Most people waste time thinking they are waiting on time. I learned long ago that the time of waiting should be utilized. An example I often give is the amount of the Word of God that I have been able to read while waiting for a doctor's appointment, or any other appointment. That is why I always carry around the Word of God in the form of a pocket New Testament. Time is valuable, and the older I get the more I value time. I try to fill up time with profitable activities, so on that morning, my only day on the Kenai, as I waited for my Kenai guide to arrive; I practiced the precept of 'redeeming the time'. Before that morning I had never heard about the Moose River, but to this day I will never forget it because it was during a down-time, a waiting-time, seemingly no time, I took advantage of the time and landed my first humpy. How many opportunities have you missed? How many firsts have you lost? How many situations have you overlooked because you didn't redeem the time? The next time you find yourself waiting, why don't you look around for something else to do, something to read (like the Bible), or someone else to help. Don't let it be said that you failed to redeem (pay back) the time the Good Lord has given you with something worthwhile. We only have so much time in this world, and on my one day on the Kenai I wasn't going to waste 45-minutes of redeemable time when I could cast a fly into a river full of fish and just maybe hook one.

## Chapter Twenty

## Kenai Surprises

Scott and I quickly returned our fly rods to the Tahoe and worked our way back to the boat landing just as Jeremy got his big Kenai fishing boat afloat. For this trip, we would be fishing with Jeremy's equipment on the Kenai. Jeremy was the same guide that had guided Scott to his trophy-size rainbows (one was over 30 inches long and weighed in at over ten pounds) in the spring, so introductions by my son were in order. After officially meeting the Kenai guide and outfitter, we were introduced to two members of Jeremy family that were in Alaska visiting from the lower 48. Andy and Aden Miller were father and son, Jeremy's brother-in-law and nephew. As we settled into Jeremy's boat, I first noticed the motor at the stern of the watercraft. It was a three hundred horsepower Mercury! I had never been in a freshwater boat with such a huge power plant. I remember some of the salt-water boats I went deep-sea fishing off the coast of Maine, but those didn't have that kind of engines in them. Where we were located at the boat landing gave me no idea just how big the Kenai River really was. I would soon understand the reason Jeremy had such a massive outboard on the back of his fishing boat.

The wide, flat-bottomed, aluminum boat looked brand new. In the spring Scott had fished from a drift-boat that Jeremy controlled with oars, but after a wet summer the Kenai was running high and heavy, so Jeremy brought out the only watercraft that could tame the mighty waterway. There were four seats in the middle of the boat, two on each side, facing toward the stern of the boat. Jeremy's seat was in the back beside the massive motor. When Jeremy stood in front of the engine, he barely stood above it.

Granted, he was a small man by stature, yet the sight of the outdoor guide and the outboard motor made for an interesting picture. As we settled into our boat seats, Jeremy took a few minutes to share the #1 rule he had for his boat mates: never place the fly rods on the deck of the boat. We were fishing with thousand dollar rods and reels (Saga-10-footers with matching reels-without doubt the most expensive fishing equipment I have ever fished with), so we needed to be careful; they were his livelihood. Then Jeremy showed us the casting method needed to fish with 'artificial eggs'! Artificial eggs? It was then I realized my dream fly-fishing trip to the Kenai wouldn't even involve flies. When Scott fished there in the spring, he at least fished with flies imitating leaches. It seemed as if that time of the year the rainbow were following the migrating salmon up the river gorging themselves on the salmon eggs drifting down the stream, so fishing was primarily with egg imitations.

At eight o'clock, Jeremy started the Mercury, and we headed up river. His plan was to motor upstream for half an hour before we even started to drift fish. The ride up was eye opening. The weather was ideal; sunny skies with the odd cloud here and there. The wind was ideal: hardly a breeze at all, but we would, before the day was over, feel a few cool gusts. The water was far from ideal, however. It reminded me of spring fishing on the Miramichi River in New Brunswick, Canada after a quick warm up, snow thaw, and rain. The river was overflowing its banks everywhere, and the water was moving at a brisk pace. The river was also dirty, and the high water made it difficult to get the bait to where the fish were. The twists and turns of the river were also much like the Miramichi and in places the river was half of a mile wide. Thirty-nine miles from the mouth of the river we ran into Class IV water at Naptowne Rapids, but the Naptowne Rapids were child's play for Jeremy's Mercury. Once above the rapids, we came into a section of river where there were a series of bays. It was in the last one near the Kenai Keys that Jeremy slowed the motor and started to rig up his four fly rods. It was then the second surprise of the Kenai River trip hit me when I noticed that Jeremy was only putting on one egg per rod, a tiny pink artificial egg as big as the diameter of your little finger.

As Jeremy worked on rigging up the rods, he told us that we were ten miles upriver from Sterling and that our goal for the days was to drift back to Sterling and be done fishing by four in the afternoon. Jeremy was the only one that baited the hooks. He changed the imitation eggs, experimenting with color and size all day. Jeremy demonstrated how to cast the lines so that we wouldn't get tangled in our companions' lines. I found the method of casting quite difficult. I had never cast as much line before with a weight. The end of the line had a small shank hook with the artificial, light pink egg just above it. Then there was as much line as the depth, which was up to twelve feet, in the place we were fishing. There were three lead-shots that would take the egg to the bottom. Then just above the trilogy of shot was a florescent orange strike indicator. This would help us know when the fish hit because in the heavy water a strike might go unnoticed, but the pull of the fish would always take the indicator below the surface. You had to cast all the line from the strike indicator to the hook, so you had to use a looping cast, swinging the line below the boat before throwing up stream above the boat or out from the boat. You also had to do this in unison with the other three fishermen in an area less than eight feet square. Needless to say, there was a learning curve to this kind of fishing! The ideal was to get the weight, the line, the egg, and the hook far enough up stream so the drift would be uniform and steady, imitating a single salmon egg drifting downstream with the current. We were trying to deceive the rainbow and any other fish in the river into thinking that our artificial egg was just one of thousands floating in the river. This was why Jeremy tried so hard to duplicate the egg color and egg size in the river. I couldn't believe that it would work, and yet it did. Another surprise!

The youngest among us showed the proper cast and drift landing the first fish in the boat on the first drift. Aden was soon into a Dolly Varden Char. I found this description of a dolly in one of the brochures I picked up on the trip:

> "Bluish gray or silver background with light spots (usually smaller than its pupils). No spots on head or tail. Easily confused with Arctic Char, but Dolly Varden occur mainly in river (like the Kenai), have a more squared-off tail, a more elongated head (especially spawning males), and a wider tail base than Arctic Char. Pelvic and anal fins often have a white leading edge."

Our first few drifts below the Kenai Keys resulted in us catching a number of char. We missed as many as we landed, however, because we were still learning the casting and setting methods of this kind of fishing. I know I missed a number of fish because I didn't have my rod and line always in a place to set the hook when the strike indicator plunged below the surface of the stream; most fish give you but a split-second to set the hook and if you don't they will spit the hook!

It wasn't long into our morning before each of us was catching fish, mostly Dolly Varden Char, but these smaller fish (15-inches being the largest) were preparing the way for bigger fish to follow. Jeremy knew well the precept of ". . .practice. . ."! (Daniel 8:24) So in the first few hours of our Kenai adventure we practiced, and what came next was worth the practice, and that was no surprise!

## Chapter Twenty-One

## Deadhead Rainbows

The pattern for our attempts to entice big Kenai rainbows from their watery depth was simple. Jeremy would motor us upstream to a suitable place, cut the engine, and let the heavy current drift us over some ideal spots. After practicing and nearly perfecting our Kenai technique on the Dolly Varden Char of the Kenai Keys, we moved down river to some other spots where the rainbows were known to wait for drifting salmon eggs. These were areas near shore where the river worked its way through narrow channels. Jeremy seemed to know exactly where he wanted to place the boat for a drift through certain spots, and if we were successful on a particular drift, we would be sure to repeat the process. If we stopped catching fish, Jeremy would change the color or the size of the artificial egg, or we would simple move off to another spot. Actually, when we started the day, Jeremy had placed different size eggs and colored eggs on our individual lines. From a large box next to his seat, Jeremy had a collection of imitation salmon eggs that he had painted himself. He told us that some of the artificial eggs got nine coats of paint for them to look just right! As the day progressed, I began to understand just how scientifically Jeremy took his profession; he was student of his craft in every sense of the word. He was a serious observer of rainbow trout fishing and the Kenai was his classroom. Sure enough, when we started to catch fish on a certain color or certain size he would change the rest of us out with the same size and color, and it often worked. One of the reasons I have always understood the importance of a fishing guide is this local knowledge, of not only the river, but also the habits of the local fish population.

Some of my greatest catches have come about because of a professional guide. A man who knows a fishing hole like the back of his hand is worth any price you pay if you want a trophy. I still remember my first professional guide. I always considered my father-in-law and registered Maine guide Stacy Meister as my best guide because we fished together more than one hundred and sixty-three times. Vernon MacNaughty, an amazing Restigouche River salmon guide, guided me to the two biggest Atlantic salmon I have ever caught: a 46-inch, 37 pound beauty and a 40-inch, 22 pound Atlantic that pound for pound gave me the best fight by a fish I have ever had. It was an hour and a half struggle with that massive fish crossing and re-crossing the Restigouche River seven times. With each crossing, the salmon would jump full-length out of the river before I hauled it back across the nearly quarter-mile wide body of water. Though our hookups were few on the Restigouche, each was spectacular. My biggest salmon took me an hour and fifteen minutes to land. Another amazing guide was Irving Vickers, my Miramichi River guide for over a decade. I might not have caught the largest fish with him, I did caught more than a dozen fish over 36 inches with him, but numbers were never the question. I always like to tell people that in the first dozen years I fished for Atlantic salmon I caught just 22 of the impressive fish on the Penobscot River in Maine, but in my first three-days fishing with Irving Vickers on the Miramichi River, I landed 26. A local guide can make a world of difference when you are fishing a foreign fishing hole and on Scott's and my one-day on the Kenai River together in Alaska, I believe Jeremy Anderson made all the difference.

As the morning stretched into afternoon our fishing successes were steady. Nevertheless, despite Jeremy's instructions and demonstrations, we lost as many fish, if not more, than we landed. But we were landing enough to satisfy the most avid fisherman among us. Along with the Dolly Varden Char, we also caught some impressive Pink Salmon, as big if not bigger than the ones we saw caught on the Crooked River the night before. Before the day was through, we would land 19 dollies and 7 pinks, but the purpose of the trip was rainbows. I had fallen in love with rainbow trout fishing in Aroostook County where a member of the Calvary Baptist Church of Westfield had a private trout pond he allowed me to fish. I had not known Herschel Smith, the man who also had a lodge on the Restigouche River, very long before he introduced rainbow trout to his private trout pond. At first I didn't think I would be converted from my beloved brook trout, but within a few years I couldn't wait for spring to come so that I could fish the 'bows'. Scott had fished Smith Pond with me as a boy. So when Scott had his reintroduction to the rainbow trout that spring, I knew I also wanted to test my skills again on the most technically challenging species in the trout family. The Kenai River would give me that chance, but my skills were honed with a fly, not with an imitation salmon egg!

Shortly after lunch, Jeremy had gotten us down river to a favorite pool where a series of deadhead logs had jammed themselves into the riverbed about twenty yards off shore. The wooden obstruction created a narrow channel causing the river to rush through the gap between the deadheads and the bank. Our very first drift through the gap resulted in a good-size (20-inches plus) rainbow on Aden's line. Jeremy quickly put the same egg (10mm Peach Fuzz) on my line. Once we were through, Jeremy motored up and took us to the head of the channel again. Because of the speed of the water, one cast and one drift was all that was possible to properly fish the rainbow run. Getting the egg to the right place so that the right drift would occur was the key, and on the next drift I made the perfect cast. Within a second of the egg getting to the bottom of the run, I had on a nice rainbow, the biggest I had ever caught. The biggest rainbow I had caught until Alaska had been a 19-incher. When we finally netted it, I was thrilled as it tailed touched the 21-inch mark on the yard stick. Around Jeremy went again and sure enough on the very next drift I landed a 22-incher; I had just broken my own record. My first rainbow record had held out from 1986 to 2014, but my new rainbow record would only survive a few minutes.

Jeremy motored his big fishing boat for a fourth time into the narrow run that created my now favorite fishing hole on the Kenai. I named it Jeremy's Gap; all good fishing holes deserve a name! Once again all four eggs went into the river, but once again my inside indicator was the only one to disappear. I set the hook and soon realized that I was into the one fish I had come to the Kenai to catch. The weight of the river combined with heavy drifting boat quickly took us below the deadheads and near a quiet place just below the obstruction. It was a pleasant place to play out my biggest Kenai rainbow and the largest rainbow of my life. Compared to the huge salmon I have caught in my life, the rainbow proved to be small, but when Jeremy finally netted the rainbow I was certain it was the longest and heaviest rainbow I had ever landed. The bow wasn't close to Scott's 30-inch spring rainbow, but at 23 ½ inches and weighing nearly four pounds I was content. If I have learned anything through the teaching of Paul in relationship to fishing it is this concept from his letter to the Church at Philippi: "Not that I speak in respect of want: for I have learned, in whatsoever state (Alaska) I am, therewith to be content (in the size of your rainbow). I know both how to be abased (no fish at Crooked Creek), and I know how to abound (I ended the day with 13 fish landed including the 3 largest rainbows I have ever caught and the 2 largest pink salmon I ever landed): everywhere (Kenai River) and in all things (fishing) I am instructed both to be full." (Philippians 4:11-12). I came back from the Kenai very full.

## Chapter Twenty-Two

## Fried Spam And Grilled Cheese Sandwiches

As four o'clock rolled around, our one day on the Kenai River ended much too quickly, and we landed Jeremy's boat back at Sterling. As the official scorekeeper, I was asked to give the final tally. After my three back-to-back-to-back rainbows, the fishing slowed because of a decision we had made as a group. Jeremy asked if we wanted to spend the bulk of our afternoon fishing for big bows or fishing just to catch fish. We opted for big rainbows, but we never caught one. My last rainbow at Jeremy's Gap was the biggest we landed. A couple of times we thought we might have hooked into bigger rainbows, but we never landed them. We spent our times drifting through sections of the Lower Kenai where large, trophy-size rainbows had been caught before. We did hook into some huge pinks! Of course, each time we thought we were into that trophy 'bow', but it wasn't meant to be. I believe our numbers would have been larger if we would have focused on more pinks and Dolly Varden Char. Nevertheless, we boated 41 fish between us: 19 char, 15 rainbows, and 7 pinks. In the end I not only caught the biggest rainbow, but the most fish with thirteen, with Andy landing twelve, Scott boating eleven, Aden hauling in three. Even our guide managed to land two between running the motor and handling the boat.

By 4:45 P.M. Scott and I were back at Gallery Lodge with plenty of fish stories to tell Coleen and Bob, the owner of the lodge. I enjoyed the rest of the afternoon getting to know this Christian pilot and hearing his stories of how he came to buy the lodge and his passion for fishing the Kasilof River. He claimed the river was the best-kept secret on the Kenai Peninsula. With the fame of the Kenai, most visitors overlooked the Kasilof for the Kenai according to Bob. Bob had a drift boat he used to fish the seven miles from his lodge to the mouth of the bay when he was home after flying some heavy cargo to places halfway around the world. His tales of massive king salmon and multitudes of humpies, reds, chum, and silvers kept me entertained while the afternoon drifted into evening. I was so challenged that I got my fly rod together and walked down the trail to Bob's drift boat tied up below the bluff. I was determined to catch a fish, and sure enough the small bay in front of the lodge was filled with rolling, jumping, swirling pinks. But none of the humpies was interested in my flies or the lures I borrowed from Bob to throw at them. Eventually Scott joined me and tried his hand, but no takers. Coleen even came down to sit on the bank and watch our attempts, which proved fruitless and futile. I think sometimes when I come home from fishing with so many stories of my successful exploits catching fish that Coleen only humors me because more often than not when she is around I rarely catch anything!

For over an hour, Scott and I took turns because the overgrowth made it difficult to fish except from Bob's drift boat. Fishing was slow, but the conversation from shore was pleasant as we visited with our hosts and enjoyed the mild weather. The picturesque scenery and the sound of the Kasilof were tranquil. The constant action of the salmon was entertaining as well as we talked well into the evening on our last day on the peninsula. About eight Coleen asked if we were hungry, and we should have been because Scott and I had eaten very little all day. I am afraid my son has followed my example and that being fishing is much better than eating. I very rarely eat while I am fishing and would have preferred to fish from sunrise to sunset on the Kenai. One of the disadvantages with a guide is that they often just work an eight to four day. I found this to be the same on the Restigouche and the Miramichi. When Stacy and I would fish the Penobscot we would fish all day; yes, sunrise to sunset. My record for my longest days fishing happened on the Penobscot. We would often be on the river by four in the morning and not off the river until nine at night. My record is 17 ½ hours! But, on the evening of our last night on the Kasilof, Scott suggested a supper menu that has always made me think twice about fishing, especially if I was striking out: fried Spam and grilled cheese sandwiches!

As we returned to the lodge, Scott told his mother and me that fried Spam had been a favorite food in Afghanistan, comfort food he called it. I couldn't believe what my son was saying because Spam has become one of my favorite foods while fishing. I still remember the first time I got a taste for Spam sandwiches. Stacy and I were fishing the Chalifour River in Northern Quebec for northern pike and walleye. One noon we stopped for a shore lunch. I can still see Stacy take that famous shaped can with the key on the bottom out of his grub bag. Using the metal key to open it up, he placed the chopped pork on a dish he had brought along. Taking out his fishing knife from the pouch on his side, he proceeded to cut the block of meat up into thick slices. Once done, he placed the pieces of Spam, two per sandwich, on slices of white bread. Bread and Spam became our lunch for the day. I can already hear some laughing, but a good Spam sandwich is not only filling but it will stick to your bones. It reminds me of an article I once read in the *Reminisce Magazine*:

> "Nothing on your grocer's shelf is more familiar than Spam luncheon meat, in its blue and gold can with that handy key on the bottom. Since its introduction by George A. Hormel & Company in 1937, nearly 5,000,000,000 (that's billion) cans of Spam have been produced. In the United States today, this mixture of chopped pork shoulder, sugar, water, and salt is consumed at a rate of 3.8 cans per second! Such popularity has made Spam a lasting symbol of American culture. But Spam has prompted some people to poke fun at this famous food. In fact, as Spam's makers themselves are fond of saying, "Spam has become the Rodney Dangerfield of the food world!" Popular comedians take jabs at Spam and not with forks. Recently David Letterman suggested a gift of Spam-on-a Rope, for "people who get hungry in the shower!" Allied troops during World War II ate so much Spam that some world leaders credited it with helping to win the war."

It is interesting to me that between World War II and the Afghanistan War one of the common denominators has probably been Spam; my father ate the stuff in World War II and my son ate the stuff in the Afghanistan War. After an amazing day on the Kenai River, I couldn't think of a more fitting meal to celebrate our catches than fried Spam and grilled cheese sandwiches.

My dear wife and Scott's beloved mother isn't a big fan of Spam, but she is a big fan of her son. On that evening, she was happy to make a classic meal of fried Spam and grilled cheese sandwiches. Sitting at the table in the dining area of Gallery Lodge, Scott and I enjoyed our supper, a fitting reward for a long day's fishing without food. For those that are still questioning the meat of the meal remember these words by Paul to the young man Timothy rebuking those that would command others ". . .to abstain from meats, which God hath created to be received with thanksgiving of them which believe and know the truth, for every creature of God is good, and nothing to be refused, if it be received with thanksgiving: for it is sanctified by the Word of God and prayer." (I Timothy 4:3-5) I have come to believe that includes a grilled cheese sandwich with a side order of fried Spam!

## Chapter Twenty-Three

## Leaving The Kenai For King's Ranch

I was up at 8:30 A.M., sleeping in a bit after a day on the water, after a wonderful rest at Gallery Lodge. I awoke to a cloudless day, but a difficult day. I have always had a hard time leaving a lodge on a river, whether Vicker's Lodge on the Miramichi River or Grog Island Lodge on the Restigouche. Now I had another experience to add to my sad-leaving list, Gallery Lodge on the Kasilof.

By 9:45 A.M. we had said goodbye to our kind hosts and we were once again on the long road that led us back to the mainland across the Kenai Peninsula over Route One to the junction with Route Nine. It would be mid-afternoon before we arrived at our seventh day's destination. As with our journey into the Kenai, we followed the mighty river out through Sterling until Lake Skilak, the headwaters of the Kenai River, was in our rear view mirror. It was then the majestic mountain landscape returned. On the day of our departure the rugged crests of the hills were totally exposed: no clouds, no fog, and no mist to block our view. The sun was revealing everything: the regal slopes, the high tundra, the stately trees, and, yes, that was an eagle we saw over a high, alpine meadow pond looking for its morning breakfast of fresh salmon. Again I was excited to travel through the mountain passes that took us from the coast of Cook's Inlet to the interior of the Kenai with it rough and rugged hills and vales. Again the phrases of the Psalmist kept whispering in my ears: ". . .. flee as a bird (like the ravens we saw) to your mountain. . .." (Psalms 11:1) ". . ..I know all the fowls (like the eagle we saw) of the mountains. . .." (Psalms 50:11) ". . ..they go up by (as we did on the Kenai) the mountains. . .." (Psalms 104:8) ". . ..touch the mountains. . .." (Psalms 144:5) "Praise the Lord from the earth. . ..mountains and all hills. . .." (Psalms 148:7, 9) The mountains and hills were certainly praising and glorifying the Lord the day we left the Kenai Peninsula!

It had been a busy two days on the Kenai Peninsula, yet I felt refreshed. We were nearing a week since we left Maine, yet I felt renewed. We had just passed the 1000th mile marker of our Alaska adventure, and yet I felt rejuvenated. It couldn't have just been the fishing or the sound of the Kasilof waters flowing by the lodge, or the companionship. I began to sense that it was the terrain, the topography, and the territory where we were and had traveled through. It was the high hills and the majestic mountains. I am not a mountain man by any stretch of the imagination, but it seems each time I have ventured into the high country I have drawn an enormous energy from the landscape, and as this day was unfolding and Scott drove on, I felt a deep peace of soul, a great surge of well-being in my spirit, and a sweet satisfaction sweeping over my entire body. The templed hills, the thick forests, the array of wildlife, the dazzling diversity of the fall colors, the changing of the season before us, the interaction of the sun off the mountains, and the wide vistas and the deeps views from the valleys we drove through that morning and into the afternoon only added to my feeling of serenity and solitude.

It was as if we were in the middle of a *National Geographic* special. The lavish displays around every corner were breathtaking and awe-inspiring. I can see why artists, photographers, writers, and ordinary men love to visit Alaska. It is the unspoiled wilderness stamped MADE BY GOD that stirs the heart into song and prose and rhyme. And if the mountain scenery wasn't enough, it was the re-sighting of the massive Cook's Inlet that turned this journey into a melodic cruise through water and wilderness. Coming out of the hills, we traveled awhile through a series of meadows. The trees were smaller than the ones we saw deep in the Kenai Peninsula, and, yes, the glaciers were back and even more brilliant in the bright sunlight of a mid-August noon. We were also coming back into civilization. For it was in these moments, the world of man is hushed and the sweet song of 'the still small voice of God' can be heard in the pristine solitude of the Turnagain Arm. This is the section of coastline we had traveled through on our trip to the Kenai. It is an arm of the Cook's Inlet that Route One must go around to get back to Anchorage. A town called Portage is at the head of the arm and a few miles up the road is another small hamlet called Girdwood, where we gassed up on our way into the Kenai. Then from Girdwood to Anchorage is a long stretch of coastal highway that causes this author to search for words enough, or sentences descriptive enough, to tell you of what he saw, let alone experienced!

The great waterway that flanked us in on the right was only matched by the high hills that penned us in on the left. Here the narrow, man-made road was the only way through this region, except by the flyer or the boater.

I was amazed with the harmony the builders of the road had placed the highway against the cliffs on the left and the sea on the right. It appeared that it had always been that way, but we know this wasn't the case. Yet in the achievement of man, the overriding majesty of what God created causes one to question whether or not one should travel through such a place. Man can make roads but only God can make a sea, a glacier, a mountain, a cliff and there on that cliff was a family of Dall sheep. Scott spotted them first because he was paying attention to the cars stopping beside the road. I was so caught up in the vista I failed to see the family of sheep on a high ridge overshadowing the highway. And there on the very edge of the cliff was the patriarch sunning himself on a narrow ledge over a 100 feet up from the roadbed. Scott quickly turned off the road, so that we could walk back with others to see the site of our latest Alaskan animal discovery. Their white coats stood out in stark contrast to the dull browns of autumn now overtaking the hills south of Anchorage. High above the huge ram were two smaller sheep walking along a ridgeline as if they were at sea level, but for them it was solid ground. As for me, you wouldn't ever catch me walking where they were strolling.

It was another one of those amazing wilderness detours, like so many we had experienced in Alaska already. Long before the locals (the sheep, not the photographers) left, we were back on the road to find King Ranch. As Phillip Keller once wrote in his beautiful, coffee-table book *Mountain Splendor*—

> "The intense excitement and deep delight of watching this take place are part of the joy in mountain interludes. I have hiked across mountain meadows and alpine flower fields, which in every truth took my breath away with their beauty. To see thousands of acres of upland slopes spangled with drifts of wild flowers, not one of which was planted by man's hand is a moving experience. It is a solemn reminder of the initial reaction God had when He looked upon His original creation '. . .and saw that it was good.' (Genesis 1:12)"

To which I can only add a hearty Amen! Such were my observations on the day we left the Kenai River for King's Ranch.

## Chapter Twenty-Four

## Combat Fishing and The Bass Pro Shop

Just before we spotted the Dall sheep on the rocky outcropping overlooking Cook's Inlet, we had stopped for a break in a public parking area just south of Anchorage. I had provoked the detour to King Ranch in hopes of witnessing one of the most amazing forms of fishing known to mankind: combat fishing. We had noticed a small stream under a highway bridge that flowed into the inlet. As we drove by, we could see a number of people along the shore of the stream with spinning rods in hand. Scott turned off Route One just north of the bridge to investigate. We immediately realized this was the parking area of a small park for those that fished this particular stream, especially when the salmon were running. There seemed to be a few walking trails in the area as well. Already in the parking area were a number of campers and family cars with their trunks opened and the fishing rods out. I had heard about the massive salmon runs in Alaska and the huge numbers of people that try to fish the best spots at the same time, but I had never seen it up close and personal, only on the television fishing channel. My only experience with this kind of fishing was on the banks of the Penobscot River in Maine when the Atlantic salmon were running in great numbers during the late 1970s and the 1980s. There were times when you had to wait a couple of hours to cast your fly, fly fishing only, into some of the best pools. Even then, you would be fishing with a fly fisherman in front of you and one behind you and sometimes one on your side casting his fly from a boat. But in Alaska, they take this kind of fishing to the ultimate extreme. Hence, combat fishing!

The sun was warm and pleasant as we took a stroll down the paved walkway to the stream. A few people were already heading to the outlet with their rods in hand, so we were hopeful to see some action. We knew we didn't have time to fish ourselves, but to watch others fight over a good spot, or to even see a salmon caught would have been nice. The ten-minute, downhill walk back alongside the highway we had already traveled twice, eventually brought us to a walking bridge over a massive gully, high above the brook. It was barely a brook. The small stream that came out of a forest valley between two very high hills was hardly twenty feet across. I immediately realized it was low tide and the stream itself was only yielding a trickle of water. The banks of the brook were muddy and slippery, and you could easily see it was only as the tide came in that any volume of water would collect in the ravine. It was this incoming tide that people were waiting for. As we took a few pictures, a man with a couple of huge spinning rods joined us on the bridge with what appeared to be a couple of his kids. We struck up a conversation and learned that what we were looking at was Bird Creek. Indeed the salmon were running, but it would be a few more hours before the tide would switch; he had come on high tide the day before and had landed seven salmon, the largest being 17 pounds. He described the shoulder-to-shoulder fishing and the countless entanglements with his neighbor. He spoke of the bad tempers and crazy people, and that at the peak of the run, there were people lined up on both shores from the bay to where the creek came out of the woods. As the tide came in so did the salmon, but there were only a few places really to fish as the water drove the fishermen back up the granite ledges of the ravine the creek ran through. You had to know the perfect spot. That is why some people were early.

There was even a billboard near an observation platform that explained the rules of combat fishing, but after talking to the local fisherman, I knew that the only rule in combat fishing was there were no rules. He claimed it was fun, but I wasn't going to wait around for the first round or the invasion of a mass of humanity with rods as rifles. Besides, Scott and I had left the spinning rods in Fairbanks. Fly fishing would have been impossible, so we took a few more pictures and slowly made our way back up the hill to the Tahoe and headed north up Route One to Anchorage. We were getting hungry after our long morning traveling out of the Kenai Peninsula, and Scott wanted to show us the OutPost, the Bass Pro Shop in Anchorage. We still had a couple more hours driving ahead before we made it to our final destination of the day, King Ranch in Chickaloon on the Glenn Highway. My final observation on the practice of combat fishing is how mankind has made combat a practice in most areas of his life.

By 12:45 P.M., we entered the city limits of Anchorage, and by one o'clock we were walking through the massive doors of the OutPost. How can I adequately describe to you what we found in this brand name sporting goods store? It seemed on every wall and post were mounted images of every fish in the Alaska fishery in each and every phase these fish go through in their spawning migrations. Yes, hundreds of fish mounts, the most I had ever seen in one place, and each crafted to the size of a trophy. All the salmon species were there: Chinook (king), Coho (silver), Sockeye (red), Chum (dog), and Pink (humpy). All the trout species were there: Steelhead, Rainbow, Cutthroat, Lake Dolly Varden, and Arctic Char. Then there were the other species: Halibut, Arctic Grayling, Northern Pile, Inconnu (sheep fish), and Burbot. And if the fish mounts weren't impressive enough, there were the animal mounts set in what appeared to be their natural habitat. We had seen wildlife in Denali, but the creators of the OutPost brought the outdoor wildlife of Alaska indoors. When you entered the massive store, your eyes were immediately drawn to the center aisle. The ceiling was a bright, cloud-dotted sky. As your eyes came downward, you saw your first Dall sheep standing high on a rocky ledge. Then along the sides, there was depicted a herd of caribou as if on migration. The images were so real you felt you were experiencing animal sightings in the wild. Throughout the store there were groupings of grizzly bear, black bear, and standing beside the fish tank (yes, there were real fish in the store as well) was the biggest polar bear mount I have ever seen. I took a picture of my wife standing in front, and Coleen was barely half its height. Wolf chasing rabbits and grizzly bears stocking moose were some of the other masterful wilderness scenes on display. Then there were the incredible mounts of Bison and Bull Moose and King Crab! Wow, is the only word I can think off besides "awesome"! Yet in this manmade world of creation's creatures, a thought fell on my heart.

How has man gotten so good at recreating the natural world? How has artificial become so deceptive? I will be honest. The imitation looked better than the original. I have been fooled before with the artificial flower versus the real flower, but the creators of the OutPost took me to a new level in their art. I stood in awe at the life-like images they had created and the artificial world that seemed so real. I know that Hollywood can do it on a screen, but these master artists did it in a store! So how? Paul tells us that the master of duplication and imitation is the Devil himself: "And no marvel; for Satan himself is transformed into an angel of light. Therefore it is no great thing if his ministers also be transformed as the ministers of righteousness. . .." (II Corinthians 11:14-15) The mounts in the OutPost were impressive, but they were all fakes, frauds, and fantasy. I wandered through that museum of mounts but left thinking I had already seen the genuine, the real in Denali and Kenai. How careful we need to be lest we are deceived on more important matters than mounts, like doctrine and ministers and righteousness.

# Chapter Twenty-Five

# King Ranch

We left Anchorage after spending $81 to fill up the Tahoe and $39 at Wendy's to fill up our stomachs; nobody said Alaska was cheap! Our travels took us north of Anchorage (a city) along Route One through Eagle River (a hamlet) and Eklutna (a village) until we came to Palmer (a town). At Palmer we came to the junction of Route Three (to Fairbanks) and Route One (to Glennallen) and the Glenn Highway. We took the right to Sutton and Chickaloon and hopefully King Ranch, which was 81 miles from Anchorage. Unlike most places in the lower 48, Alaska seems to have only one way to get anywhere and King Ranch was no exception. Our only fear is that we might pass it by.

Our quest to find King Ranch took us on a two-hour trek into another section of wilderness similar to what we drove through from Fairbanks to Anchorage. The trees were smaller than the Kenai, but the valley and hills were exactly like the Kenai, especially as we started to travel along the banks of the Matanuska River. This grayish waterway originated from one of the greatest glaciers in Alaska and, in fact, the world. It was a sight we would get to experience up close and personal the next day. Once again we were engulfed by the sheer size and powerful vista as we wound our way through the narrow roadway carved out of the hillside that was the Talkeetna Mountain Range. There was no easy way through this section of central Alaska, but the engineers managed to build a safe, slow road through Sutton and then Chickaloon and Glennallen far beyond. The afternoon of our exploration to find King Ranch was bright and sunny, so every curve and corner revealed another picture-perfect landscape. Sometimes we were low in a dip and close to the Matanuska while at other times we were high on a bluff and the river was blocked by a thick stand of trees. We felt like we were driving through a tunnel at times, and then the highway opened up so we could see for miles up the riverbed. As with the other highways we had already traveled in Alaska, the Glenn Highway was another momentary excursion into a mountainous dominion dominated by granite hills and a glacier river.

Knowing the mile marker near the lane that lead to King Ranch, Coleen and I kept our eyes on the few, passing signs as Scott kept his eyes on the road. The sudden twists and turns required your full attention, as we would soon discover when we arrived at the ranch. Then, after nearly seven hours on the road from Gallery Lodge to King Ranch, Coleen cried out, "There it is!" Sure enough, a sign announcing the road to the ranch. What I thought would be more miles was less than a mile. I had known Dwayne and Caroline King for over twenty years and had imagined many times how it would be to visit them in Alaska, seeing where they lived and what it looked like. I had seen a few photos, but as we all know what we imagine is nothing like the real thing. So it was as Scott turned off the Glenn Highway onto King Lane. A dirt road, that was typical, but within two turns there was the ranch. Instead of miles along a fire lane, over a creek or two, and washouts and difficult terrain, the path into King Ranch was short and smooth. We drove into a cleared area with a massive hangar on our left and a dining-hall lodge on our right. In front of us was an airstrip lined with old aircraft. On the other side of the airfield, there was a view of seven mountain peaks, the Chugach Mountain Range, all taller than the tallest mountain in Maine.

There to greet us in his happy-go-lucky manner was Dwayne King. A crushing bear hug embraced me, an almost to the ground frolicking from this old friend. Despite being in his seventies, Dwayne King has always had a youthful countenance and an infectious demeanor. He is a guy you like immediately. Over the half dozen times Dwayne had visited the Emmanuel Baptist Church since I became pastor, our talks and interactions have resulted in a mutual appreciation for each other and our ministries. Despite the decade between our ages, we had both been in the service of the Lord for nearly half a century. We are kindred spirits in every sense of the meaning of that phrase. His first words to us were how our travels had been and how we found the road from Sutton. It was then Dwayne went into one of his typical stories of how just that spring he had traveled from Palmer and fell asleep at the wheel. When he woke up, he was at the bottom of one of those ravines we had passed by. Unhurt, a major miracle in my book, Dwayne walked away without a scratch. You might think this amazing, but if you know Dwayne King that is typical for him. One might say even normal!

After his hair-raising story of surviving a Glenn Highway accident, Dwayne started to show us around the grounds. After a lifetime of ministering with the mission organization of SIM in Alaska and Russia, Dwayne had always dreamed of developing a program to train Christian pilots to reach the most difficult regions of the world with the Gospel through flight. In 1999, Dwayne's son David, an Alaskan helicopter pilot, began clearing land in Chickaloon to establish what would become known as King Ranch Airport, a place where David's planes and helicopters could fly people into the back corners and bush areas were only a plane or helicopter could go. Over the years that business had grown to include two airports and eight helicopters. David invited his father to join him, and so King Ranch Airport also became the home for Kingdom Air Corp, Dwayne's retirement ministry. Upon his retirement from SIM, Dwayne now gives full time to the training of missionary pilots in mountain flying and bush operations and proper maintenance of planes. For fifteen years, the program had grown in numbers of trainees; twenty-five in the summer we were there, and the ranch had also grown in the number of planes, over a dozen now, and facilities. Besides Dwayne and Caroline's home at the end of the runway, David had his home and a large hangar for his helicopter. There is the mission hanger, the dining hall, five guest cottages, a trailer park for those that visit with a camper, a saw mill, and a new (completed after we left) firehouse and conference room.

As we walked the grounds, all I could think about was the use of this pristine place for the service of the Lord. Granted, there was a business there, but the primary business was using the tools of flying for spreading the Gospel of Jesus Christ. Kingdom Air Corps' purpose statement reads like this: "To train up people who will carry the good news of the Gospel to places that are difficult to reach; to prepare pilots and mechanics to fly in remote areas, and to work and develop relationships in order to bring the message of salvation, and to bring vision and inspiration to new missionary pilots." These words remind me of Paul's challenge to the Ephesian Christians: "I . . .beseech you that ye walk worthy of the VOCATION wherewith ye are called." (Ephesians 4:1) We forget that our Christians lives have a vocation connected with it: to some doctoring, nursing, teaching, construction, pastoring, and, yes, flying. But how many see their vocation as a way of sharing the Good News of Jesus Christ? Dwayne has always been an example of the individual that had a passion. Dwayne learned to fly in Ellsworth, Maine, in the early 1960s while attending the church I am currently pastoring. As a matter of fact, it was a group of men from my church that first paid for Dwayne's original flying lessons and bought him his first plane. Dwayne has used that passion to proclaim the Gospel. So what is your vocation? What is your passion?

## Chapter Twenty-Six

## A Kansas Wheat Farmer and a German Cook

As Dwayne took us on the guided tour of King Ranch, he also introduced us to some of the individuals scattered around the complex.

At the heart of the property was the 1600-foot airstrip totally cut out of virgin territory in the late 1990s and early 2000s. I remembered seeing an aerial photograph in one of Kingdom Air Corps' brochures of the ranch site, but now that I was walking the site I could really see how much labor it took to cut the airstrip and the surrounding fields out of the forest that once stood on the bluff overlooking the Matanuska River with the Chugach Mountains to the south and the Talkeetna Mountains to the north. The cleared land shaped like a lower case "r" was still surrounded by forestland, but with the opening of the airfield, one had an open view both east and west. Most of the buildings on the property were made of native logs, while all the wood had been harvested on site and cut on site. I was introduced to a man who had for many summers come to Alaska and King Ranch just to help Dwayne on the various building projects. He was a master cabinetmaker. When I met him, he was manufacturing a set of cabinets for the newest guest cabin that had been built that summer. His wife was varnishing the porch on that cabin when we meet her, and their story became a continual theme of our tour.

Our tour took us to the plane hangar were three airplane mechanics were trying to work out a problem in the gas tanks of the only twin-engine plane on site. I began to realize that Dwayne had a big staff at Kingdom Air Corps, but all of them were retired believers, giving their summers to the work of the ministry. It was then one of the youngest men, a local from the Russian community in the area, we had met came to Dwayne as he was explaining how one of the deacons of Emmanuel Baptist Church, Bud Clark, had spent two summers at the ranch trying to get the grass to grow on the airstrip. Bud was a gardener by profession turned firefighter in middle age, but used his talents to help make the property of King Ranch look more appealing. Besides sowing grass, Bud planted flowers, made flowerbeds all over the property, and planted a few flowering shrubs and bushes here and there. I began to see how Dwayne was using anyone with any kind of talent to help support the work. Back to the young pilot. It seems he had to make a practice flight for his certification, so very-Dwayne-like-quickly-distracted, our tour guide was off to do his instructing and we were left waiting.

It was fun watching the preliminaries of flight as the young man gassed up the plane and with the help of a few of his friends push the two-seater, orange Piper out of line and onto the airfield. Fifteen minutes after Dwayne left us, he was in the backseat of the aircraft as the young pilot taxied to the east end of the field and then took off at the west end of the strip. As we watched the small plane grow smaller against the height and hills of the Chugach Mountains, we struck up a conversation with the young pilot's two friends. It was then we discovered that the two young men standing beside us watching the aircraft floating over the Matanuska River couldn't speak English; they too were from Russia. An interesting aspect of Kingdom Air Corps was its Russian connections. When the Iron Curtain came down in the late 1980s, Dwayne King was the second American pilot to fly into Siberia. As Dwayne tells the story, he had for years, remember he had been flying in Alaska since the late 1960s, flown along the border between Russia and Alaska in the middle of the Bering Straits praying someday he might be able to take the Gospel into Siberia. So if you want to know one of the reasons why the Iron Curtain came down, it was because of the prayers of an Alaskan missionary bush pilot! Over the years Dwayne had gone back and forth opening up contacts in Russia, and now he is training Russian Christians to take the Gospel into the remote villages of Siberia, just like he took the Gospel into the remote villages of Alaska. We couldn't share much with the Russians because their translator was in the plane with Dwayne, so we moved on and explored a few more areas of the ranch on our own, including the King ranch junkyard.

Behind the hangar was a big area that would have made the best hoarder happy. Besides the junk in the open, there was a long narrow building full of stuff, anything you might need to repair a plane including two complete planes in pieces. Dwayne gets donations from all over the states, and if he thinks they can be used, they are shipped to King Ranch. Instead of the car graveyards we see in the lower-48, this is a plane graveyard, but I was told every piece of junk was a treasure to Dwayne. It was when we came out of the yard that we had our first, and certainly not our last, encounter with the wildlife of King Ranch—rabbits. Two of the tamest, wild rabbits I have ever encountered were eating grass under one of the parked planes. Dwayne told us they had been eating Bud's grass ever since it came up, and each summer they returned and had become domesticated, ranch pets. The rabbits held our attention until we heard a bell ringing. Beside the dining hall stood a tall post with an old-fashioned iron bell on the top and under that bell was a tall, thin man pulling the rope attached to the handle of the bell. Walking towards him, we were greeted warmly by a German accent. The cook of the campus was calling people to supper, and yes, he was another volunteer. From all over the area, we watched as groups of one and two and three people flocked to the log-cabin hall. I didn't realize just how many people were at King Ranch until that first call to supper. At the same time, Dwayne and his student made a smooth landing on the airstrip and soon joined us for supper.

After a prayer to bless the food, we all dug into moose stew with rice. My dear wife reluctantly ate some of the moose stew; she is not a fan of wild meat. For me the most amazing aspect of that first meal at King Ranch was not the menu, but the men and women gathered around the tables. I soon meet people from all over the lower 48; people whose sole purpose for being there was not to tour Alaska, as my wife, son, and I were doing, but to give their time and talents to the furtherance of the Gospel through Kingdom Air Corps. I was impressed with the wheat farmer and his wife from Kansas, who had made the pilgrimage to King Ranch an annual affair. But they had never flown to Alaska, but each year brought a tractor-trailer loaded down with supplies for the ranch. As soon as the wheat was planted, they were on the road for Chickaloon. As I heard story after story, the tale was basically the same: all volunteers there to cook, to build, to fix, to clean, and to paint. One volunteer who impressed me was a retired preacher who came to the ranch just to paint the newest building, the firehouse. Why a firehouse, you might ask? There are numerous forest fires in the summer, one while we were at the ranch, and the nearest fire station is miles away. Dwayne felt it wise to create his own firehouse. The more people I meet, the more I thought of the words of a favorite old church hymn:

> "A call for loyal soldiers comes to one and all; Soldiers for the conflict will you heed the call? Will you answer quickly, with a ready cheer; will you be enlisted as a volunteer? A volunteer for Jesus, a

soldier true! Others have enlisted, why not you? Jesus is the Captain, we will never fear; will you be enlisted as a volunteer?"

Isaiah overheard the Lord ask, "Whom shall I send, and who will go for us?" (Isaiah 6:8) To which the volunteer Isaiah replied, "Here am I send me!" I met the ones sent to Alaska as I toured King Ranch and Kingdom Air Corps.

## Chapter Twenty-Seven

## Mother Moose And Her Baby

AFTER A SUPPER OF moose stew in the Kingdom Air Corps dining hall, Scott and I went exploring while Coleen returned to the King's residence with Dwayne's wife, Caroline. We were going to stay with the Kings in their home at the end of the runway for the next two nights. As Caroline and Coleen got reacquainted, Scott and I got acquainted with some other residents of the ranch.

As Scott and I left the log cabin dining hall, we watched as the staff of Kingdom Air Corps scattered in all directions, back to their appointed tasks. The sun would not set for another three hours, so there was plenty of daylight to work for a few hours. The mechanics went back to the hangar. That twin-engine aircraft was still giving them fits over leaking fuel tanks; the carpenters and painters went back to the new fire station building to put on more siding and to slap some more paint on the eaves; Dwayne went back to the airplanes along the side of the runway for another lesson with one of the trainees from Russia; the cabinetmaker and his wife returned to the woodshop by the sawmill and the small cabin by the trailer park. Scott and I headed back up the camp road to the highway looking for wildlife. Dwayne had told us during supper that the rabbits we saw before dinner were not the only creatures hanging around that summer.

I told Scott to get his camera from Tahoe just in case, and sure enough, we hadn't walked a hundred yards when I looked up a narrow tote road leading into the forest just behind the King's junkyard. Scott was a few steps behind me when I turned. Less than seventy-five feet away was a medium-size female moose grazing on the tender grass growing along the lane. Because of her size, I was focused on her and failed to see just in front of her and to my left her calf. Scott spotted the baby in his lens; its camouflage being its dark coat in the darkening shade of the canopy of trees that stretched over the tote road. Using a series of hand-signs, Scott was able to get my attention away from the mother moose onto the mini-moose. The pair seemed to be unaffected by our presence. I was even able to take a few steps into the lane and walk within forty feet of the calf and fifty feet from the mother. Moving very slowly, one deliberate step after another and waiting until their heads were down, I shortened the distance between us. Only one other time had I been able to get that close to a mother moose and her baby.

A number of years before my Alaskan trip, I was fishing with my good friend Mike Hangge in a narrow trout stream called Malcolm Branch Brook. The creek was deep enough to fish it from a canoe. More often than not we usually encountered a moose in our travels up the stream and, on this particular morning, we found a female moose standing in one of our favorite trout holes. The stream itself narrowed to just the width of the canoe leading into the wider pool, so slowly, ever so slowly, Mike paddled us to within a hundred feet of the feeding moose. Like the Alaskan moose, this moose acted as if we were not even there. Our movements were limited, and we spoke in whispers as we watched the moose's head drop into the water for another tasty mouthful of stream-bottom grasses. We were about ready to back our way out of the compromising situation. If the moose had decided to charge or walk at us, we literally had no place to maneuver or go. Mike was in the stern of his twelve-foot Old Town canoe, and I was in the bow. When Mike touched my shoulder, I turned to see what he wanted when I came face to face with an infant moose. I was less than four feet away. It was a newborn calf tucked in the alders and bushes by the stream. The baby still had it light tan coloring, and the tiny moose stood up, thinking it was time to get back to mother. It was the smallest moose I had ever seen. We suspected the moose had placed the baby in the spot for protection while she ate out in the open. Both Mike and I knew we were really in a dangerous circumstance now that we knew we were between a moose and her baby. There is no worst place to be in the wild.

The baby moose stumbled its way along the bank of the brook as Mike quietly backed us out of the dilemma. While I kept one eye on the mother to note any aggressive changes in her behavior, I kept my other eye on the baby. I could tell the way it was struggling to move through the thick underbrush it had only been walking a short time, another sign of just how newborn it was. Mike had even managed to snap a few photographs of the toddler before he started our retreat. It was one of those glorious times with wildlife in a wilderness area that will stay with you for the rest of your life; much like the evening in Alaska when Scott and I found ourselves joining a mother moose and her baby during their supper. The only difference between those two events was the baby moose was months older, and we had our feet under us with a broad way of escape if things turned nasty. In both situations, the mother moose and the baby moose were more interested in each other and dinner than us. Scott and I watched the pair for a good twenty minutes before our venturing into their domain was too much, and they both slipped into the thicker woods behind them. They were there and then they were gone, like a shadow, a mist in the forest, but we have the pictures to prove it really happened!

Our walk back to the King's home was the conversation of two men enriched in body and soul as they returned from a great adventure. Such encounters are beyond the bounds of the human spirit to measure and comprehend at the time. There is no scale to measure such events in the weight of delight they bring. They are the essence of a shared experience between two people, in this case a father and son, and the enrichment they bring to a relationship. They cannot be gauged by anything less than the God-given standard of "This is the Lord's doing" (like meeting a mother moose and her baby in the woods outside Kingdom Air Corps in Chickaloon, Alaska); it is marvelous in our eyes. "This is the day (event) which the Lord hath made (allowed); we will rejoice and be glad in it!" (Psalm 118:23-24) So it is that in the natural presence of such pristine animals, we will quietly bow our hearts and utter in thankful sincerity and grateful simplicity: "Thank you, Heavenly Father, for such an experience to share with my son (father)!"

By 7:45 P.M., Scott and I had returned to the King's house overlooking the Matanuska River. We were not as close to the Matanuska as we were to the Kasilof at Gallery Lodge, but the view was breathtaking just the same. I spent the rest of our seventh day in Alaska on the King's back deck reading an old history book on Alexander the Great and realizing that our Alaskan adventure was half over. By dusk Dwayne was back from his flight lesson and continued telling his amazing missionary tales of his experience in Alaska and in Siberia. We eat cold ice cream around a warm fire. When the sun sets in Alaska, even in August, it gets cold. We dreamed of tomorrow because two events would classify it as one of the best days of our trip. The first was a four-wheeler ride to the Matanuska River. One of the desires on Coleen's wish list for Alaska was to four-wheel, her most favorite outdoors activity. The second was an airplane ride over the mighty Matanuska Glacier.

## Chapter Twenty-Eight

## Devotions At Kingdom Air Corps

Our first night at Kingdom Air Corps was filled with wonderful stories by our host and hostess and a wondrous rest in their guest bedroom. Our week on the road was beginning to take its toll on my traveling companions and a good night's sleep was just what the doctor ordered. While Scott and Coleen slept-in, I was up early to do something that for me is far better than an extra few hours' sleep: an opportunity to share the Word of God.

Dwayne had asked me the night before to give a few spiritual thoughts to his staff and him during their daily devotional time after breakfast and before another busy day at Kingdom Air. I was hoping for such an opportunity, so I brought along a challenge I had been saving for just such a situation. By 6:30 A.M., I was walking the short distance from the King's house to the dining hall in anticipation of my one chance to preach in Alaska. Over my nearly fifty years of preaching, I have been granted unique occasions, new situation to share God's Holy Word. Those occasions have included preaching in two Canadian provinces (Quebec and New Brunswick), five states (Maine, New Hampshire, South Carolina, Georgia, and Alaska), and four countries (Australia (two provinces-Western Australia and New South Wales), India (five states in India—Kerala, Orissa, Andrah Pardesh, Tamil Nadu, and Punjab), Canada, and America. I have preached in wilderness camps: both undercover and out-of-doors, straw-thatched roof churches in India, but this would be my first, and hopefully not my last Alaskan message. I had tucked a few messages in my traveling Bible before I left Maine praying I would be able to use them. On the morning of August 20, 2014, my prayer was answered as I pulled a sermon titled "God Puts You In The Way" from my Bible and prepared to share.

Before any message I like to get alone and work over the notes I have compiled for a certain message in my mind. That morning on King Ranch was no exception to this lifetime practice, since my first sermon in 1966. I had gotten up a bit early so I could take a walk around the ranch and pray and meditate on what I wanted to share with the staff at Kingdom Air Corps. The sun was already up and the cool dawn air was warming as I made my way along the runway south of the dining hall. I noticed immediately I wasn't the only one up. There beside the helicopter hangar were three men. I decided to stop my meditation for a few minutes and see what was going on. The first man I said hello to was David King, Dwayne's son, the owner of King Ranch Airport and the pilot. I could see I wouldn't get much information out of him because he seemed busy getting the helicopter for flight, and I could also see he was having a few problems getting the 'bird' started. I walked over to the other two men who seemed to be waiting more than working. I introduced myself and quickly found two friendly Joes. The men were from a local engineering firm that often rented the King helicopter for trips into areas where cars cannot go or it takes too long to get there by truck. That morning they were heading into a mining camp about 150 miles north of King Ranch. David would take them in and stay with them all day while they did what they were there to do, and then David would fly them back later in the day. What made the encounter even more interesting was the fact that one of the men was originally from Portland, Maine. My third Maineaic!

Leaving the engineers and the pilot to their day's work, I headed towards the dining hall again thinking what I might say to challenge the missionaries at Kingdom Air Corps, when I ran into a man whose son was at the ranch learning to fly. There he was with Dwayne at the end of the runway getting ready for an early morning instructional flight. Deciding I had to wait for the director to return before devotions started, I was again distracted from my message as I listened to the story of how Zack made his way to Alaska. We watched as Zack made a perfect take-off with Dwayne seating in the backseat of the Piper cub. We watched in awe, as the small plane was lost against the size of the mountains south of the Matanuska River. We chatted as Zack and Dwayne flew up the river for half an hour and then came back to make a perfect landing. We watched as they taxied back to the plane's concrete pad, and it was then I heard the booming voice of Dwayne shout out, "Time for devotions!"

After a breakfast of bacon and pancakes, I was introduced to the thirty plus individuals that were there that morning, basically the people I had meet the day before with a few new faces. Dwayne introduced me as the pastor of his home church, the church that had given him his start. I was pleased with the connection as well, even though I had only been pastor of the Emmanuel Baptist Church for half the time Dwayne and Caroline had been supported by the church. It was then I had the floor and was able to share with the assembled staff, volunteers, and guests my thoughts on the doctrine of 'the Opportunities of Service' based on Luke 10:31-33:

> "31 And by chance there came down a certain priest that way: and when he saw him, he passed by on the other side. 32 And likewise a Levite, when he was at the place, came and looked *on him*, and passed by on the other side. 33 But a certain Samaritan, as he journeyed, came where he was: and when he saw him, he had compassion *on him*."

Using the classic Good Samaritan parable of Jesus, I shared these thoughts with the gathered workers:

1. CHANCE AND CIRCUMSTANCE ARE OF GOD—when God puts you in the way, like he did the Levite, the priest, and the Samaritan. I shared how each had an opportunity to help the robbed and beaten man, but only one took the opportunity. God is constantly putting such situations and circumstances in front of us, and we have a choice: will we walk by, will we look and go by, or will we stop and help the man in the byway?

2. CHIRST HAS SHOWN US WHAT WE OUGHT TO DO—Jesus was always having encounters with those who needed help, and what did he do? I shared three illustrations out of the life of Christ: Bartimaeus (Mark 10:46-52), Zacchaeus (Luke 19:1-10), and Lazarus (Luke 16:19-21). Each time Jesus stopped what He was doing and where He was going and helped; the lesson is clear. So should we!

3. CONCEPT TO CONSIDER IN THIS DOCTRINE—"The steps of a *good* man are ordered by the LORD: and he delighteth in his way." (Psalm 37:23) The conclusion seems to be clear; no matter whom or what you come across the encounter is God-ordained, and the rest is up to you. The key to the Good Samaritan story and the other stories we shared seemed to suggest if we are to do right we need to keep our eyes open, keep our minds open, and keep our hearts open. Our victim, our lame man, our blind man, our poor man is probably near us, but are we even looking or listening for their cry?

The audience was attentive and respectful, and I finished with a deep sense of satisfaction that my thoughts and observations of Scripture were heard by a group of fellow servants that were only looking for opportunities to serve the King of Kings by serving His people.—"And the King shall answer and say unto them, Verily I say unto you, Inasmuch as ye have done it unto one of the least of these my brethren, ye have done it unto me." (Matthew 25:40) When we help others we are really helping out the Lord.

## Chapter Twenty-Nine

## Four Wheeling To The Matanuska River

By mid-morning, the activities at Kingdom Air Corps were humming. Everybody seemed to sense the summer was drawing to a close, and if they were going to finish the 2014 project list, they had better put the pedal to the metal. Speaking of metal, one of the exciting things that happened for Scott after breakfast that first morning at King Ranch was Dwayne letting him drive his fully-restored 1947 Chevy pickup, Dwayne's pride and joy and the lawn ornament of the ranch. The old but new 'wheels' was fire engine red in color, and though I got to go along for a ride I never got to drive it myself. Maybe next time?

When Dwayne found out that Coleen wanted to go on a four-wheel ride through an Alaskan wilderness, he lent us the two four-wheelers at the camp. Over the years of clearing the land for the airstrip and the ranch, the wood to build the buildings was harvested from the nearly 1,000 acres connected to the ranch, owned by Dwayne's son David. To get the logs out of the woods for cutting and milling, the process resulted in numerous tote roads being created and scattered throughout the forest that surrounds the ranch on both sides of the main highway. Dwayne gave us the keys to the two red four-wheelers and simply said, " Have fun," and he went back to teaching his students how to fly in the bush.

With Scott in the lead, we first headed for the woods roads behind the ranch sawmill. The trails after that were your typical paths through any wood, Maine or Alaska, where a skidder had been used to haul out tree-length logs. We started downhill almost immediately after leaving the sawmill. Our goal was to try and find the trail that would eventually lead us to the Matanuska River. We had traveled beside that river from Palmer to

Chickaloon, and we had seen it from just about every angle on the ranch plateau, but we wanted an up close and personal look at the mighty river created by the melting snow of one of Alaska's biggest glaciers.

Within a short time, we started to come across the various cross trails created by the logging enterprises of King Ranch, and the ultimate decision—which way to go? We had all morning to explore, so we would try one trail and find its end and turn around and find another to motor down. Within 45-minutes, we had come to another bluff overlooking the Matanuska River. Were we getting closer?

Along the way we would stop and take a few pictures, and I could see that my dear wife was having the time of her life. It had been since we inherited my uncle's home in Aroostook County and with it a four-wheeler that I found out just how much Coleen loves the sport. In the spring and summer and fall months, we enjoy running the numerous RV trailers that criss-cross throughout the County around our cottage in Perham. Coleen is a cautious driver who enjoys the scenery not the speed, and the trails on King Ranch were built for logging not speed, so Coleen was in seventh heaven as we wound our way back and forth, trail by trail to the Matanuska River.

It took us nearly an hour over unfamiliar trails to finally find one that brought us to the riverbank. A slight drop over that bank got us to the rocky, river bottom below. As with the other glacier river we had seen in Alaska, the Matanuska River was broad, but nearly empty of water. The river we were looking for was on the far side of the riverbed, so off we went working our way around drift-wood and large boulders and deep channels craved out by the water when it flowed high and heavy down the length of the Matanuska. Eventually we arrived at a stream no wider than twenty yards; grayish in color, very cold (remember it was the water from a glacier-a landlock iceberg) and lined with smooth stones. The four-wheelers did well over the rough terrain, and once again we stopped often to take in the size and scenery from below versus above King Ranch. Besides the ranch, we could make out other houses on the 1,000-foot bluff, including one that had a staircase down the entire length, from ranch house to riverbed!

After an hour of exploration, we headed back hoping we could remember the maze of trails that had brought us to the river. Once again Scott led the way as we motored over fallen limbs and through mud holes and around countless branches that attempted to block our homeward flight out of the engulfing forest between the Matanuska River and King Ranch. Coming around a sharp corner, Scott suddenly and unexpectedly stopped. Both his hands immediately went into the air, but Coleen and I couldn't see why he stopped until we slowly pulled up beside him. Within fifty feet was a yearling moose grazing on a patch of grass created by an opening in the dense canopy of trees. It was the closest Coleen had ever come to a moose, and she was thrilled. Besides four-wheeling at the cottage in the northern most county in Maine, Coleen and I enjoy traveling around the back roads of Perham looking for wildlife. Especially in the spring, we normally get to see whitetail deer and moose just about every time we ventured into the side lanes of my hometown, but never had my dear wife gotten closer than on her four-wheel ride through King Ranch.

As with the moose the night before, this moose seemed to be at home with spectators. We watched the small moose for ten-minutes, and it was only as we revved up the engines of the four-wheelers to continue on did the moose lumber into the ravine beyond. It was a thrilling climax to our morning adventure traveling the trails back and forth to the Matanuska River. Near noon we reemerged from the forest south of the ranch and took our time exploring all the side roads and lanes that cut through the edge of the woods from David's home and hangar to the sawmill and trailer park and the King's home on the southern side of the airstrip. We even crossed the airfield, careful that no planes were landing and went across to the main road and side lanes north of the airstrip. We also discovered that there were some trails on the other side of the highway; trails Scott and I would explore later in the day.

As we turned off and parked the four-wheelers by the hangar and headed across the road to the dining hall for lunch, I thought of the wonderful family morning we had shared. The Psalmist once wrote, "He turneth rivers into wilderness...." (Psalms 107:33) It is on such days as I spent riding the back of a four-wheeler with my wife that I realized just how amazing the diversity of the creative hand of God is, and perhaps most exciting of all, is the sudden appearance of wildlife. Granted, we only saw one moose in our river trip, but it might as well been a hundred for the thrill it brought my wife. God had given Coleen the desire (Psalms 37:4) of her heart. If she were writing this story, she would remind me that she had looked into renting a four-wheeler in Alaska and even looked into a tour by a four-wheeler in Alaska online. Either would have cost her hundreds of dollars, but instead she waited on the Lord and He gave her the whole experience for no out-of-pocket expense, and for my thrift-conscience wife that was the best of the best the morning she went four-wheeling into the wilderness of Alaska.

## Chapter Thirty

## Flight Over A Glacier

THE MENU FOR LUNCH before our epic plane ride over the Matanuska Glacier was fresh tuna sandwiches, homemade pizza, and meeting a man that would lend us his boat to go fishing. Our arrival to King Ranch the afternoon before had shown us that there were very few fishing holes in the area. We knew our only hope was to connect with a local, and during our third meal at the King's dining hall, we meet such a man. A transplant from the lower 48, but a native by general standards, he had been in Alaska over thirty years. He was a part of the King's church family and often volunteered his spare time to the mission. He had a flat-bottom boat on site, and we were welcomed to use it. Immediately after lunch, Scott took off in the Tahoe to checkout a couple of ponds he suggested. I stayed behind to calm Coleen down. She was still having second thoughts about the afternoon plane ride that was scheduled. Coleen has never liked flying, even in the big planes, and our flight over Matanuska Glacier would be in a 6-seater. Dwayne also became an encourager to his reluctant guest. His plan was to get Coleen use to being in the plane and talk her through her initial fright before the flight.

Talking all the way to the plane, Dwayne explained where we were going and how he would give Coleen the smoothest flight possible. Coleen's Achilles' heel was motion sickness. She can get sick on a winding road if she is sitting in the back seat, so a bumpy ride in a light aircraft with downdrafts and updrafts wouldn't be pleasant, and that is all Coleen could think about was getting sick on the flight. Dwayne put Coleen in the plane first letting her get use to the closeness of the small plane, and all the while he talked while washing the windshield and checking the plane out from top to bottom. His actions and calming tone seemed to relax my nervous wife. I was simply listening and keeping my mouth shut because I knew the less said for me was best. I would let our pilot deal with my cautious spouse, but I knew this would be the only opportunity for such an experience. How many get to come face to face with a massive glacier while flying over its back, up its sides, and around its face?

My mind was on the adventure ahead when Scott returned from his exploration of the local fishing holes. I could tell by the smile on his face that he had found something, but it wasn't what I had expected. I quickly asked, "Can we go fishing tonight?" to which he replied, "No holes, but!" Scott went on to tell of a close encounter with a family of moose. He was checking out a small pond just off the Glenn Highway when he heard something coming down off a steep hill by the pond. He tucked himself into a stand of small trees and waited. Sure enough within minutes a mother moose with twin calves emerged from the undergrowth on the edge of the body of water. Undetected, Scott watched and photographed the mother moose teaching her twins how to swim. In a series of spectacular pictures, Scott caught the exercise on film; next to the set of photographs he took of the mother grizzly and her twins, the set with the mother moose and her twins were the best animal pictures of the trip. He was able to watch the entire process from a reluctant baby to the three swimming across the pond. Such are the thrills one may encounter when you venture out looking for a fishing hole.

By the time Scott finished his story and showed me the pictures, we were strapped into the middle seats of Dwayne's plane with Coleen comfortable in the front seat beside the pilot and the man whose son I had watch take off that morning before devotions in the back seat. Dwayne tries to give every one of his guests this tour, and our time had come. Starting the engine Dwayne taxied us to the end of the airstrip. Pointing the light craft into the wind (not much that day), he revved up the engine to full capacity, let up on the brakes, and we were off down the runway. Despite the rough airfield, it was a relatively smooth takeoff, and before we knew it we were out into space. I have never thought of being a pilot myself, but I, like many, have been fascinated with flight since I saw my first bird do it. Big planes don't give you that sensation like little planes, and it was in a small aircraft I took my first flight in 1972. Each time I have repeated the marvelous mystery I have been thrilled, just like the day Dwayne took us into the Chugach Mountains south of King Ranch.

Of all my small planes flights, our trip through the hills and valleys toward the Matanuska Glacier was the most bird-like flight I had ever taken. Dwayne flew us so close to the cliffs and ravines looking for wildlife, that you felt you could reach out and touch the rocks and trees above the timberline. At the same time, you felt as if you were not even moving. It felt like we were suspended in space, hanging on a string, just floating over this incredibly beautiful terrain, and there in the distance was a white river coming out of a vast canyon. Scattered along our flight path were strips of forest, open burns, glades, mountain meadows, marshes, ponds, and streams but no wildlife. Dwayne's lecture before our flight spoke of the possibility of seeing bull moose, black bear, grizzly, mountains goats, Dall sheep, and who knows what else. Actually, in the evening flight Dwayne took that same day, his passengers got to see the whole array, but we didn't see one creature—the difference between an early afternoon and evening flight, perhaps?

Every type of terrain we had seen during our week in Alaska was directly before and below us as we worked our way along the seven mountain peaks to the glacier. The interplay of the high sun on the landscape gave us an entirely different angle of observation. It was amazing to see the world from the edge of the sky versus the edge of a road. Despite the roaring of the engine and our soaring above the valley below, there was stillness there, solitude as we edged our way up the headwaters of the Matanuska River. It was here that the ramparts of ice and rock and snow meet. Our first few miles up the glacier were where the glacier was dying, melting away. Amid such grandeur, I was stirred to hum, "This is my Father's world, and to my listening ears. All nature sings, and round me rings the music of the spheres. This is my Father's world; He shines in all that's fair!" And I was witnessing one of the fairest sights I had ever seen. Soon we were in the heart of the massive Matanuska. Below us, beside us, and before us was a sheet of white unmatched by anything I had ever seen. We were now flying into mountaintops that reached thirteen thousand feet, and the ice below us was four thousand feet thick. Dwayne took us to the very face of this huge glacier flying us within feet of the snow-covered cliffs and crags. Occasionally, we could see a patch of deep blue (spots were the glacier was melting, forming small pools of water), but mostly it was the snow of centuries clinging tenaciously to the rock-face of the mountains of the Matanuska.

As we cut our way through the high hills and low valley of the Matanuska Glacier, my mind once again returned to the hymn: "This is my Father's world; I rest me in the thought of rocks and trees, of skies and seas-His hand the wonders wrought!" After my flight over the Matanuska Glacier, I had another stanza to add to Maltbie Babcock's hymn and Franklin Sheppard's melody and the Psalmist's precept: "For the world are mine, and the fulness thereof." (Psalms 50:12) This is my Father's world and to my wondering sight, a glacier's white, the bright sunlight, a wondrous afternoon flight!

# Chapter Thirty-One

# The Splendor At The Summit

Life at the sky edge of a glacier's edge is a rare realm indeed. On August 20, 2014, I got to share a memorable experience with my son and wife in a small plane as we roared and soared along the massive Matanuska Glacier for nearly an hour. The most experienced pilot in the region guided our flight and tour over this spectacular glacier. As Dwayne tenderly directed his plane from site to site through canyon and ravine, by mountaintop after mountaintop, he answered all our questions and inquires and filled in what we didn't even consider or imagine. Dwayne had made this glacier flight hundreds of times before, but as he said on our flight: "Each trip is unique, and it never gets old!" This was the statement of a man who has found his destiny, his final destination. Mountain skies blending with glacier snows have a grandeur and glory all its own. The scenery is unparalleled because of the high altitude, the high flight. Instead of observing the various changes in the topography, the high hills and deep snows create their own environment that has drawn people from all over the world. Dwayne told of individuals he had flown to the glacier who spent weeks just hiking and studying the changes in the glacier. I enjoyed my flight, but I can't see making Matanuska a destination. What fascinated me most was the sheer volume of snow that remained in the Matanuska Glacier. Over twenty miles long and in some places three quarters of a mile thick, the buildup of thousands of years of snowstorms has left a lasting terrain that despite all the screaming of global warming will never melt, until the Lord returns and truly ushers in a millennium warming.

As we made the turn to return to King Ranch, Dwayne told us that it was only four miles to the sea over that last ridge, and that would make it the greatest drop (from mountain top to sea level) in the world (13,000 feet to zero feet in 4 miles)! The flight back was just as impressive as the flight out. Once again Dwayne took us around the snow-covered valleys and up the sides of snow-covered mountains before we exited into the colorful autumn of the Matanuska River Valley. The contrast was awesome. We had taken our flight on a nearly cloudless day with barely a breeze. Dwayne would say it was the smoothest flight of the season, to which I can with confidence say it was because of my wife's prayer. Some might ask if God cares whether or not a flight is smooth or rough, but I would say with Paul: "Be careful for nothing (including a flight to the summit of a glacier); but in everything (including not getting sick on a trip up a glacier) by prayer and supplication with thanksgiving let your request (my wife's) be made known unto God." (Philippians 4:6) Never underestimate the power of prayer, or a wife's petition when it comes to taking a glacier tour in the air, over a snowfield and through a snow valley along mountainous, coastal Alaska.

As we slowly worked our way back to the airfield, Dwayne flew us by all of his favorite animal spots. He talked about taking in moose hunters to remote airstrips, for the big, bull moose that inhabit the area. Some of these moose weigh nearly a ton! From high above, we wondered how he managed to land in such places, but he talked of it as a pilot would land on a long, wide concrete airstrip in the desert. Our amazement for this bush pilot only grew as we witnessed firsthand his tremendous skills in handling his light plane in rugged terrain, through narrow canyons, and by snowy outcroppings. Part of the splendor of our trip to the summit of Matanuska Glacier was the admiration of our 72 year-old pilot, and his unchanging enthusiasm for not only what he does but also where he does it. I have meet few men who have held their passion for something for a lifetime, but Dwayne King is one of those men. With each turn of the plane wheel, Dwayne would bring our attention to something new, even if it weren't an animal. The barren mountain-sides, mountaintops, and mountain crags and cliffs didn't diminish his excitement for where he was, in God's unspoiled nature. Despite traveling that flight path for nearly two decades, Dwayne believed that he had found the summit, the zenith of his life and that it didn't get any better than what we were doing that afternoon: the splendor of the summit of one's ministry and mission; even if it was simply sharing his backyard with visitors from Maine.

Our final approach took us back down the Matanuska River, but this time along the bluffs of the Talkeetna Mountains. As we winged our way towards the plateau airstrip, I thought again of just how blessed we had been on our trip. Whether traveling by land or by air, the Good Lord had given us a safe trip to the summit and back. Never before had I made such a trip and perhaps, will never again, but I had at least for an hour experienced the flight of an eagle, a hawk, a bird in the mountains, and I was reminded of a favorite poem "High Flight" by John Magee, an American pilot with the Royal Canadian Air Force, who died in aerial combat on December

11, 1941. That poem best describes the afternoon I spent in a plane with Dwayne King flying to the summit of the Matanuska Glacier:

> "Oh! I have slipped the surly bonds of earth
> And danced the skies on laughter-silvered wings;
> Sunward I've climbed, and joined the tumbling mirth
> Of sun-split clouds-and done a hundred things.
> You have not dreamed of-wheeling and soaring and swung
> High in the sunlit silence. Hovering there
> I've chased the shouting wind along, and flung
> My eager craft through footless halls of air.
> Up, up the long delirious, burning blue
> I've topped the wind-swept heights with easy grace
> Where never lark, nor even eagle flew-
> And, while with silent lifting mind I've trod
> The high untresspassed sanctity of space
> Put out my hand and touched the face of God!"

Landing safely on the Talkeetna side of the Matanuska, we all knew we would be eternally richer for the unforgettable, unbelievable flight we had just experienced with a man who loved what he did and loved even more the One who gave him the place to do it in. When one writes of 'the splendor of the summit', one has to be speaking about more than mountain summits covered in snow, but also of the summit of one's existence. Dwayne King is a missionary that has only one focus and that being the sharing of faith and flight with anyone who will enter his cockpit and go for a ride to a snowy summit. The splendor is just as much the pilot as the place, the missionary as the mountain, the guide as the glacier.

*Chapter Thirty-Two*

# Dwayne King, Bush Pilot Extraordinar

After we returned from our amazing flight over the Matanuska Glacier, Scott and Coleen decided to take a nap while I hung around the hangar to see if I could get a few minutes alone with Dwayne. I had been fascinated with Dwayne King ever since I heard his story from the people of Emmanuel Baptist Church. A New Yorker turned Mainiac in the 1960s, Dwayne had lived a life only dreamed about by ordinary people.

Once Dwayne learned to fly over the coastline and hills of Downeast Maine, he took his young family to Alaska to reach the natives and the transplants with the Gospel of Christ. His passion was to get into the isolated villages and towns of rural Alaska. Over the years he did just that, flying into the remote hamlets where only a plane could go. He established an early reputation of being an amazing pilot, an interesting communicator, and an extraordinary visionary. Despite all the outreach he could handle, Dwayne was always looking west into Communist Siberia. His heart was drawn to the dark, North Country of Eastern Russia and the lack of missionary opportunities, so between 1960 and 1990 he prayed and sought opportunity to fulfill a lifetime passion to take the Gospel of Christ into Siberia. That opportunity finally arrived, and on the afternoon of our glacier flight, I got a chance to sit down in Dwayne's hangar office and see the pictures and talk of the open door that now exists in Siberia, Russia.

In a cedar-paneled office with each wall containing some chart or map or photograph of Dwayne's life, I sat spellbound as story after story came flowing from Dwayne's lips. He told of that early flight into the unknown and how over the years he became best friends with the governor of Siberia and just about every important Russia official in that land. He talked of how the Lord

God opened the doors for establishing contracts with the native people and finding, that despite seventy years of Communist oppression, the Church in Russia had survived. Dwayne found a remnant of believers and was able to encourage them and help them and now he was training some of them to fly, so they themselves could reach more isolated villages and town, and, yes, even huge cities with the Good News of Jesus Christ. His eyes would glow when he spoke of getting the first plane into Russia for that purpose, and he showed me the airfield that would be home to those flights. You could hear the pride in his voice as he talked of his pilots, Russian pilots that he had trained not only to fly but to care for the missionary planes; yes, planes, for a second one was being prepared for early next spring to make the long flight from the States to Siberia. It was all about more opportunities to share the Gospel.

Dwayne opened a book he had on a table that contained pictures of him at official ceremonies in Siberia with the governor, and his work with a group that was documenting the connection between Siberia and the United States during World War II. This documentation would include the countless planes that were flown from of all places, New York to Siberia to help the Russians fight the Nazis. Dwayne had even helped with an archeological mission to find one of those planes that had gone down, so that it could be resorted and put in a museum in Siberia. The more Dwayne talked about his harrowing stories of God's marvelous protection on numerous occasions and how God had opened the doors to reach the loss of Siberia and Alaska, all I could think about was the promise God gave to the Church of Philadelphia: "I know thy works: behold, I have set before thee an open door, and no man can shut it. . .." (Revelation 3:8) Even the Iron Curtain wasn't shut tight enough to keep the Gospel of Jesus Christ and Dwayne King out.

I know that I am writing as if Dwayne King is a superman, a man with exceptional skills and abilities, but he is just Dwayne King. A small man by stature, but a man that yielded to the Almighty and was willing to go and do whatever God wanted. His life reminds me of the words to a little know Church hymn by Mary Brown: "It may not be (or it may be) on the mountain's height, or over the stormy sea (Bering Sea); it may not be at the battle's front (Cold War) my Lord will have need of me; but if by a still, small voice He calls to paths I do not know (Dwayne did not come from a flying family), I'll answer, dear Lord, with my hand in Thine, I'll go were you want me to go. Perhaps today there are loving words that Jesus would have me speak; there may be now, in the paths of sin, some wanderer whom I should seek (in Alaska or Siberia). O Savour, if Thou wilt be my Guide, though dark (Communist Siberia) and rugged the way (the wilderness of Alaska), my voice shall echo the message sweet; I'll say what you want me to say. There's surely somewhere a lowly place (it doesn't get any lowlier than the Eskimo villages of isolated Alaska) in earth's harvest-fields so wide (no wider missionfield than Siberia-from the Ural mountains to the Pacific Ocean, a distance of 4000 miles, 4,956,868 square miles), where I may labour through life's short day (nearly fifty years now for Dwayne) for Jesus, the Crucified. So, trusting my all unto thy care (Dwayne is the only man I know that over the years has simply trusted his God for so much. I love the story of a year he was getting ready to fly his team to the Brooks Range Bible Camp, but he didn't have the money for the fuel. As he pondered what to do a man came up to him and gave him his credit card and told Dwayne to put all the fuel he need on it-thousands and thousands of dollars!), I know Thou lovest me! I'll do Thy will with a heart sincere (one of the best I've meet); I'll be what you want me to be (even a bush pilot). I'll go where you want me to go (Alaska, Siberia), dear Lord, over mountain, or plain, or sea (and Dwayne has); I'll say what you want me to say (even telling Communist leaders the Gospel of Christ), dear Lord, I'll be what you want me to be!"

Our little talk only lasted about 45-minutes before Dwayne was called away to a pressing need, but it was a joy to share those few minutes in the presence of a man who has given all for his King! Before we separated, I did mention to him about a young man in my church (Liam Brennan) who had been so impressed with Dwayne's last visit that he has decided he wants to learn to fly (Liam has started his journey through the Civil Air Patrol), and that someday (Liam was only 13 at the time) he wanted to come to Kingdom Air Corp and learn to be a missionary pilot. We do not know how this will all turn out, but what impressed me about Dwayne were his responses to my story of Liam. You could tell by the tone of his voice and the sparkle in his eye that his greatest joy is to hear others getting the same passion and desire he got a half-century before. To pass on his extraordinary skills and knowledge of flying in the wild is what makes Dwayne press on, push on in the very difficult and expensive ministry of flying at 72! As Dwayne left for another training flight, I remembered again the words of Paul when he wrote: "For seeing your calling, brethren, how that not many wise men after the flesh, not many mighty, not many noble, are called, but God hath chosen the foolish things of the world to confound the wise; and God hath chosen the weak things of the world to confound the things which are mighty; and the base things of the world, and the things which are despised, hath God chosen, yes, and things which are not, to bring to nought things that are: that no flesh should glory in His presence." (I Corinthians 1:26-29) Dwayne King is one of these men.

# Chapter Thirty-Three

# Overlooking Kingdom Air

After leaving Dwayne to his afternoon ministries, I headed back to the King home to check on the family. I found Scott just getting up from a nap and my dear wife still sleeping. Unknown to me, Coleen had kept it to herself that despite the smooth flight she had gotten some motion sickness and her stomach was upset. She shared this with Scott on their walk back to the house. We decided to let her sleep it off while we went exploring for our evening fishing hole, so Scott and I took his Tahoe to a couple of spots he had checked out earlier. After further examination, we realized even with the flat-bottom boat promised by Tom Cobb a transplant from Wilmington, NC, we would have a very difficult time getting into the pond we found. The lake we discovered was too big to know where to fish. After further consideration, we decided that maybe another four-wheel ride along the trails of the Talkeetna foothills would be just as much fun.

Returning to the ranch we found Dwayne and asked if we might borrow the four-wheelers again. The answer was a hearty, yes, and within minutes we were crossing the Glenn Highway to the four-wheeler path beyond. Sure enough right in front of us was a RV trail leading up into the steep hillside north of the ranch. We would learn later the trail was cut out of the hill to make a way for the ranch's fresh water supply and system. Taping into a spring located halfway up the hill, the Kings had run a pipe from the spring to the ranch. All gravity feed, the natural water source had been running for years, giving the ranch all the water it needed. I was impressed again with the ingenuity of Dwayne and his staff, but our purpose wasn't to find the ranch's spring, but to explore the ridgeline north of Kingdom Air Corp.

The first phase of our late afternoon tromp through tree lined, granite steep paths was to make our way to a power line that weaved its way about half-way up the ridgeline. Scott led the way as I followed his ATV, working our way through switchbacks up the very, steep slope. The four-wheelers were up to the task as we eventually made the electric power line. Once we saw where we had come out of the thick forest below, we decided to follow the trail along the power line to a high knoll in the far distance. The trail was full of dips and turns, but slowly and surely we gained the height. At last we broke out above the valley below. Finding a narrow trail to a bluff, we eventually came out on a cliff overlooking King Ranch. My judgment of height isn't good, but I believe we were more than a thousand feet above the ranch and two thousand feet overlooking the Matanuska River. We had a bird's eye view of the valley, the river, and the seven mountains beyond, including the tallest, King Mountain! The sun was bright and unobstructed by the few clouds in the Alaskan sky. The ranch complex looked so small against the size of the hills, the width of the river, and the massive forest that surrounded it. It was as if we were suspended in space, hanging on air, over the whole scene.

Somebody had found the spot before us because we found a small lean-to and a campfire pit. Others had seen the observation post for what it was, a marvelous vista and a direct view of the ranch. Shutting our four-wheelers off, Scott and I took seats under the lean-to and just grazed out into the vastness of space surrounding the ranch. The flight in front of the seven mountains to the south of the camp gave us the size of the mountains, but sitting on that Talkeetna Ridge gave us the splendor of the mountains. It was as if for a moment we were transfixed, breathless before the spectacular scenery. Reverence and respect came to mind as neither of us spoke. It would have been a desecration, a sacrilege, and an insult to what lie before us. Sometimes we forget to stay still, be quiet and just take in the interlude that is found sometimes in the hills and nature. Moments that two can share without saying anything, because all that needs to be said is already being said by the site and the sights before them!

As we sat and watched a few drifting clouds emerging from the mountain valleys across the river, nothing could dampen the experience my boy and I were having that Alaskan afternoon. We sat for a few more minutes before we knew we must return to the valley below and supper. I felt like Peter who suggested to the Lord that they ought to make three tabernacles and stay (Matthew 17:4)! The afternoon was coming to an end, and our exploration into the Talkeetna foothills had allowed us to found what we were looking for. Granted, a few animals would have been nice, but the overlook on the overhang was certainly enough. We followed the slope back the way we had come. At least we didn't have to search for another trail, so we could enjoy the trip back. The pristine forestland combined with rugged granite veins appeared periodically along the path. Huge boulders sometimes obstructed our way, but a few twists here and turns there got us through. The air was crisp and clean, and as I maneuvered my machine slowly behind Scott I thought again of the amazing trip I was on with my son. Our time together was adding up with fishing experiences, flying experiences, wildlife experiences and just plain being together experiences. Everywhere we turned on the high hill to the north of Kingdom Air, we saw evidence of others having been there before us, but for Scott and me it was if we were the first, the pioneers, the explorers that cut the trail and explored the path to that Talkeetna Bluff; our own secret hideout that will remain long after we departed on the morrow. What had been a disappointment in not finding a fishing hole had turned out to be a wonderful time together just the same. Isn't that just like the Lord? It is true: when God shuts a door, He does open a window. For Scott and me that afternoon north of King Ranch, it was the closed door of fishing, but the open window of seeing the world of the Kings from a high hill and a narrow cliff.

Our second four-wheeler ride on King Ranch ended a little after five on August 20, 2014. It was just another experience that only Scott and I shared together. We had already had a few before the ride up the Talkeetna, and we would have plenty more before our travels back to Maine finished, but for me that hour and a half ride was symbolic of the reason I had come to Alaska. Truly, I had come to see the State in all its glory and to fish a few of its pools, but ultimately I had come to get reconnected with my son. Throughout my fatherhood, I have lived by the admonition of Paul: "And ye, fathers, provoke not your children to wrath: but bring them up in the nurture and admonition of the Lord." (Ephesians 6:4) Over the years I learned that 'nurture and admonition' didn't just come from the Bible or Church. God's lessons of grace and mercy and faith can also be learned out-of-doors as well as indoors. Sunday School and Awana are not the only places to find instruction in the things of Christ, so that is why I have taken seriously these verses from the Book of Job: "But ask now the beasts, and they shall teach thee; and the fowls of the air, and they shall tell thee; or speak to the earth, and it shall teach thee: and the fishes of the sea shall declare unto thee. Who knoweth not all these that the hand of the Lord hath wrought this?" (Job 12:7-9) It is my prayer that our jaunt to that bluff overlooking Kingdom Air was another lesson. He might be in his mid-thirties and me in my mid-sixties but we still have a lot to learn from God through his creation, especially a creation as inspiring and instructional as Alaska.

## Chapter Thirty-Four

## Fire On A Mountain

We had just gotten back from our four-wheeler adventure into the Talkeetna hills when we saw Dwayne rushing towards one of his planes. He quickly took off and headed due east. It wasn't until supper that we learned that he was going to help fight a forest fire near Victory Bible Camp. This was the story Dwayne told us later that evening.

The same year Dwayne and Caroline King moved to Alaska to minister through SIM (Sudan Interior Mission), Arctic Mission was established. One of their longest lasting ministries was Victory Bible Camp, a Christian summer camping ministry located about ten miles down the road from King Ranch off the Glenn Highway. As Dwayne told the story, he relayed how forest fires are a clear and present danger in that part of Alaska. This was one of the reasons he was building his own fire station on the ranch. Because the population is spread out along the highway, mutual support is necessary but because of the distance often the fire has to be fought by the locals, not professionals. Virtually every mountain in that region had been scorched and burnt over by fire one time or the other. Even as we travelled through the few miles of forest in our four-wheeler rides, we could see sections of forestland that still bore the scars of an old fire. Most had healed over, but the marks were still visible. Most fires in Alaska start with a lighting strike, especially the mountain peak fires, but the one near Victory Bible Camp happened through the carelessness of hikers. Dwayne had fought plenty of fires in his day, but on this day he simple acted as an aerial observer to point the fire fighters, young men from the camp, to the hot spots.

I sat at the table as Dwayne and his son David, back from carting those two engineers I had meet in the morning to the mining camp, and debated the uselessness of the Federal Forest Service in fighting forest fires like the Victory Bible Camp fire that afternoon. By the time the professionals arrived, the fire was either out or out of control. Dwayne spoke of the long hot summers when gigantic cumulus clouds would build up over the ridges. Out of those clouds at times massive thunderheads form, and in time their intense, electrical energy is let loose. Lightning flashes exit and find their way to the highest hill. The high voltage electrical charge goes to ground and sometimes finds a tender spot to ignite. As the echo of the thunder rattles down through the wide valley, the fire has begun in a dry root or a rotten tree. Sometimes it is hours later before any sign of a fire is noticed, and then it must be taken seriously because a fire on a mountain can find its way to the valley and at the bottom of a hill might be a summer camp for sharing with kids the Good News of Jesus Christ or a ministry to train missionary pilot.

Truly, one of the grandest shows in nature is a thunder and lightning storm, a thousand times more majestic than any manmade light show or fireworks display, but there is always a danger especially if woods surround you. A lightning bolt crashing to the earth will explode a dry forest into flames. It has been for thousands of years God's way of controlling forest growth and regulating the plants on the forest floor. Even the native people of Alaska came to understand and grasp the importance of nature burning off part of itself every year as beneficial. The raging flames remove and consume the grass and weeds that invades and ultimately hurts the forestland. The heat and the fire destroy ravening insects that harm the forest as well. The emergence of new foliage and fresh grass fertilized by the cinders and ash only stimulates more growth and healthier trees. We discovered in our trip into Denali that forest fires are allowed to burn themselves out versus man's involvement. Controlled burning has become a standard in the modern forest management strategy of the United States. Denali, however, has land to spare, but the people of Victory Bible Camp and Kingdom Air Corp know that one fire on a mountain can wipe out years of labor, so fighting a fire on a mountain or not fighting a fire on a mountain is not option: it must be fought. Dwayne told of five men climbing the mountain above Victory Bible Camp to fight the fire with simple shovels and sharp axes.

The good news about the Victory Bible Camp fire was the small size of the outbreak and early detection before it could gain ground. Another factor was the abnormal wet season the region was having. The fire didn't get a head start and the moisture in the trees, shrubs, bushes, and grass kept the fire at bay until the fire fighters could arrive. Within a few hours, the young fire fighters from Victory Bible Camp had gotten the fire under control and before supper Dwayne felt he could come home; the fire on the mountain was under control if not out. I have thought much about this phenomenon in natural, just how it is like man has built within its being the ability, most of the time, to take care of itself. Granted, there are times when all of nature and us needs a helping hand from five young men and an old man in a plane. But there is something profound about a fire on a mountain. One of the repeated themes of the Bible is mountains and fire and the presence of God: God on a mountain in fire! Remember these words from Moses' remembrances from Mount Sinai: "And Moses brought forth the people out of the camp to meet God; and they stood at the nether part of the mount. And Mount Sinai was altogether on a smoke, because the Lord descended upon it in fire: and the smoke thereof ascended as the smoke of a furnace, and the whole mount quaked greatly." (Exodus 19:17-18) We have all seen pictures of the tops of hills or mountains aflame, so a natural forest fire can give us an image of our God. Why is fire so often used in the Scriptures as a description of the Almighty?

Whether "our God is a consuming fire" (Hebrews 12:29) or the Holy Spirit as "tongues like as fire" (Acts 2:3), we Christians are children of fire just as John the Baptist predicted: "I indeed baptize you with water unto repentance: but He that cometh after me is mightier than I, whose shoes I am not worthy to bear: He shall baptize you with the Holy Ghost, and with fire." (Matthew 3:11) As I listened to Dwayne and David talk over their moose meatloaf, I thought how the Church needs a lightning strike to set us afire again. We need a fire on a mountain. Paul, quoting Psalms 104:4, says that we ought to be "His ministers a flame of fire." (Hebrews 1:7) Jesus taught that we are supposed to be "a city that is set on an hill" (Matthew 5:14), so a flame on a hill is the image given of the burning, hot believer igniting his world; seen because of the smoke and the flame, a "light of the world"; (Matthew 5:14). Just like the fire on the hilltop next to Victory Bible Camp couldn't hide or be ignored, neither should we (Matthew 5:15-6). Only the burning, raging fire of God and God's Holy Spirit can clear away the cheapgrasses of sin, the weeds of wickedness, the thorns and thistles of transgression, and the undergrowth of iniquity! Unless it is done here and now by a belief in the redemptive work of Christ on Calvary, the next destination of the wicked and the world will be the flames of the Lake of Fire (Revelation 20:14-15). There needs to be a fire on a mountain again, and there will be, but will it be too late for some?

## Chapter Thirty-Five

## A Night In Chickaloon

OUR SECOND SUPPER AT Kingdom Air Corps ended with a few more hours left of daylight on our last day at King Ranch. Dwayne was off to pilot another flight over the Matanuska Glacier for a family of five. The staff of KAC returned to their summer projects. Scott, Coleen, and I thought we might take another four-wheeler ride, but instead opted for a drive around Chickaloon in search of more wildlife. Mountain country is generally rich with animals as we had experienced, so we thought a drive into Chickaloon and maybe a few side roads might avail us of a few more exciting sightings!

Scott turned the Tahoe onto the Glenn Highway heading back towards Sutton and Palmer. Chickaloon has no city-center; as a matter of fact, we passed through Chickaloon on our way to King Ranch and failed to see it. We were determined to at least say we had been into Chickaloon. As we retraced our journey from two days before, we watched for Chickaloon signs and wildlife. Sometimes it is a paradox when looking for wild animals; more often than not it is the times you are not looking for them that you see them, and it is the times you are looking for them you don't see them. Such was our experience on our evening exploring the village of Chickaloon, Alaska. No animals and really no town. We did find the post office, an isolated building beside the Glenn Highway, but no other structures. I took a photo of the post office to prove we had been there. We did find a few houses together on a side road by a feeder stream of the mighty Matanuska, but that was it. We lamented the scarcity of animal sightings. Little did we know that those sightings were taking place on Dwayne's evening glacier flight. By eight o'clock we had returned to the King house and were settling in for the night. We decided that our night in Chickaloon would have to be with the Kings, and what an evening it was!

At quarter to nine, Dwayne returned from his flight, and what a flight it was. They saw 8 mountain goats, a family of Dall sheep, 6 black bear, and a couple of big bull moose! Our timing was off by one flight for animal sighting, but neither Coleen nor I were complaining about our ride, and I heard no murmuring from my son either. Such is the results of seeking to find wild animals in a wilderness area. You can hike, four-wheel, drive for miles and see nothing, yet unknown to us how many eyes were watching us in our travels. We know the animals were there, but they also know we were there and sometimes the animal kingdom proves to be very inhospitable. However, that was not the case in the King's home as some of their friends came to say goodbye and to visit a bit.

Dwayne had barely gotten his animal flight story over when a knock came to the door. It was Arvin and Kathy Bouisnett, the Kansas wheat farmer and his wife I have mentioned in a previous chapter. I can't remember the last time I spent an evening laughing as much as I did that last evening with the Kings and their friends. Arvin, like Dwayne, was a storyteller and what stories he told. Each and every one had a comical punch line; needless to say, our funny bones were hurting before the evening was through. Besides a wheat farmer, Arvin was a Gideon, the ministry that puts Bibles in motels, prisons, and hospitals around the world, and a lover of John Deere tractors. Besides planting wheat, he is also a soybean farmer and a lover of *Duck Dynasty*, the reality show of 'duck-call' millionaires. Isn't Christian fellowship a wonderful benefit of the brotherhood of Christ? Whenever I share a night in Chickaloon like I did at the King's home, I am reminded of this verse in the epistle of Peter: "Use hospitality one to another without grudging." (I Peter 4:9) A translation called "God's Word" renders this verse: "Welcome each other as guests without complaining!" The Kings showed this kind of hospitality to us and we witnessed that same kind of hospitality to the Bouisnett's and no doubt to any others that came into their home. The New Living Translation uses these words that could also describe our time at the King's home: "Cheerfully share your home with those who need a meal and a place to stay!" They certainly did!

The night ended with the topic getting around to Dwayne's favorite subject: not flying or Siberia, but the Brooks Range Bible Camp, Dwayne's pride and joy. It is the longest ministry the Kings have had in Alaska. In a brochure of the ministry, this paragraph best explains the camp:

> "Each summer a group of our trainees (from Kingdom Air Corp) fly with us 60 miles north of the Arctic Circle to the Brooks Range Mountains where we hold a Bible camp for the children living in the surrounding villages. This camp is only

accessible by small aircraft and these villages have no roads to connect them with the rest of Alaska. Through their experience, our students gain a vision for the importance of flying, to reach the people living in the isolated places of the world who have little or no access to the Gospel!"

What a testimony, not only to the ministry of Kingdom Air Corp, practicing what they preach, but the ability to reach children from remote Alaskan towns through the miracle of flight. Not only have they created this camp out of an isolated region in northern Alaska, but also they year after year bear all the cost of such a camp. Remember, everything (food, fuel, staff, campers-the camp itself) has to be flown in, but the benefit of the enormous amount of work is another opportunity to train and motivate the next generation of missionary pilots not only in the skills to fly in such places, but the burden that comes that no matter how difficult it is to reach someone in a wilderness area they too are a part of Christ's great commission.

When I read again the blueprint of Christ's mission of His great commission I see a certain piece of it now in bold letters: "But ye shall receive power, after that the Holy Ghost is come upon you: and ye shall be witnesses unto me both in Jerusalem, and in all Judea, and in Samaria, and unto THE UTTERMOST PART OF THE EARTH." (Acts 1:8) Luke never could have dreamed that the power Christ was speaking of also included the power of flight. How could any imagine the 'uttermost' being isolated, remote, rural villages in the heartland of Alaska, or Siberia? To be witnesses to Eskimos and Siberians would be beyond thought or imagination! I have just finished a book I titled *The Uttermost Part*. (This book was published in 2015 through Resource Publications-an imprint of Wipf and Stock Publishers.) It is the story of my 4th short-term mission's trip to India and my second mission's trip in India, to one of those 'uttermost' places, Dangul, Orissa. It took me five days by plane, train, and taxi to reach an isolated Christian community in the mountains of central Phulbani. This group of believers was just recovering from a massive persecution (2008) that saw their homes and house of worship burnt to the ground. Some might ask is the time, the expense, and the labor worth it, and we must answer that if we are to fulfill the Lord's commission we must spend time reaching the remote, the out-of-the-way. Any soul, every soul is valuable to God, so they ought to be important to us. I have been drawn to the 'uttermost' for most of my life (the Gibson Desert in Western Australia in 1972) and now I know of another 'uttermost' place I would love to visit. I have been a summer camp pastor also for most of my ministry, I am nearing my 50th camp, but most of them I have only had to travel a few hundred miles. One of my first was to an isolated camp with the Boy's Brigade out of Stockholm, Maine held in northern Quebec Canada in 1975, but someday I wouldn't mind being the camp pastor at the Brooks Range Bible Camp.

## Chapter Thirty-Six

## Valdez Waterfalls

Our stay at King Ranch had come to an end. It had been a wonderful two days with fellowship, flight, and fun. Our time with Dwayne and Caroline King will remain some of the most cherished memories of our Alaska trip. The hospitality was exception, the food was traditional Alaskan, the flight over the glacier was awesome, and the animal encounters were memorable. We left mid-morning for our next destination, Valdez, but we left with a feeling that we had experienced something both on an emotional level as well as on a spiritual level that would not be matched on the rest of our journey. As Scott turned the Tahoe onto the Glenn Highway for Glennallen, I looked back for one last glimpse at the miracle that was King Ranch and the miraculous ministry that was Kingdom Air Corp.

For our morning travels, we followed the Matanuska River eastward. On a high bluff overlooking the river, we also got a final glance of the mighty Matanuska Glacier. Its wide valley of moving ice and snow was shining in the late morning sun, and from the angle of our observation, we could see deep up the canyon of white. Compared to our looking down on it the day before, our last distant view was anti-climactic. The Glenn Highway weaved its way along the bluffs and ridges of the Talkeetna Mountains for a further 122 miles from King Ranch. We did pass through a few very small towns, but mostly we drove through another Alaskan wilderness. We eventually lost sight of the Matanuska River, but just before us was another huge watershed: Tazlina Lake and the Tazlina River. The water from the lake and river eventually flow into the mighty Copper River just south of Glennallen. Our journey to Glennallen was pleasant as the weather warmed. We woke at the King home to autumn temperatures that reminded me of early spring in Maine. By eleven, we drove into the town of Glennallen where we stopped for gas. $4.41 a gallon was the most expensive gas we brought during our travels. Glennallen is a junction town: 253 miles back to Fairbanks or 117 miles to Valdez. We were heading for Valdez so we took a right hand turn.

Alaska Route #4 runs from Delta Junction to Valdez, but the road from Glennallen to Valdez is also called the Richardson Highway, and "High Way" is a good description. I thought that after nine days in Alaska its scenery wouldn't surprise me again, but the hundred plus miles up and down to Valdez did just that. The Richardson Highway literally cuts through a mountain range, part of the Chugach Mountains, and around every corner of that mountainous roadway is a picture beyond description. Our first stop was to take a few photographs with the family standing before another massive glacier: the Worthington and it was worthy of that name. Our guide was a wealth of information as he had trucked the road many times. Our first goal was Thompson Pass, the top of the ridge before we made the final descent into Valdez. But before we could reach the pass, we had to climb nearly 3000 feet through cutbacks and curves lined with mountaintops and more glaciers. It was along the early section of our climb that Coleen spotted her first black bear, and our first in Alaska. The midnight black creature streaked across in front of us as we were navigating one of a hundred twists in the road to Valdez. It was also at this time our tour guide made one of the funniest observations of the trip.

Traveling along at a great speed, Scott's lead foot was ideal to get us to our destination in record breaking time, but could be a bit hairy on an Alaskan curve! On one of the few long and straight sections of the Richardson Highway, Scott spotted what he thought was a small moose walking beside the road in the far distance. In seconds we were close enough to realize instead of a moose it was an old man with a walker slowly making his way up the side of the road. Needless to say, we all got a good laugh out of Scott's miss-observation and for a great while thereafter we didn't let him forget his mistake. Even the best of guides can be fooled at times, but a geriatric senior citizen for a moose is a bit of a stretch.

It was high noon by the time we made the top of the pass. The weather had cleared nicely, and we could see, as they say, 'forever'. We stopped at a turnout just through the pass and took some amazing photographs of the region. What a wonderful and incredible diversity laid before us! We had seen the landscape before, but we took a few minutes to take in the site and the sights of the tumbling terrain. From all directions, the land simply fell away. Our descent out of Thompson Pass (2678 feet) was steep and long. I was impressed with the granite peaks, and I marveled how man had conquered what seemed to me an impregnable ascent. With Scott's Tahoe it seemed to be an easy climb, but Scott told of the days he drove into Thompson Pass with a tractor-trailer in tow. Both the ascent and descent were dangerous, especially in the cold and snow of winter, not to mention the ice. The mighty ridges combined with the beautiful sky edge only made our moments in Thompson Pass that much more impressive. From everywhere we looked, we could see small patches of white in and around the peaks, more glaciers. It took us nearly half an hour to work our way down out of the Pass, but at the bottom was one of my top five natural, wilderness sites we saw on the entire Alaskan trip.

Passing through a very steep and narrow, twisting canyon called Key Stone, we came upon the first of two spectacular waterfalls. Pulling off the highway, we got out to enjoy what the locals call The Bridal Veil Falls. I have been a lover of falls ever since I witnessed a few in my early years in Maine. I have seen wondrous falls in Quebec, Canada on fishing trips, a vacation with my wife to Niagara in New York, and the very impressive falls in Munnar, India. From little trickles of water falling off granite boulders to rivers of water flowing over rocky outcroppings, a waterfall is like a log fire, it is mesmerizing. You focus your eyes upon one, and it is hard to look away. It is just water falling, like it is just wood burning, but there is something in the process that draws your attention and fixates your eyes. Bridal Veil Falls outside of Valdez, Alaska is one of those places. Scott had warned us before we arrived, but his description never came close to the majesty we saw. It reminded me of this phrase by the Psalmist: "He watereth the hills from His chambers. . .." (Psalm 104:13) For any good waterfall, you need a water source, but that chamber must be located higher than the hill it will flow down. Because the hills of the Key Stone Canyon were so high, we never did see the water source: glacier, or pond, or just run-off?

Getting back into the Tahoe, we hardly travelled a mile when Scott stopped again. This time the waterfall was on our side of the road. The Bridal Veil Falls was across the Richardson Highway and between the road and the falls was a deep ravine so we couldn't get up close and personal with it, but Horse Tail Falls was different. It was accessible and if there is anything I love better than looking at a waterfall it is climbing a waterfall. I still remember my first waterfall climb outside of Quebec, Canada on a vacation with my wife to that elegant city. Just north of town was a small waterfall that I was able to climb up the side. Such was the case at Horse Tail Falls. My family got some wonderful pictures of me against the grandeur and glory of that massive waterfall!

## CHAPTER THIRTY-SEVEN

# OUR FIRST VALDEZ EAGLE

THERE IT WAS SITTING in a short, leaf-less tree beside the Lowe River: our first Valdez eagle. I have been fascinated by the bird Adam called eagle (Genesis 2:20) for most of my life. Living in a state where there is a healthy population of the majestic fowl, I have had the privilege of seeing countless eagles over the years. Each sighting has been a thrill whether over the massive Penobscot River while Atlantic salmon fishing, or the snow covered Branch Pond while ice fishing, I have enjoyed every encounter with an eagle. After hearing Scott's stories of eagles as thick as seagulls in Valdez, I couldn't wait until we got to the Alaskan port. I just knew I would see more eagles than I had ever seen before.

Thirty-four times in God's Holy Writ the eagle is mentioned: God's favorite bird? Granted, I know that the eagles named in the Bible are not the same as our famous North American Bald Eagle. According to my research, there are at least fifty-nine species of eagles worldwide, and this magnificent bird is found on every continent except Antarctica. Haliaeetus Leucocphalus is the scientific name for the Bald Eagle, and by some estimates, there were half a million of these birds flying over America when it was named the national bird in 1782. Surely you know by now that Ben Franklin wanted the turkey! The very demeanor of the eagle speaks of high flying freedom, and despite the decline, only 417 pairs in 1963, of the population in the lower 48 states, the Alaskan Bald Eagle has always been free-wheeling and numerous in America's 50th state. Alaska is home to over 20,000 pairs, but on the afternoon of my first Valdez's sighting I only saw one eagle, not the multitude of eagles I expected to see! I was hoping I would witness a verse that I had read since childhood: "For wheresoever the carcass (and there were plenty of carcasses of dead salmon on the shores of Valdez Bay and the rivers that flowed into that bay) is, there will the eagles be gathered together!" (Matthew 24:28) I still haven't seen good evidence of the verse.

Created for the Alaskan environment, bald eagles have several layers of feathers including a layer of down that insulates the eagle and makes it possible for the bird to live in the harsh climate of Alaska. Fish is the eagle's primary source of food, so it is not surprising that in Valdez where fish are plentiful the population of eagles would also be plentiful, but on the day (August 21, 2014) we pulled into Valdez the eagles were few and far between. We only spotted a half of a dozen fishing along the Lowe River leading into town, so my first impression with Valdez was disappointing because of our lack of spotting numbers of eagles, and then we ran into another difficulty. Arriving at the Best Western we found out that the reservation we had made months before had been cancelled. Our Valdez side trip wasn't starting out very well. There would be a room eventually, but we would have to wait, so we decided to go exploring for a fishing hole and maybe, more bald eagles?

Edwin Way Teale once wrote, "Above all other birds, it is the soaring eagle that gives the most abiding impression of power and purpose in the air." The wisest man ever to live agrees when Solomon wrote of the four most wonderful things he had ever seen, and first on that quartet was "the way of an eagle in the air..." (Proverbs 30:19) We would eventually see 22 eagles in our Alaska adventure, far fewer than we imagined, but enough to fill our quest to see the world's greatest bird. Besides the eagles along the Lowe River, we saw a number flying over Valdez Bay and a few soaring. God created (Job 39:27) the eagle with broad, long wings ideal for conserving energy while in flight. Its very makeup reduces air turbulence and makes gliding easier. The experts say an eagle can attain speeds of up to 30-50 mph and that eagles are known to travel upwards of 180 miles in a day. The eagles we saw in Valdez were not travellers because everything they needed was below them in the massive pink salmon run that was happening in Valdez Bay.

As we watched and watched for eagles, I knew from my study (I have a whole series of messages on God's use of the eagle in Scripture to teach us many lessons) that the eagle was watching us. The eyes of the eagle are one of its most amazing features. A second eyelid slides across their eyes every few seconds, wiping airborne dust away, and because the lid is translucent, it allows the bird to see even in mid-blink. The eagle also was created with a two-fold focusing system: one for looking sideways and the other for looking forward. As a result, the eagle's eyesight is the sharpest of any other animal and eight times sharper than the human eye! I read once that an eagle flying at a thousand feet can oversee an area of three square miles and identify a prey moving at a mile. Whether flying high or perched on a tall tree, the eagle is always on the alert for its next meal. I have seen them in tall spruce trees along the shores of Big Lake in Downeast Maine waiting for a bass to come to close to the surface of the lake, and I have seen them in tall fir trees along the banks of Grand Lake Stream waiting patiently for a landlock salmon to make a mistake. One of the great thrills of the out-of-doors is to watch an eagle leave its perch for an attack, or a free meal. One of the joys I had while ice fishing was the late afternoon arrival of the local eagle to get the insides of the lake trout we caught; I was looking for a similar event from the eagles of Valdez.

While in Alaska I learned that one of the greatest concentrations of eagles takes place along a ten-mile stretch of the Chilkat River near Haines, Alaska. This is one of the primary wintering grounds of the Alaskan Bald Eagle in the months of November and December. At times as many as 4,000 eagles gather to take advantage of the late Chum Salmon run. Scott spent his first winter in Alaska running supplies from Fort Wainwright in Fairbanks and to other military based scattered around southern Alaska. A number of his winter runs were to Valdez, and though he never saw the number like in Haines, he did see the gathering of eagles that Christ foretold (Luke 17:37). It was a bit early to see such a sight for us. Because the salmon runs were going on everywhere in Alaska in August, the Bald eagle population was spread out. They would gather in a few months.

Over the day we were in Valdez, I was reminded again of my favorite Biblical eagle verse each and every time I saw one of these spectacular birds: "But they that wait on the Lord shall renew their strength; they shall mount up with wings as eagles; they shall run, and not be weary; they shall walk, and not faint." (Isaiah 40:31) My mind goes back to that first Valdez eagle as it sat on it perch keeping an eye on its feeding grounds, no doubt a pool in the Lowe River were the spawning salmon congregate. It looked healthy as food was plentiful and little energy had to be expended to find a meal. Harder and harsher days were just around the corner with the coming of autumn and the dark winter thereafter, but for now it was paradise and heaven rolled up in one season. It is with this picture I would have you ponder Isaiah's verse, a verse I have had in my memorized memory since my early twenties. It was the verse my college society chose as their motto, and yes, our mascot the eagle! Isaiah wants us to see the power of an eagle taking to flight as we recognize the strength we receive when we 'wait on the Lord'. The Bible is clear that as our days are so shall our strength be (Deuteronomy 33:25) from the Lord. Paul taught that we can do anything through the strengthening of Christ (Philippians 4:13).

## Chapter Thirty-Eight

## Valdez Pinks And Valdez Fishers

As we waited to get into our motel room in the village of Valdez, we explored the small coastal town for a place to fish. The town was crowded with the summer people. The clerk at the Best Western told us the population triples in the summer months, much like the Maine coastal community of Bar Harbor, with the motels and hotels full and the RV and trail parks scattered around town also flashing 'No Vacancy' signs. We quickly got out of town heading for the road leading to the gigantic oil terminal on the other side of the bay. The informative clerk also said that one of the most popular fishing spots was also along that road: Allison Point.

On the way to Allison Point we passed a fish hatchery and the largest flock of seagulls I have ever seen in my life. Living on the coast of Maine for the last thirty years, I have seen my fair share of seagulls and even a large flock here and there, but at the most, a few score at a time. But as we drove beside Valdez Bay there were hundreds upon hundreds of seagulls milling around in the air over the small stream by the hatchery. The tide appeared to be going out and large sand bars stretched along certain sections of the shoreline. On these sand bars were hundreds of more seagulls just sitting or feeding on dead salmon. We eventually arrived at a large parking area, and we could see from the roadside a sandy beach below a small bluff. There were a few fishermen casting into the bay, so we decided to check the situation out. Coleen stayed in the car while Scott and I walked down a narrow path to the beach. It reminded me of a few places along the coast of Maine, except for the "Beware of Bear" signs!

Interestingly, the first person we talked to was a transplant from Maine. She was a lady who had been married in Caribou, Maine, the town I had been born in. As I looked up and down the long shoreline, I noted that the lady in front of me was the only lady I saw in a group of about two-dozen fishermen. Each was casting a large spoon??? into the bay along a sandy shore that was about a football field in length. Periodically there was a small boulder or two, but most of the shore was flat and sandy. The beach went down the shoreline until a large rocky outcropping jutted into the bay. Up the shore the beach stopped at a small stream that flowed into the bay from under the roadway. I struck up a conversation with the lady because she had at her feet what I was looking for, a silver salmon. She had just caught the 15-pound beauty and was actually about to leave with her prize. When she found out that we were from Maine she stopped to give us the lowdown on Allison Point. She had moved to Alaska with her husband and enjoyed catching dinner. She told Scott and I that we had arrived at ebb tide and that the incoming tide might hold some silvers, but most of the fish in the sea were pinks. She kind of laughed at us when we said we were going to fly fish. Everybody there that day was spin fishing, but she gave us a hearty good luck as she headed up the bank with her salmon in hand.

It was then I noticed just how many fish were swimming along the shore in a few feet of water. What was even more impressive were the hundreds of dead fish washing up on shore. I had seen a few at Montana Creek, but nothing compared to the numbers along Allison Point Beach. I learned from another fisherman that Valdez Bay has one of the largest Pink (Humpy) Salmon runs in Alaska. What made this particular section so populated with pinks was the hatchery above the beach. Most of the salmon returning had been hatched in that hatchery, and they were returning to the place they had been released. I stood amazed at the volume of fish before me, and I was even more determined to fish. We returned to the car and once again Coleen told us to fish. We couldn't get into our room until 4 o'clock, so we still had a couple of hours to fish the incoming tide. We geared up and left Coleen reading a book.

To say fishing Valdez Bay for pink and silver salmon was a unique fishing experience would be an understatement. I had never fished were the fish were so thick that they were constantly hitting your legs while you stood in the water. Scott and I waded as far into the bay as he could to get away from the dead and dying salmon near shore. Once again our biggest obstacle was the lack of aggressiveness of the salmon. Most of the fish we saw were dying. Our hope was that a few long casts further out in the bay might attract a passing silver. We could see the boats far off shore trolling, and we surmised they were looking for silvers not pinks. Scott was fishing a floating line, but I had put on a fast-sinking line with a huge Miramichi spring salmon fly: a favorite, a Copper Renus. Within minutes I had on my first Valdez Bay pink. It was sluggish in its fight, but heavy against the strong tide that was switching and the deep water I was fishing in. Over the next two hours I landed about 10 salmon all about 25 inches long and weighting 4-5 pounds. Scott didn't get a strike! It was then Scott decided to take his mother back to the motel and have some supper, but I made a different choice.

I was determined to stay and fish the complete tide, six hours' worth, in hopes the new tide would bring a few silver salmon near shore. Leaving me with his bear repellant, (the lady from Maine said they had seen a mother and two cubs over the last two days feeding on the dead salmon washing up on shore) just in case, and promised he would be back in a couple of hours to see how I was doing. As they drove off back to Valdez, I went back to fishing along Allison Beach. We had started fishing at two in the afternoon, and as the afternoon slipped away, I noticed that with each passing hour fewer and fewer fishermen there were. I began to think that the lady had mislead me because by the time there was just a thin strip of sand life on Allison Point Beach, I was the only fisherman still fishing that I could see. Granted, I was periodically catching fish (I would catch 54 pinks (John 21:11-far fewer than the disciples) between 2 and 9 P.M), but no silvers. I did enjoy the alone time as I always have. Fishing alone is a pleasant experience if you're catching fish as I was, and the scenery was interesting and I was hoping, as I regularly looked around, to see that mother bear and her kids, but no visits from the local bear family happened.

When everybody left me to the fishing hole of Allison Point, I was joined by a pair of fishers that entertained me for the rest of the afternoon. As I casted my heavy fly into the bay and slowly retrieved it, I looked around to see what else was happening in my line of sight. It was then I saw a fish jump into the air far out in the bay. I was excited at first thinking it was an incoming school of silvers. Upon closer observation, I realized it wasn't jumping salmon but salmon being thrown by a harbor seal that was playing with his supper. As I watched closer, I spotted one seal and then another as they worked their way off shore fishing as they swam, but every once in awhile I would see an airborne salmon and watch as the throwing seal caught his cast before it hit the water. I had seen the feat on television, but in Valdez Bay it was amazing, and when I thought I had seen everything I saw something else in the water just beyond me, sea otters. Again I had seen the creature on television, but this was my first sighting in the wild. Between landing Valdez pinks, I was entertained by two very colorful sea creatures. I will never forget the afternoon that my only fishing companions were a couple of seals playing toss with pink salmon, and a sea otter who was having just as much success fishing as I was!

## Chapter Thirty-Nine

## Eagles In The Wind

Around six o'clock in the evening of our only day in Valdez, Scott returned alone after getting his mother settled into our motel room. He had also taken her out to supper (two sandwich dinners for $40) before returning to see if bears had eaten me. I must admit when he returned I was ready for a break, but not before fulfilling one of my Alaskan dreams: standing in a stream of salmon!

By the time my son returned, I had fished every inch of Allison Point Beach. The tide had made a complete recovery, but because it hadn't reached the tree line I was able to cast my fly without getting caught in the branches and underbrush along the shore. Step by step and foot by foot I had worked my way along the shore until I came to a small stream that was flowing under the roadway through a culvert from a small creek that came out of the hillside just beyond the parking lot. When I arrived at the brook, I couldn't believe the number of salmon trying to swim up the shallow (barely a foot of water) stream. I walked out into the flow and kneeled down. I then had Scott take a few photographs of me surrounded by salmon. They were all pink salmon, but it made a nice picture for my Alaskan fishing collection. But, where were the silvers?

It was after this that Scott and I decided to explore a bit more before returning to the beach for some late evening fishing. We first drove down the road to the entrance of the Alaska Pipeline Terminal, but the gate was closed and there were no super tankers being loaded. We reversed our direction and returned to the hatchery to see what was happening there. Just in front of a small bridge that crossed the hatchery stream was a parking lot. We got out and decided to walk the beach on the bayside of the pink salmon hatchery. As we crawled down the small bank to the beach we saw them: two huge bald eagles. That late afternoon and early evening was wrapped in

August warmth. The air was filled with seagulls soaring over the cliff behind us and in the bay before us. The smell of dead fish was everywhere, yet at the same time the strong salty air gave off a fragrance that made the walk towards the eagles pleasant. The eagles we sought had landed at the seaside no doubt looking for a fresh meal. The seagulls, on the other hand, were looking for salmon eggs and fish eyes. One of the observations I noted on my sea edge fishing trip was just how many of the dead fish on the shore had their eyes plucked out. Seagulls only eat what they like the best, and fish-eyes were high on their menu.

Scott was determined to get a few up close and personal pictures of the eagles on the shore, but it wasn't long before he went too close and into the wind the pair went. At first they circled the sandy shore barely twenty feet in the air. I think they liked their fishing spot and didn't really want to leave, but our intrusion into their territory was bothering them. More often than not, they sit quietly and patiently waiting the right time to liftoff, but when provoked by invaders like my son, they are soon off into the one domain in which no enemy can follow, the wind. Ever since my first eagle sighting an eagle in the wind has captivated me. With powerful strokes of their massive wings and despite their exceptional weight, it doesn't take an eagle very long to get into the air even from a sandy beach. Granted, taking off from a cliff or a tree is easier, but a flatland start is just a doable as it was that evening across the bay from Valdez. An eagle takeoff starts with a shaking of itself, fluffing its plumage, and a lifting of its massive wings. I judged the wings on the eagles were at least five-feet wide. As with all other takeoffs I have witnessed over the years, the regal bird simple starts walking along the shore until enough air is under its wings for takeoff. Its only help was the slight breeze blowing up the bay that evening. Yet, within seconds, the pair was flying over our heads heading for the cliff on the other side of the road.

Darkness was approaching, and, in the cool of the night, the pair would rest on some old branch on the Lowe River, or perhaps, on a crag overlooking the hatchery. Whichever, I knew the eagles would be back the next day to fish and bulk themselves up for the long, cold Alaskan winter. The glorious flight of any eagle (Jeremiah 49:22-"Behold, he shall come up and fly as the eagle. . ..") is a cherished experience, but in Valdez that evening it was more special given the surroundings we were in. The last we saw of the pair of eagle in the wind was when they gained height and disappeared over the small ridgeline on the other side of the road. Their departure allowed Scott and me to continue our exploration of the stream by the hatchery. You might ask me why the eagles had taken so much of our attention when we were surrounded with the vastness of an Alaskan bay. The answer is a simply one for me. In the wilds of Maine or the wilderness of Alaska, I have yet to find any creature that has demanded my attention more than the bald eagle. Granted, if I were in India it would be different. In India I have had the privilege of seeing an Indian eagle, much smaller than our eagle and, in my opinion, not as beautiful: white head yes, but more of a brownish body. Yet in that same park were White and Royal Bengal Tigers and, of course, Indian Elephants.

Working our way up the shore to the small stream that feeds the hatchery and eventually dumps into the head of the bay, I got to do something I had also dreamed about doing in Alaska: fishing with my hands. Since my boyhood, I have been fishing and, yes, on a few occasions I have tried to catch a fish with my hands. What boy doesn't! The fish of which I speak were small minnows because no respectable fish would ever allow anyone to get close enough to be caught with one's hands, yet in Valdez that opportunity happened. I have photographical proof that I have done just that. The pink salmon were so thick in the stream by the hatchery that I literally stepped into the water and reached down and started pulling four to seven pound salmon up out of the water with my hands. Scott stood on the shore with his camera as he took picture after picture of a half dozen salmon I picked up with my hands, but you can't really call it fishing. I had heard of fishing in a barrel, but this was easier than that. Perhaps, that is why I don't think my fishing in Valdez was really fishing. It was just plain too easy!

Scott and I returned to Allison Point and fished a couple more hours but no silvers. We were back to the Best Western in Valdez by dark (10 o'clock), and it was nearly eleven before I had my journal caught up. Our ninth day in Alaska was over, and on the morrow we would be heading back to Fairbank, one of our longest days on the road. I shut the light off at 11:30 P.M., but I didn't go right to sleep. Despite the number of fish I actually landed on Allison Point and the number of fish I actually picked up out of the hatchery stream and the chance to literally kneel down in a stream of salmon, the highlight of my trip to Valdez wasn't the terminal, the terrain, or the thousands of salmon I saw; it was the eagles in the wind, the eagles in the trees, and the eagles along the bay that highlighted and underlined my Valdez adventure. To see just one of these amazing birds would have been enough. Without a doubt, I can write that I saw more eagles in one day than any other day in my life. Up until Valdez, to see a pair if not a trio was the best I had witnessed, but in my one day in Valdez I saw nearly two-dozen of God's greatest birds.

## Chapter Forty

## The Turning Of The Tide

I woke in Valdez, Alaska to a thick fog. It reminded me of my five years in a small, island community off the coast of Downeast Maine: Eastport on Moose Island. After spending more than twenty-five years in Ellsworth, I know Coastal Maine has a climate and a culture all its own, but coastal island life is entirely different from the mainland, or as they say in Eastport 'inland'. It is a way of life that can only be understood if you live there for a while, maybe, a lifetime? If you're not from there then you will always have a hard time knowing why things are done as they are done and be accepted as one of them, for as the locals will tell you, it all has to do with the turning of the tide.

The Good Lord had once again been good to us on our tour of Alaska. Our plans were to spend only one day in Valdez, and the day before, the weather had been perfect. If we had come to Valdez a day later we would have seen nothing because of the thickness of the fog. Our arrival on the 21st of August instead of the 22nd made it possible for us to see the site and the sights in all of their majesty. The high mountains along the coastline create a small pocket of land for the residents of Valdez to live on. The Gulf of Alaska, and in particular the Bay of Valdez, cradles the citizens of Valdez on the other side. The sheer size of the hills to the north and the sea to the south was scenic to say the least, the bigness of Alaska on display once again. Having lived in such a coastal town in Maine, I could understand the geography and topography as well as the attitude we found in Valdez; isolated, coastal living creates a self-reliant, hard-hearted, suspicious people. More often than not they will blame it all on the turning of the tide.

The day before I had spent most of my allotted time in Valdez fishing the tide of Valdez Bay hoping to land a silver (Coho) salmon, but to no avail!

## THE TURNING OF THE TIDE

It was a mighty tide I felt on my waders because of the huge volume of water and the wide bay, but small (maybe twenty feet) compared to some I had experienced. The greatest tides in the world, averaging between 20-50 feet, but 70 feet at the mouth of the Petitcodiac River, are found in Fundy Bay, 32 miles wide at its entrance and 96 miles long, in New Brunswick, Canada. I have seen them up close, and they are impressive. Even my little ministry town of Eastport has more spectacular tides, 30 plus feet in places, in Passamaquoddy Bay than I witnessed in Valdez Bay. Though not all tides are created equal, there is something about the turning of the tide that affects those who live by its power, its timing, and its movements. So I had lived another day in my life under the influence of a strong tide. As I walked along the waterfront of Valdez on the morning of our departure, I felt it again. Despite the ocean fog that cut my visibility to a few hundred feet, I could sense the moving of the sea. I like to explain it like the ocean taking a breath, exhaling is the outgoing tide and inhaling is the incoming tide. It is at that moment of transition that the tide turns.

That turning is called the ebb. The laws of the sea are quite simple and there comes a time, the lowest time, when a dramatic change is going to happen. It is hard to see, it is so subtle, but the ebb is the turning point when the tide takes charge again; so rhythmic, so regular, so reassuring its pattern and process can be timed, clocked to the exact second, for the lowest ebb of the sea is the turning of the tide. I stood gazing out into the fog of Valdez Bay and I thought we too had come to the ebb of our trip. We had reached as far as we would go in Alaska, and it was time to head back to Fairbanks. Six days on the road and it was time to finish the circle. It was like the tide. We were returning to the place we had started. At the writing of this remembrance of our time spent in Valdez, I have just finished a wonderful devotion by Vance Havner under the title of "Turn of the Tide" in which he gives a marvelous application to the precept of the tide:

> "The lowest ebb is the turn of the tide. It is true of more than the ocean. We have an old proverb that says just about the same thing: The darkest hour is just before the dawn. We have seen it happen again and again. Maybe it was a crisis in serious illness. Someone almost died, then came a turn. The patient touched bottom and then started up. Or it was a low ebb in the family fortune or failure in a career. Everything was lost, we thought, but no-when everything was darkest, came the dawn. . .Civilization stands today at low ebb. Never has there been such scientific advancements, such material wealth, such intellectual brilliance, but the soul of humanity is sick. America flies the skies, but also flounders in the slime. Such

low ebb does not guarantee a turn of the tide, however, for history does not operate like the ocean. Nations die, civilizations rot, and kingdoms pass away. We learn from history that nobody learns history. The world is awash today in tidal waves of revolution. Other lands are surging in worldwide ferment. There is no certainty that our American low ebb means a turn in the tide. The church is at low ebb today. Religious leaders wring their hands and beat their breasts. Of course there have been low ebbs before. . .but this does not justify such a state. God never intended it. Low ebb and high tide are orderly processes of nature but Christianity was never meant to fluctuate up and down. There is no justification for malarial Christians, living from fever to chill. Low-grade religion is a consequence of sin. However, there will be an incoming tide of some sort one of these days. Will it be our Lord's return? Or revival? Or retribution? One thing is certain; the tide never stays out! And the lowest ebb is the turn of that tide. . .And Jeremiah in his fifth lamentation turned from a dark picture of the times as pen can write, to say, 'Turn thou us unto Thee, O Lord, and we shall be turned; renew our days as of old.' (Lamentations 5:21) With him the lowest ebb was the turn of the tide."

Truly we live in an age where the fog is so thick we can't see clearly, but despite our lack of vision, the tide is turning. I find it fascinating that even while on vacation the spiritual side of me is always looking for a lesson, a teaching, and an instruction into something more important than a day fishing the tide in Valdez Bay. I think now I see why the Lord gave my family and me such a day. Another day living with the turning of the tide, another day experiencing the ebb tide, whether the ocean ebb, a trip ebb, or just maybe, a life ebb (Little did we know this would be our last trip with Scott; his life too was ebbing, he was turning toward heaven!). One of the reasons my wife and I took this trip was to be with our son, to support our son as he too came to an ebb time in his life. The military life he had known for eight years was over. A new tide in his life was beginning, and we wanted to be there to encourage him and help were we could as he made the transition back into civilian life. Such swings in one's life are not always easy, and the surge and redirection can be daunting and dangerous. We know that Scott has been in an ebb time in his spiritual life for a long time, and it was and still is our prayer that he might be at his lowest that the tide isn't still going out, but that the turn has happened. As with any ebb tide, it takes a while to see the change. As I fished Allison Point, I couldn't tell exactly when the ebb passed and the tide started to come in, but as the afternoon passed I did notice the tree line coming closer and closer as I moved with the tide up the shoreline. So it is with life. My prayer is that we are in that turning time, that transition time, that the ebb is passed and that the tide has turned for our son. My supplication is the intercession of Jeremiah: "Turn thou us (son) unto Thee, O Lord!"

## Chapter Forty-One

## Eight Days On The Road

We woke in Valdez to a thick fog. After a sit down breakfast, we headed back to our Alaskan home base: Fairbanks. This would be our second longest day on the road since we left Fairbanks a week before. It was 364 miles back to Fairbanks by way of Glennallen and Delta Junction; our eighth day on the road would be filled with more Alaskan adventures!

As we talked to the locals before heading out of town, we discovered that Valdez has a year-a-round population of about 3500 residents, but in a day like we spent in Valdez that population can double. Most come for the fishing, but others come to enjoy the sights and sites of coastal Alaska. We too enjoyed the village of Valdez because it reminded us of Bar Harbor, a coastal tourist destination near home. As we left Valdez, Scott point out the terminal where he used to travel to pick up ammo for the various military bases scattered around Alaska, but as usual, my focus was more on the God-made versus the manmade.

Our trip up the Richardson Highway took us over familiar territory because there is only one way in and one way out of Valdez, at least by land. We hugged the shoreline of the Lowe River in the first section of our trip northward. We saw again the majestic Alaskan Bald Eagle perched in the trees along the banks looking for breakfast or maybe lunch. We counted five of these marvelous birds as Scott's Tahoe took us into the mountain canyon toward the heights above. My last eagle of the trip left an immeasurable impression on me. The lone sentinel of the Lowe River was sitting stately in the branch of a weather-beaten tree revealing its enormous vitality, fabulous strength, and noble grandeur. We were traveling through its domain, and no matter how often I would visit, or if I would ever visit again, it would always be the eagle's world. The eagle, despite its retiring habits and demands for greater and greater space in which to thrive, deserves to survive; not just because it is our national symbol, but because it is one of God's greatest handiworks created on the fifth day of creation. The eagle is a magnificent and noble expression of God's wild world, and it is an emblem of the untamed, free spirit that mountain creatures symbolize. We lose them and how far are we from extinction?

It was a joy to see the falls of the Key Stone Canyon again. Both the Bridal Veil and Horse Tail Falls were flowing full. The cascading water was impressive even in a light fog. Our first views were on a sunny day with only the shadows of the canyon to restrict the vista, but the low hanging fog gave the gorge an eerie feeling. This didn't dampen my second look; if anything it only enhanced my thanks for the privilege of seeing such an unblemished sight. I am acutely aware of the plundering and pillaging of the planet by those who care little about the earth. The greed of mankind is legendary, and I have travelled far enough afield to see the appalling ruination wreaked on a hillside or mountainside by the callous indifference of humans. But in places like Key Stone Canyon, one has the opportunity to witness how it was intended to be. The world can have its desert wastelands, polluted rivers, raped forests, and impoverished grasslands. As for me, give me the waterfalls of the Key Stone Canyon. One does wonder just how long such places will exist or how long it will be before the greedy, grubby hands of man will violate such pristine spots. For me, it was my rare privilege to have enjoyed the beauty and majesty of untamed Alaska on our day traveling back to Fairbanks from Valdez.

Quickly we climbed to the summit of Thompson Pass, and just as quickly descended off the slopes of Chugach Mountain Range. We passed the Worthington Glacier for a second time, and it wasn't far beyond it we caught another fabulous glimpse of wild Alaska: three beautiful swans paddling in a small pond by the Richardson Highway, a few fleeting, intimate glimpses of three creatures in a natural habitat worthy of a whole book, but I am afraid just a few lines in a passing chapter in an Alaska recollection. I hate even to stop describing the trinity of swans, but the road is long back to Fairbanks and I must press on if I am to share with you the rest of our eighth day highlights.

We stopped twice before we reached Glennallen. A marvelous section of the Alaskan Pipeline came into view suddenly as we rocketed (remember my son's lead-foot) around one of the countless corners on the Richardson Highway. Scott brought the Tahoe to a stop as he had promised early in the road trip, and I got a wonderful photograph of the pipeline as it rose from a small hilltop only to disappear into a tundra vale. Our second stop was to take a picture of three mountain peaks behind a massive Lake Kenny. A turnout with roadside picture boards told me that at 13,009 feet, Mount

Drum; at 14,163 feet, Mount Wrangell, and at 16,390 feet, Mount Blackburn of the Wrangell-Elias National Park was what I was looking at. We had left the coastal fog on the other side of Thompson Pass, so the skies were clear and we could make out the tops of the mountains despite the distance. The combination of high, snow-covered peaks against the backdrop of Lake Kenny was a great use of our limited minutes.

By eleven, we drove into Glennallen were we gassed up ($81.00), and I had the worst five dollar hotdog I ever ate. Granted, I haven't eaten too many $5 hotdogs in my life, but by far that was the worst. The highlight of the pit stop for me was a stuffed wolf I saw in a small tourist center by the gas station. I had never seen a wolf in the wild, and the ones on television don't give you the dimension properly. The creature on display was huge. I determined then I wouldn't want to meet one in the wild. By 12:30 we drove into the town of Paxson and within a few miles were following the shoreline of the biggest lake we had seen in Alaska: Summit Lake. It wasn't long after the lake we saw another section of the Alaskan Pipeline suddenly come out of the ground as if by magic, and we watched it cross a small brook and then disappear again over a small range of hills. By 1:30 we were passing another huge military base, Fort Donnelly, were the 'arctic warriors' do their winter training. Scott showed us a rugged mountain he had climbed (not for training just for fun) with a few of his army buddies earlier that year.

Four and a half hours after we left Valdez we drove into Delta Junction where Alaska Route 4 and Alaska Route 2 intersect. We had travelled 265 miles, and it was still another 100 miles to Fairbanks. We stopped so Coleen could have lunch. She didn't find anything she liked at Glennallen, so she got some chicken and fries at an IGA in Delta Junction. Coleen ate on the fly because Scott and I were focused on a fishing hole Scott had fished before, Lost Lake. This small pond would give us a two-hour break from a very long day in the Tahoe. It was here Scott got his mother fishing again, and though it was mid-afternoon, not the best time to fish, we did catch a few rainbows: the biggest about a foot long. We were still an hour out from Fairbanks, so by five we were back in Scott's Purple-Heart car on the Purple-Heart Highway leading into Fairbanks. (The story of how Scott earned his Purple Heart medal in Afghanistan is in another chapter.) By six we were pulling into the Best Western Motel, and our second longest Alaskan road trip day was done. For me, the best part of the day was the hours spent watching the Creator's creation pass by me: "Hast thou not known? Hast thou not heard, that the everlasting God, the Lord, the Creator of the ends of the earth. . ." (Isaiah 40:28)

## Chapter Forty-Two

## Gold Dredge #8

We finished our grand tour of Alaska on the evening of August 22, 2014. The 1730-mile trip took us from Fairbanks to Denali to Kenai to Chickaloon to Valdez and back to Fairbanks: what I like to call the Alaskan Circle. We had made reservation at the Best Western before we left Fairbanks, so when we returned, tired from Valdez, a room and a shower was waiting for us at a familiar spot. After a wash up, we were on the road again to a famous restaurant just outside the city limits of Fairbanks for supper. Meeting us at the Silver Gulch were the Lloyds, Hailey and Brandon, Scott's friends from Fort Wainwright. After the best $29 steak I have ever eaten, it was early to-bed for me!

Our last Saturday in Alaska was meant to be a rest day after a fast-paced, world-wind tour of central Alaska. Scott knew we would be exhausted, so we didn't have anything on the schedule but to kick back and rest. The next day we were going to put Coleen on a plane for California to see Marnie and Josue. We did sleep in that morning, but Scott was up early to help Hailey and Brandon pack for their move out of Alaska. They would be leaving in two weeks for their new home in Louisiana, but they were going by way of California and Arizona to visit family and friends, so they had to have their belongings ready to be picked up by the shipper during our last weekend in Alaska. I got up around mid-morning but Coleen was fast asleep; we had done her in! I walked down to the lobby to verify our stay in the motel until Monday when Scott and I would leave for Maine. Once those reservations were confirmed I found a quiet place to sit, not wanting to disturb Coleen. She had a hard day ahead of her the next day, so I wanted her to sleep as long as she could. I watched the world news on the motel's lobby television and was shocked to see our dear president golfing while ISIS marched through Iraqi. I was especially sad because I knew what my boy, and many sons like him, had sacrificed to liberate Iraqi and keep the peace only to see it all destroyed after a few short years. The newsmen were already calling it the Third Iraqi War.

I was also touched by the story of the Americans who had contracted Ebola while trying to help the West Africans with an outbreak of Biblical proportions. The spread of that terrible plague was all over the news, and I felt fortunate to be on vacation, resting, without a care in the world. After an hour of terrible news, I returned to our room with Coleen's breakfast to find my wife up, but Scott still away. While Coleen ate and got ready for the day, I watched an old movie, *Torpedo Run*. By the way, watching old war movies is one of my favorite downtime activities. By the time Coleen was ready, Scott had returned with his friends. Brandon and Hailey were still two weeks from leaving, but they had to empty their military apartment. The Army was putting them up in a motel for their remaining stay in Alaska. Only the government would think that was economical! Coleen wanted to do a bit of shopping, so Scott took us back on base. This was the same military base where Coleen and I started our great adventure in Alaska together.

One of the items on Coleen's bucket list for Alaska was to pan for gold. Ever since we got hooked on the reality TV show, *Gold Rush*, Coleen wanted to see if while we were in Alaska we might be able to pan for gold ourselves. Searching the flyers and brochures in the places we stopped Coleen discovered such a place just outside of Fairbanks. We had a 1:30 Saturday appointment with Gold Dredge #8. Scott didn't think that was something he was keen on, so he would drop us off and pick us up after the tour. He had a few things to do before he could leave Alaska on August 25, 2014. I must admit I was very skeptical about the whole affair. The possibility of actually finding gold would be rare I thought, but to fulfill my wife's desire I went along. She had been a good sport when it came to letting Scott and me go fishing while she was left alone, so she deserved at least one afternoon doing what she wanted to do. After Scott dropped us off at the staging area for the gold mining tour just off the Elliott Highway, I wondered what we would find in the way of gold, and what was a gold dredge anyway?

About a hundred other folks were waiting for us as we walked into the Gold Dredge #8 National Historic District and gave the attendant $80, which included two bags of dirt, for the three-hour tour. I will be honest with you. I had never heard about a gold dredge until we started looking into this afternoon excursion. I knew about panning for gold, and digging for gold and mining for gold, but dredging for gold? The tour started actually with a small lecture on the Alaska Pipeline because of a section of the pipeline past through the historical site. I was actually a bit disappointed at first thinking I had come for gold, and they were going to tell me something I had already learned in my nine days in Alaska. However, the talk was short, and we were soon on a small gauge railroad car that would actually take us to Gold Dredge #8. So far the tour had been quite a letdown, a disappointment, but as we would soon learn, the best was yet to come!

The miniature train with a dozen passenger cars got started a bit late because of road construction work near the entrance; we had to wait for a tour bus to arrive. Once we got started a well-informed man told us about all the methods used in gold mining in the history of Alaska. Along the sides of the tracks were various displays of gold mining techniques, like sluicing and water cannon. We found out that we were traveling through a section of the district called the Davidson Ditch. We could see that vast areas of the region had been dug up or washed away through the various methods employed over the years. The ditch was actually a 48-inch pipeline that carried water 91 miles from the headwaters of the Chatanika River to the Fox region, or the Goldstream Valley, where vast amounts of gold had been discovered. With gold at the ready, the dredge system was developed to mine gold on a massive scale, a means to move large volumes of gold yielding dirt economically and efficiently.

After about a fifteen minute ride through a series of washed out vales, we came around a corner and there it was: Gold Dredge #8. My mouth dropped. It was a huge mechanical machine unlike anything I had ever seen before, and there it was floating in a small pond. This is what we learned about the history of the dredge:

"In 1928, after years of planning, Gold Dredge #8 arrived in the Goldstream Valley. The dredge has a ship-like steel hull, 99 feet long and 50 feet wide. In its day it was considered a masterpiece of engineering because of its incredible efficiency in recovering gold. It actually targeted gold left behind by earlier generations that couldn't reach the gold the dredge could. Vast amounts of overburden (non-rich soil) had to be removed so that the underlying gravel beds near to the bedrock could be thawed. The dredge would then use its 'bucket-line' to dig up the gravel on top of the bedrock. The 'bucket-line' consists of 64 massive buckets pinned together by chains; each bucket weighed in at 1,500 pounds and could carry 6 cubic feet of gravel. As the dredge floats in its man-make pond, the bucket line would dig into the bank of the pond scooping up loads of gold-bearing gravel, and then haul each bucket load into what is called the 'hooper'. The bucket would then travel down the ladder to pick up another load."

Time had proven that like the proverb of old says: "There is gold. . .." (Proverbs 20:15) 'in them there hills'!

# Chapter Forty-Three

# An Ornament Of Gold

As the instructor of the Gold Dredge #8 told us about the dredge and its history, he also took time to tell us how we were going to pan for our own gold. In a demonstration on the deck of the dredge, he got out a tub of water and a panning dish and a small bag of dirt. He dumped the dirt into the pan and started moving the pan through the water allowing the dirt to wash away. Slowly and surely he removed all the dirt while the heavier flakes of gold stayed in the bottom ridges of the pan, and sure enough there was gold; he showed us, but was it a trick?

After the demonstration, the train, a replica of the original Tanana Valley Railroad, moved out traveling around the massive dredge to the other side of the pond. As we travelled, our host told us more about Gold Dredge #8:

"The floating gold miner worked from 1928 until it was decommissioned in 1958. Once the dirt was picked up by the bucket and dumped into the hopper it then emptied into a trommel (36-feet long and 6 feet in diameter) that separated by water the larger pieces of gravel from the smaller pieces that dropped into the sluice boxes which continued the process of separating the gold from the gravel. The bucket could dig as deep as 28 feet and at a top speed of 22 buckets a minutes over 6,000 cubic yards of dirt could be processed in a 24-hour shift. The left over gravel (called 'tailings') was picked up by a conveyor belt that brought the remains to the rear of the dredge where the 'stacker' would pile the dirt into piles behind the dredge. The dredge was shut down for a 'clean up' once every two weeks to remove the gold trapped in the sluice boxes under the trommel. The average cleanup, that only took a few hours, was nearly 4,000 ounces of gold (in today's money that is over 5 million dollars every clean up)!"

Once the train stopped at the station, a tourist attraction if I have ever seen one, we were all allowed to pick up a two-pound bag called 'poke sacks' of dirt from a large bin. We were then directed to a series of long tubs filled with water under a canopy roof. There were long benches beside the water tubs where we could set and sluice out our gold as the narrator demonstrated. Everybody got to work, but I was very skeptical still despite the informative lecture which to me was very interesting. I decided to take pictures while my wife and others panned for gold. The process took Coleen quite a while because she was afraid she might be sluicing gold out with the water, but a friendly attendant came along and re-demonstrated and with confidence Coleen went back at it. By this time I too had decided to take my two pounds of dirt and see just how much gold I could find? For ten minutes, I played the Alaskan gold miner role!

As I watched my gravel slowly float away from my gold pan, I was left with a small amount of fine dirt. It was then my wife shouted, "I have some!" Sure enough in the bottom of her gold pan was about a dozen small pieces of gold dust. I couldn't believe it. The lady who had given us the bag of gravel also gave us a small black plastic bottle to collect our gold in. I thought how optimistic can you be, but as Coleen put her gold into the bottle I began to hope. I placed my gold pan back in the water and slowly moved the water over my final pile of fine dirt and speck-by-speck the dark pieces were washed away. To my utter surprise, there in the bottom of my pan was more gold than was in Coleen's pan. We began to compare with the tourist that was panning next to us, and we soon discovered that everybody was finding gold. As matter of fact, we didn't find a single person that didn't find at least some gold. Some more than others, but we were all very content with our experience. Finding gold is an amazing feeling!

Pooling our haul, we headed into the visitor's center to get our gold weighted. Sure enough, the instructor had told us the procedure but my pessimism had doubted such an event, but now we were the proud owners of our own gold, so how much had we panned on our first attempt? The line was long at the counter, so we looked around the enclosure. The main building contained a gift shop, exhibits of mining artifacts including a gold nugget worth $75,000 that they allowed us to touch and get our pictures with. They even had a complimentary beverage and freshly baked cookies for us in a side room. Very nice! After looking at animal furs, photograph history of the region, and gold mining equipment, we were ready for the verdict on our afternoon as gold miners. A lady at the end of a counter was lonely, so we approached her and she was glad to weigh our gold. I must admit it was a thrilling experience to shake the small black plastic bottle and hear the small pieces of gold rattling around, banging the side. They sounded like something! The lady dumped the golden flakes into the tray and in a moment she said, "You have found $25 worth of gold!"

We couldn't believe it! Twenty-five dollars? We were gold miners after all. It was then the lady said that if we wanted to we could get the gold put in a souvenir locket on the other side of the store. Sure enough, there was a guy doing a brisk business selling golden chains for small round lockets in which the gold we found could be placed in a clear, plastic container. Coleen's mother had given her some money for the trip, so Coleen decided to treat herself with a keepsake of her Alaskan trip. Within minutes the young man had the gold, about 25 flakes, in the locket and Coleen had it hung around her next. That souvenir is for Coleen, one of the best reminders of her days in Alaska, a testimony to the wealth that is in the ground of our 50th state.

We spend another hour walking around the area, including a tour of the dredge itself, which was fascinating to me. We got to see the massive sluice-boxes that caught all the gold, and the trommel that separated the gold. We got to go up to the wheelhouse to see the brains of the dredge, including the complicated electrical system that ran everything. It was here that I learned that the dredge had been built at Bethlehem Steel in Pennsylvania and had been shipped in pieces to Alaska and reassembled. The walk back through time was really amazing, and since our return to Maine Coleen and I have continued to watch Gold Rush, and it has been especially interesting to us that in the past season a man on the television program has been trying to be rehabilitate an old gold dredge. These episodes have allowed us to revisit our time at Gold Dredge #8.

My final observation of this Alaskan adventure was the realization the wisdom of the owners of the dredge in relationship to shutting Gold Dredge #8 down. Somebody discovered a few years ago that there was more money above ground than below ground. Granted, there is still gold in the gravel around Fox, Alaska, but the real gold is in the pockets of the tourist that flock to places like Gold Dredge #8. We did discover $25 of gold in our panning, but to get that twenty-five dollar we paid out nearly $150 between the cost of the tour and the purchase of Coleen's locket and necklace. Who wouldn't give $25 to get $150? Despite the cost, it was a grand experience that Coleen and I will not soon forget. I find it interesting that gold is mentioned so often in the Scriptures. "As an earring of gold, and an ornament of fine gold, so is a wise reprover upon an obedient ear." (Proverbs 25:12)

## Chapter Forty-Four

## The Wonder Of Autumn

Coleen and I got done our gold panning adventure about twenty minutes before Scott was supposed to pick us up. While the rest of the tourists and staff drove away in their buses and cars, we waited in the gold park parking lot for Scott to return. Coleen talked to the young man who had made her necklace, for it seemed his ride was late as well. Neither Coleen nor I complain about the delay because we were enjoying the bright sun that was still casting its warm rays on our faces. As we waited, I looked around at the advancing fall colors in the trees and terrain surrounding Gold Dredge #8 National Historic District, and the wonders that autumn was bringing into the region just north of Fairbanks.

Only a person, who has spent a hot summer anywhere, can comprehend the true breathtaking beauty and the attraction of autumn in the northern latitudes. A popular misconception is that it doesn't get hot in Alaska or Maine, which is not the truth! People use to cold weather usually have a hard time with heat and humid; I know I do. That is why there is no other physical experience in the world that can quite match the miracle of the changes of seasons, especially from summer into autumn. Nothing is so designed to stimulate the entire person and quicken the natural senses like the return to cooler temperatures and the changing of the landscape from green to golden. What a better place to see that change than in the topography of a gold mining region! The gold around Coleen's neck was not the only thing shining that late afternoon outside of Fox, Alaska.

No matter how adaptable man can be, nothing prepares the human being for the long winter nights, the deep freeze of unrelenting cold, the unmerciful winds bearing blizzards of ice and snow, that is, except autumn. Autumn is God's preparation period for the human soul to get ready, and He does it with the most brilliant of all His seasons. As spring liberates the soul and summer captivates the soul, autumn insolates the soul to the reality of what is coming, and it does it with Indian summer days and spectacular colors. There is an aura and awe in the ever-increasing colors. Granted, I didn't see the variety in Alaska that you would see in Maine, but the contrast with the evergreen and the brownish hills still brought a smile to my face and a joy to my heart. As we sat at the gate into the gold mining park, I looked northward into the low flung hills toward Fox. The autumn color of Alaska is mainly yellow, golden. The vibrant reds and oranges of Maine are missing, but the variations of yellow are there. We began to see the change in our trip into Denali in the shrubs of the tundra. Even down into the Kenai we saw the odd tree with a few leaves changing color. Around King's Ranch, the forest was turning a lighter green with the occasional leaf already turned. The final triumphant display would be witnessed as Scott and I left Alaska and crossed Canada. But in the backdrop of Gold Dredge #8, the first complete changes in some of the foliage could be seen. It was these sights that inspire me to write of the wonders of autumn.

For those of us who love seclusion over the madding crowd, the quiet parking lot and the surrounding forest only added to the vista that afternoon. From where I stood I could gaze out upon hundreds of acres of colorful plants and shrubs in the Tanana Valley. The ridges on both sides of the vale were untouched and unmatched except for a section of the Alaskan Pipeline that weaved its way over a small hill to my right. To my left was an exquisite beauty of golden bushes. The park had planted a myriad of varieties of flowers to cover a drab wall between the parking lot and the park. Still in full bloom, like the flowers at their visitors' center, the flowers only added to the stunning scenery. If I didn't know better, it looked like the brush strokes of an artist's hand. To be honest, I have never seen a sight better depicted on an artist's canvas in any museum I have ever visited. Maybe that is why I prefer God's nature museum to man's inside museums! This total transformation of the area around Fairbanks from a summery green to an autumn gold was simply magnificent. This total transfiguration is a moving experience that makes one stop and ponder the divine spark that sets natural into such a dramatic change. This total transfer of color and cooler air is a thrill to the soul and brings a chill to the body that no other season of the year can bring.

I find nothing haphazard in the change from summer into autumn. About the only thing I found strange in my Alaskan experience was the fact that it was happening in August instead of September. We think our summers are short in Maine; we have nothing compared on our fellowman in Alaska; perhaps, this is one reason why few people live in the 50th State. Autumn is not a fickle affair that just happens. It is a pattern, programed by God Himself, to happen every year at a certain time depending on His timetable, not ours. Its advent is sure; its affect is complete, and its impact is enormous. If you don't think so then you need to talk to the young man Coleen was conversing with. I overheard him tell my wife of the length of their season, basically just three months, and that within the month they would be packed up and leaving Gold Dredge #8 to its wintry fate. The advent of autumn had caused everybody involved with the enterprise to realize that their summer ministry was over and a long tough Alaska winter would have to unfold before they could get back at the work in the spring. Autumn always brings on incredible changes. Everything in life is dying, and in Alaska so is the business of teaching tourists how to pan for gold! Despite the beautiful summer flowers in the pots, the white, warm cumulus clouds overhead, and the golden sun high against the sky edge of space, the end of summer had come to Alaska and with it the end of my wife's Alaskan adventure with me!

A very long, long-time ago God promised Noah after a devastating flood: "While the earth remaineth, seedtime and harvest (autumn), and cold and heat, and summer and winter, and day and night shall not cease." (Genesis 8:22) Whether in Maine or Montana, Alaska or Alabama, the promise of God has been being fulfilled with each passing season. In the year 2014, I had the privilege of experiencing the wonders of autumn twice. My twenty-minute interlude with an Alaskan autumn was cut short when Scott showed up in the Tahoe and picked us up for the fifteen-minute ride back to our motel in Fairbanks. But as you can see, I have not forgotten the simple pleasure of looking out into the transition from summer to autumn and marveling one more time in the visions and vistas I saw.

## Chapter Forty-Five

## A Beer Commercial Hymn

We got back to the Best Western in Fairbanks around 4:15 on Coleen's last afternoon in Alaska. Coleen was scheduled to catch a flight to Seattle, Washington and then one for San Jose, California near eleven, so what to do with the rest of the evening? I wanted to look for another fishing hole, but Scott had a headache; I should have gone fishing! I think the stress of all the details with leaving the army and moving south was getting to my son. It could also have been the 10 days he had spent with his parents driving them around Alaska (over 2000 miles to date)! Coleen caught a two-hour nap before I took her out to supper at KFC while Scott grabbed a nap. After we returned we still had a couple of hours before heading to the Fairbanks's airport just a few miles away. It was then I had one of the most exasperating experiences of the trip, and it all had to do with a simple television commercial.

I have been exposed to old Church hymns since I was a lad; I was part of a singing church and a singing Christian family. Over the years I have learned hundreds of the traditional Church songs and choruses. In my longest running ministry (celebrated my 45th years in 2014) in which I have conducted thousands of church services in boarding homes and nursing homes, I have sung more than ten thousand solos, duets, and trios for the folks living in twenty different homes. In my longest current ministry, I just passed twenty-three years. So it will not be surprising to you to believe that it is not very difficult for me to recognize an old tune connected to an old hymn. This experience took place as I was watching television while waiting to take Coleen to catch a plane for California. What shocked me that evening the most was the context in which the Church hymn was being used!

Sitting on a bed at the Best Western in Fairbanks, Alaska, I was watching the national news when the newscast switched to a commercial. Normally I would switch to another station because I despise commercials, but on this occasion I was distracted by a conversation between my wife and my son. Instead of flicking, I left the station I was watching on paying more attention to my wife and son than what was happening on the television. However, within seconds my mind recognized the music being played on the TV. Turning my head towards the television at the foot of the bed, I listened more carefully. There were no words, but the tune was undeniable. It was the music to the 19th century Church hymn "Leaning on the Everlasting Arms". To my utter amazement, the music was being used to sell Guinness Beer! I went ballistic. At first, Scott and Coleen couldn't understand what I was so upset about. It took them a few seconds to catch the context and realize my anger. A sacred song being used to sell the Devil's brew was and still is a sacrilege to me. When the commercial ended a few second later, probably only thirty-seconds long in its entirety, I turned the television off and began to rage. In a short sermonette that would have made Billy Sunday proud, I preached to the choir of two of the many wrongs, the sheer wickedness we had just witnessed. My companions were speechless as I stomped around the motel room cursing Guinness Beer and their ignorant marketing staff for allowing a favorite hymn's melody to be used to sell beer. Surely there were countless other tunes they could have used to promote their product of death and misery. But they didn't; they choose Anthony J. Showalter's wonderful refrain! The commercial was simple: a glass of Guinness on a table with the sweet melody of "Leaning on the Everlasting Arms" playing in the background!

One of the joys I have experienced with Church hymns is the research I have done over the years in the story behind the song, or the history behind the hymn category. I have read numerous books on this topic that has brought the hymns alive for me and given me a deep respect for anything connected to these hymns. The case in point is what was in my mind when I was listening to the sweet music of Showalter, because with the music I heard the words of Elisha A. Hoffman in my mind:

> "What a fellowship, what a joy divine, leaning on the everlasting arms;
> What a blessedness, what a peace is mine, leaning on the everlasting arms.
> O how sweet to walk in this pilgrim way, leaning on the everlasting arms;
> O how bright the path grows from day to day, leaning on the everlasting arms.
> What have I to dread, what have I to fear, leaning on the everlasting arms?
> I have blessed peace with my Lord so near, leaning on the everlasting arms.
> Leaning on Jesus, leaning on Jesus, safe and secure from all alarms;
> Leaning on Jesus, leaning on Jesus, leaning on the everlasting arms."

For me you can't separate the music from the message. Then when you add what I knew of the making of this hymn my rage and anger had no bounds.

On the same day, the successful author, businessman, and Presbyterian layman Anthony Showalter received sad letters from two of his dear friends telling him of recent deaths in their families. In sending bereavement letters, Anthony included this wonderful promise from Moses' book of Deuteronomy: "The eternal God is thy refuge, and underneath are the everlasting arms. . .." (Deuteronomy 33:27) After he sent the letters off, Showalter thought to himself that there must be a hymn in that verse somewhere, so he immediately began to jot down some words and music for the refrain. The music came easier to Anthony, so he decided to get his friend Elisha Hoffman, a pastor and hymn writer himself, involved in the creation of a new church hymn. The collaboration of these two fine Christian men resulted in a memorable song that was first published in 1887. Still sung today around the world as an example of God's steadfast care and unerring guidance and a confident peace in a difficult time, this hymn allows us to enjoy the intimacy of Jesus' fellowship no matter what we are going through, and a beer company thinks it has the right to use it for selling a diabolical drug, an additive product?

After a few minutes of expressing what I thought of Guinness Beer, my son tried to calm me down by telling me I should tell them what I thought by logging onto their website. I had never done that before, but I was mad enough to try. Between my wife and son they found the site and allowed me to write of my displeasure. The more I wrote the calmer I became. Eventually, by the time I finished my rebuke and reproof of Guinness, my blood pressure was back to normal and my anger had subsided. I was still mad and as you can tell from reading this chapter I still am, but the matter has gone unresolved. I have yet to hear the commercial again, and I hope I never do, but I suspect it is still being aired somewhere in the world. What is more tragic to me is the fact that most people who hear it won't draw the connection I did. It is just another example of the desensitizing that is taking place especially in the Christian community. There was a time when such a blatant act of sacrilege would have been met with an outcry from the Christian community, but today we have sheepishly yielded the field to the beer industry. I suspect a good many Christians today enjoy a Guinness over a gospel song? Jesus told us to be 'harmless as doves' (Matthew 10:16), but we are to be 'wise as serpents' and every serpent I know has a bite.

## Chapter Forty-Six

## On A Plane For California

Needless to say, it took me until we headed to the airport to really settle down from the beer commercial sacrilege. I knew of the ignorance of man and the disrespect of man for the things of God, but for me it was a new low. Even my e-mail to the Guinness website was a drop in a deep bucket of wickedness, and how much can a single drop of clean water cleanup a cesspool of filth? The beer industrial complex is one of the richest and most influential lobbies in the entire world. One e-mail from a no-account pastor from Maine, texting from Alaska, would not stop the breweries from pumping out their poison; I knew that, but it felt good to register my feelings! It is my hope that this second piece of protest will reach a wider audience.

As Coleen finished packing for her side trip to Salinas, California, I took stock into why this separation three-quarters of the way through our Alaska adventure was happening. The original plan was to help Scott relocate to North Carolina after his eight-year stint with the United States Army. Coleen was all in until she realized that a very difficult cross-continent road trip was part of the package deal. I began to feel my wife's reluctance and hesitation and made the suggestion she might prefer a side-trip to see our daughter and new son-in-law to a 4800-mile car journey back across America. Coleen jumped at the suggestion, despite her dislike of flying alone. When we finally booked our Alaskan flights, we added a series of hops from Fairbanks to Seattle and then on to San Jose, so when Scott and I would be still on the long road home, Coleen would be flying into Bangor, Maine.

It seems customary that most flights in and out of Alaska happen at night. We had gotten into Fairbanks early in the morning of August 14, and Coleen was scheduled to leave early in the morning of August 24. The short trip to the Fairbank International Airport got us there mid-evening on the 23rd. The traffic was light, and so were the lines at the check-in counter. We got Coleen's bag checked, her seat booked, and her gate number confirmed. We were able to visit a bit before we had to drop her off at screening. My dear wife has always had a hard time flying, especially alone. I still remember our first flight together in the 1990s to Florida. Our church family had given us a ten-day vacation to the Sunshine State for a Christmas present. Coleen's nervousness was showing as we got on her first plane out of Bangor. She survived the ordeal, but her opinion about flying was unchanged. Since that first flight, she has flown over the Atlantic twice. She has made numerous flights within in the lower 48s to California, Texas, North Carolina, and Kentucky, but each flight has been difficult for her. Every take-off and every landing has taken a toll on my dear spouse's countenance, but the one thing that has kept her flying is her dislike of driving long distances. When I married Coleen in 1973, one of the first things I learned about her was her susceptibility to motion sickness, especially in a car. Coleen needs to drive or sit in the front of a car on every trip. The backseat of a car is torture, a torment every time for her. So despite her fear of flying, she realized that a week in a car travelling across the North American continent would be a greater agony.

The other thing that has kept my wife in the air is the love of her kids. Ours is a typical American family. There was an age when children stayed close to mum and dad, but with each passing generation distance has become the norm; take my family? Of my four brothers and sisters three of them still live within fifteen miles of their parents, but my kids live afar. Scott's military career took him away, but his choice for permanent residence will keep him away in North Carolina. Marnie's choice of husband took her away and will probably keep her away in California. A love of family will always trump a dislike of flying every day, and now that our first grandchild (born August 18, 2015 Judah Alan Legaspi) is on the way "California Dreaming" is all that matters (in a ten-month period in 2017-2018 we made the trip from Maine to California and back four times!)! So as Coleen made her way slowly through screening, Scott and I watched and waited as she pressed on because she knew at the end of her flying ordeal would be Marnie.

The last Scott and I saw of Coleen was the back of her head as she passed beyond the personal scanner. We knew she would do ok despite her fears, for she had managed a couple of times before to fly alone. The reality was she wasn't alone really. One of the many beliefs of our family is the belief in the continual presence of our Lord and Saviour Jesus Christ. He promised his followers two thousand years ago: "Lo, I am with you always (even in flight), even unto the end of the world. Amen." (Matthew 28:20) I remember years ago hearing the story of a young Chinese student who had taken his first flight across the Pacific Ocean to attend a college in the

United States. It was a difficult move having to leave his family and the only life he knew behind. It was frightening in every way. Added to his fear was the fact that he was a new Christian and still was facing those early years of doubts. The Bible was also new to him and he knew few of God's promises. However, he had barely gotten settled into the dorm at his new college when he opened his Bible and began to read the 28th chapter of Matthew. By the time he finished his reading, his faith had been strengthened, his fears had been dispelled, and his face had a sweet smile on it. Oh, I forgot to tell you, his first name was Lo!

Postscript: Coleen did just fine on her trip to California and back to Maine. She had a wonderful week with our daughter Marnie and son-in-law Josue. She enjoyed the California warmth, ate fresh strawberries every day, and basked in the ocean breezes of Monterey Bay. She got to see with her own eyes where her newly married daughter had settled. She also got to meet more of Josue's large family. He comes from a family of fifteen siblings of which he is the youngest. Coleen got to read her romance novels and cook Marnie's favorite meals and help Marnie decorate their new dwelling. While Scott and I were logging nearly 5000 miles in his Tahoe, she was resting in the thought of only three more flights. (One flight included a first-class seat upgrade.) For years we have teased each other with the thought that one day we would fly first-class because of a change in our ticket. This happened to Coleen when she got to the San Jose airport on the first leg of her trip back to Maine. Her original flight had been cancelled, and she was re-routed through LAX in Los Angeles. As compensation for the inconvenient she was upgraded to a first class seat. It was a great blessing of God to help her through her trip back home alone. Often the best way to get rid of a fear is to find something far more satisfying, like a week with a special child or a first class seat. Granted, Coleen missed out spending another week with her beloved son, but after a week and a half it was time to give her other child some quality time. Besides, Scott was going to spend a month with us in Maine before he drove to North Carolina to settle.

## Chapter Forty-Seven

## Beading For Graying

I woke to my last full day in Alaska with the hopes of a grand fishing day. This would be only the second full day of fishing Scott and I would have together on our Alaskan adventure. Up to the 24th day in August 2014, we had already fished ten different places and had caught five kinds of fish, four species I had never caught before. We certainly had some fun fishing the streams, ponds, and rivers of Alaska. Today our fishing destination was the North Fork of the Chena River for big grayling and 45.5 Mile Pond for rainbow trout. Yes, there are so many ponds in Alaska they have run out of names so they simply call them by the mile marker on the road they are located. I was looking forward, as I always am, to fish a new hole and perhaps have a new fishing experience. We left around 7:30 on an hour-long trek to an area east of Fairbanks on the Chena Hot Springs Road. I found this about the Chena River from a fishing book Scott had bought in Alaska:

> "The Chena River provides an easily accessible fishery to the residents and visitors of Fairbanks. This river has runs of both king and chum salmon, and hosts one of the most reliable grayling fisheries in the state. The king run begins to show the first part of July and continues to build throughout the month. Much of the king fishing takes place near the mouth of the river, which can be accessed from Chena Pump Road. The river is closed to salmon fishing above the Chena River Dam. The chum run materializes later in July and provides an exciting fishery for some extremely hard-fighting salmon. The grayling fishing on the Chena is excellent due to regulations that require their release, providing for many large specimens in the mix. Anglers seeking trophy grayling of twenty-inches or more need to look no further than the Chena. With an average size of 12-14 inches,

fishermen can reasonably expect to catch grayling much larger. Grayling are a fly-fisherman's dream, as they are primarily insectivores that usually respond aggressively to a wide range of dry flies. Popular patterns include the ubiquitous Mosquito, Black Gnat, Elk Hair Caddis and various attractors like small Humpies. Please handle these unique northern beauties with care so they may live to fight another day. The lower Chena is a big, powerful river and should be approached with care. The wading angler should exercise caution and not take unnecessary risks. The upper river can be accessed via Chena Hot Springs Road, where all an angler need do is watch for promising water then pull over to fish it. The upper stretches of the Chena, including the forks (north and south) are much tamer than the lower river and more suitable for safe wading. The grayling also tend to run bigger here and the scenery is magnificent."

It was to that 'more suitable for safe wading' and 'where the grayling also tend to run bigger' and 'where the scenery is magnificent' that Scott and I were heading, and by 8:30 we were on the North Fork of the Upper Chena River.

We stopped at a small campsite near one of the many bridges that had crossed over the Chena since we left Fairbanks. The Lower Chena River actually cuts straight through Fort Wainwright; we had seen it on our trips on to the army base. The section of the Chena that lay before us was an easy-flowing stream at best barely sixty feet wide in places. We quickly got our waders on, and in the cool air of that August morning, headed down stream for what we were expecting as non-stop grayling action. Few topics stir up more imagination and expectation than fishing. I can honestly tell you that every time I have gotten in a boat or waded out into a stream, I have expected to catch a lot of fish. I have always been an optimist when it comes to fishing. However, over the years, after fishing a certain site time and time again, I have been able to understand when and where those best catches happen, but in a new fishing hole every cast I had expected a strike. Such was the case when I entered the waters of the Chena River, but it wasn't long before I realized my dreams for a big catch and a big fish were not going to happen.

For two hours Scott and I systematically worked our way downstream fishing every pool and slick along the gently flowing river. The conditions looked ideal. The water was cold, the sun was warm, but with each cast I knew the fish were not there. The water was crystal clear and not deep except for the pools, and the runs were ideal, but there were just no fish. Not until we came to a small eddy far downstream did we see our first fish. There in a small pool were three spawning chum: two females and one male. I would eventually hook the male three times, but each was not a bite but a snag. The fully colored male made a good picture, but I was after grayling, and sure enough after a few casts to the lower part of the pool my orange fly attracted a foot long grayling. At the time, it was the largest I had hooked, but it was not the mega-grayling I was looking for. Scott and I played around with the spawning salmon awhile hoping a school of grayling might be around, but that was the only one hooked. Our trip back up stream resulted in no other hookups, so our disappointment was clearly growing.

Arriving back at the bridge, I decided to try the Kenai River technique of trout beads. I figured if they caught rainbows, why not grayling? Scott and I had rigged a few beads and weights with a strike indicator during some downtime. I told Scott of my decision and he said, "What have you got to lose?" I was thrilled when after casting upstream and allowing the bead to drift naturally downstream with the current that I hooked my very first grayling on a bead. The pool just below the highway bridge was deep and the water was swift, ideal for holding a big school of grayling. Scott had fished the pool before and had good success. Working the grayling to shore, I saw it was about the same size, 13 inches, as the one I had caught downstream, but I was sure I would be on a fish with every drift, so I quickly let the grayling go and worked my way back to the spot that gave me the most productive drift. Again and again I cast the bead into the flow but I never caught another grayling. For a second time I thought, "Where are all the big grayling?"

Returning to the campsite, we meet another transplant from Maine. He and a few of his buddies had camped on the river and had fished it for a few days, but had little luck. Our hopes were dying quickly that the Chena would give us the numbers and sizes of grayling we were looking for. Deciding to try another spot, we drove up the Chena Hot Springs Road to a favorite rainbow/grayling pond that Scott had discovered with his friends, Brandon and Hailey. Despite our success at 45.5 Pond, Scott and I returned later in the day to try the North Fork of the Chena again. Hope stays eternal in the heart of a fisherman. But once again we were disappointed though I did manage to land another foot long grayling on a pink bead. For thousands of years men have expressed their ideas about fishing with word and pen. One of the oldest are these lines from the pen of the Hebrew prophet Isaiah: "It is written, the fishers also shall mourn, and all they that cast angle into the brooks shall lament. . .." (Isaiah 19:8) It seems that fishermen in Isaiah's day also were disappointed after casting their hook. The good news about a discouraging result in one fishing stream is that the next fishing hole might just produce big numbers and big fish: once again the eternal optimism of a fisherman, even in Alaska!

## Chapter Forty-Eight

## Making The Local Newspaper

I have believed all my life that fish came from the creative hand of God: "And God said, Let the waters bring forth abundantly the moving creature that hath life. . ... And God created. . .. every living creature that moveth which the waters brought forth abundantly after their kind. . ... And God said, Let us make man in our image after our likeness: and let them have dominion over the fish of the sea. . .." (Genesis 1:20-26) God simply created every species of fish by simply uttering His mighty word (Hebrews 11:3). I know the flimsy and confusing theories of evolution that now fills the minds of mankind and appear in fishing journals. But for me, God said He did it and that is good enough for me! For me the presence of fish in a small pond east of Fairbanks is a marvelous and undeniable proof that there is a God and that He desires to make Himself known to us and a reproof of all those that believe rainbow trout and grayling just evolved. Consider the great kindness of God in giving mankind fish to eat, and for those of us who don't need fish to eat, but He gave fish as a source of pleasure as well. For a chance to spend a few hours with my son and two of his friends simply fly-fishing is a joy beyond compare for me.

Before Scott and I left the North Fork of the Chena River, Brandon and Hailey had arrived for a mid-day fly fishing trip to 45.5 Mile Pond. It was one of the favorite places for the three to fish. They had made the trip up the Chena Hot Spring Road many times and had always found the small pond productive. As we headed up the highway to the pond, Scott told me of the other times he had been there. The rainbow trout and grayling were small (6-12 inches), but there were always plenty of them. The other good thing about the pond was the fact it could be easily waded, and the fish came to both dry and wet flies, two of my favorite kinds of fishing. In the increasing pressure on the world's fisheries, the places one can go and catch big numbers of fish are shrinking. My best days numbers wise have been in Maine and Canada were I have caught fish in the hundreds. My record is 181 brook trout on June 19, 2008. I have had eleven occasions when I have landed over 100 fish in a day on a fly. I have enjoyed some of the glory days of fishing, but I fear for fishermen in the future. My generation has seen a decline over my father's generation, and I suspect the same will happen to my kids and especially my grandkid's generation. My day at 45.5 Mile Pond did get recorded in my fishing record book, because I did catch over thirty fish; the number needed to get into my fishing record book for a day's fishing!

Scott and I fished from eleven in the morning until three in the afternoon. The pond was just like Scott described it, wadeable and filled with small rainbows and grayling. Brandon and Hailey stayed for about two hours, but after Brandon fell in they left. Brandon caught 12 fish and Hailey landed 4 fish including the first. They all ran between 6 and 9 inches. Scott would eventually land 17 fish including the two biggest rainbows of the day, both 12 inches in length. Before I was through I would land 35 fish total, which put that total 47th on my list of good fishing days by the numbers. That it even got on the list was a positive event, only the third day in Alaska that is on my best catch by numbers list. Remember I had caught 45 fish on our first day in Alaska, and I caught 54 fish in Valdez. But for me, the revelation of our hours at 45.5 Mile Pond was when a local newspaper reporter showed up and began hanging around my son.

I first noticed the young lady as I was fishing on the far side of the pond. She drove in shortly after Brandon and Hailey had left. She first started up a conversation with a young family that was camping and fishing at the site. We had met them after we had arrived. They told us the fishing was slow, but they were catching a few. They were fishing from a canoe they had brought along. While the mother fixed their meals, the father and the two children were out in their canoe worm fishing. Scott, by this time, had worked his way back along the right side of the pond and was catching a few fish near the campsite of the couple and their kids. The reporter had a camera hung around her neck and was soon taking pictures of Scott landing a few average size rainbow trout. It wasn't until later in the day when Scott and I reconnected that he told me the lady was a reporter with the *Fairbanks Daily News,* and she was doing a feature on the topic of the Chena River and recreational fishing. She told Scott that he ought to pick up the paper the next day because he probably would be in it. Sure enough, when Scott came back the next day from picking up supplies for our trip home, he had the *Fairbanks Daily News* in his hand, and in the Interior section a quarter page picture of Scott's hand lifting out of the water of 45.5 Mile Pond a rainbow trout and underneath the photograph this caption:

"Scott Blackstone catches a rainbow trout while fishing with his father at 45.5 Mile Pond in the Chena River State Recreation Area on Sunday. Blackstone caught multiple rainbow trout and arctic grayling throughout the day. Four ponds in the Chena River State Recreation Area and one on 25 Mile of Chena Hot Springs Road, just before the recreation area, were stocked by the Alaska Department of Fish and Game in May. The Chena Hot Springs Road runs through the area and at mile 25, 30, 45.5, and 47.9 ponds are stocked with arctic grayling and rainbow trout, and the pond at 42.8 Mile at Red Squirrel Campground is stocked with arctic grayling. Rainbow trout do not naturally occur in the area. Arctic grayling are known for their diverse colors and can be good fish for beginning fly anglers to learn with because they are not picky about how flies fall in the water. Erin Corneliussen/news miner."

It was nice to think that Scott and I made the papers on our last day in Fairbanks, but I must admit the picture and the caption brought a bitter taste to my mouth in what I thought was a good day's fishing. I must admit I am a purist when it comes to fishing. I prefer fishing native fish, not stocked fish! Stocked fish for me is like cheating. Don't get me wrong, I have fished places before where the fish had been released, but I still think there is something more sporting than stocking a fish. Native fish, put there by God himself, is the best kind of fishing! One of the reasons I have been so proud of my great numbers catches is the fact that all the top catches were accomplished with native fish, not stocked fish. Once again it goes back to the concept highlighted at the beginning of this chapter. I thought it was God who put the fish in 45.5 Mile Pond, but it was only after I read the newspaper I discovered I was fishing a man-stocked pond, God created the pond, but man created the school of fish. Granted, at first 45.5 Mile Pond was probably God-made, fish and all, but through over fishing the numbers had dwindled to the place that man felt he had to step-in and replenish the pond. I had fun seeing the rainbows or the grayling coming up and taking my Red Tag and Royal Coachman flies, but not as enjoyable as the God-made fish of other places!

My fishing days were over in Alaska and the final totals were in. I ended up fishing in a dozen fishing holes with the most memorable being Montana Creek. I ended up catching 59 pink salmon, 48 arctic grayling, 41 rainbow trout, 10 chum salmon, and 4 Dolly Varden, for a grand total of 162 fish. My largest fish was a 29-inch chum salmon, but my best fish was the 23-inch rainbow I caught on the Kenai River. I must admit I dreamed of bigger numbers and larger fish, but the best was sharing it all with Scott.

## Chapter Forty-Nine

## Shaking The Dust Off His Feet

My last full day in Alaska began in a steady rain. One of the wonderful blessings of our Alaskan adventure was the great weather we enjoyed throughout the trip. Other than an isolated shower, the trip around central Alaska was mostly dry. It wasn't too cold and it wasn't too hot, so the rain on our day of departure wasn't a big deal. All the sites we wanted to see and experience were in our rear view mirror and picking up a U-Haul in the rain wasn't going to be a big deal, or was it? I could tell that morning that Scott had an extra skip in his step as we got out of bed!

Between 7:30 and 9:00 A.M., Scott and I cleared out of our Best Western Motel room, paid our bill ($468 for three days), and headed for the U-Haul rental place on the other side of Fairbanks. I waited in the Tahoe while Scott got the paper work done for our cross-continent companion, a twin wheel, medium size, U-Haul trailer. After about fifteen minutes, Scott returned and I could tell by the look on his face that he wasn't a happy soldier. Sure enough, no U-Haul! It seems the U-Haul that had been set-aside for Scott hadn't been brought back to the rental center. A problem, according to the attendant, not so uncommon. That explanation didn't go over well with my son. It was just another negative on a very long list of negatives about Alaska, according to Scott. No problem, I thought, because we were not scheduled to leave until later in the day anyway. Scott had promised Sergeant Greely that he would pick him up at the airport later that day. The sergeant had been down to the Lower 48s visiting family and was scheduled to fly into the Fairbanks Airport around nine. It was my hope that after filling the U-Haul we would park it and do a bit more fishing before hitting the road. I still had two days left on my Alaskan fishing license, and I wanted to use it until it ran out. However, the setback of not getting the U-Haul when planned sent my son into one of his troubling times.

# SHAKING THE DUST OFF HIS FEET

Coleen and I had noticed after Scott's Afghanistan tour that he was very edgy, (PTSD) especially when things didn't happen as he thought. We attributed it at first to the three concessions he had received on his combat tour, but the more we talked to him the more we realized it was also the friends he had lost, the things he had seen, and the horrors he had to endure in the deserts of southeast Afghanistan. What concerned us was the fact that by his very nature Scott is a very laid-back kind of guy, not much has ever really bothered him. He has been that way since birth. Before his two wars (Iraqi and Afghanistan), Scott had taken things as they came, but after three tours, seeing four friends die before his eyes, and Alaska in eight years, we found our son could be on edge at times. On the morning of August 25, 2014 Scott was on edge and mad.

Scott was visibly upset as we drove over to the Wal-Mart to pick up a few supplies for our road trip; our plan was to eat as we drove. I tried to calm him down and reassure him that something would turn up before the day was through, and sure enough, shortly after we left Wal-Mart, Scott got a call from the U-Haul rental center that a replacement for his missing U-Haul could be found at a gas station at 3245 College Road. I could see the change on his face and in the tone of his voice almost immediately. As we drove over to the new site, we talked of the day ahead and our plans. It was then I realized that Scott was really ready to leave Alaska; the missing U-Haul had been the last straw. If he could work it out, he wanted to leave the minute we had the trailer loaded, but there was still that obligation to Sergeant Greely.

By 10:30 A.M., we had the Tennessee trailer attached to the Tahoe and were working our way over to Fort Wainwright to pick up Scott's stuff from Sergeant Greely's garage. These would be things he had collected during his two-year assignment with the 539th Transportation Unit. On the way, we had to stop at a weighing station to weigh the Tahoe and the trailer. Scott would get reimbursed by the Army according to the weight of the things he would be carrying back to North Carolina, so we had to weigh the Tahoe and trailer before and after we loaded the stuff: fishing rods and poles, clothing, an extra set of tires for the Tahoe, extra gas cans for the trip, golfing equipment, and the odds and ends one picks up over time. Unloaded we weighed 7040 pounds and when fully loaded 8960 pounds, but what was best was we were able to keep the back of the Tahoe relatively clear of too much stuff. We were able to make a bed for sleeping on the long road home.

By eleven we were all packed up and heading off base for the late time. An interesting thing I noticed as we left was a board on which were different colors: green, pink, red, and black. Scott told me those were for the wintertime to tell drivers of the road conditions on base. I could tell by Scott demeanor that he wasn't sad as we left the base for the last time. Alaska had been a tough deployment for Scott, despite the fact he was stateside. For him it was another overseas assignment, and in some respect as tough as Kuwait, Iraqi, or Afghanistan. Granted, he didn't have to fight IEDs or snipers, heat or dust, but Alaska had its own set of difficulties for my son. In his oversea tours he had been with friends. Scott had actually volunteered for Afghanistan simply because he wanted to go over with former comrades from Iraqi. Scott is a sociable fellow and friends are very important to him, so despite the dangers on the battlefield he was among friends, but in Alaska he was in a new unit with, as he would say, a bunch of idiots. Scott had told us countless stories as we drove around Alaska of the stupid things he had to live through with the men of the 539th; he would call them kids. Most were young and inexperienced, just too immature for him; he was ready to get out, not just out of Alaska, but out of the regular Army as well. On our way off Fort Wainwright, Scott symbolically shook the dust of his feet (Acts 13:51). If you are not aware of this Biblical practice, it was given by Jesus as an instruction to His disciples (Matthew 10:14) to symbolize a place that wouldn't receive God's word. For Scott, Alaska was a nice place to fish and the scenery and wildlife were exceptional, but the climate and his comrades in the Army were far from what he had enjoyed at Fort Bragg, North Carolina. There also were the friends he had lost in the wars, and the friends that had been assigned to other bases. He had endured and tolerated Alaska for nearly two years, and now it was time to leave.

One of our last stops was to visit two people he had become friends with: Hailey and Brandon. They were still clearing out their military apartment waiting their departure in two weeks. While we were visiting, it was decided that Brandon would pick up Sergeant Greely at the airport that evening so that Scott and I could get on the road earlier than planned. Isn't that what good friends do? We had also stopped by to pick up some Alaskan fish that Hailey and Brandon had been keeping in their freezer since an early spring fishing trip off the coast of Alaska. Scott had come back with a sample of just about every fish caught off Alaska's shoreline, including halibut and silver salmon. Yes, Scott did catch the elusive fish I had been hunting since I arrived in Alaska two weeks before! Once we got our fish loaded into the cooler and said our goodbyes to Hailey and Brandon, we headed out of town. Before we actually left Fairbanks, we had a very important phone call to make: a special man to honor, and a sober anniversary to recall.

## Chapter Fifty

# A 90th Birthday And A 3rd Anniversary

It was the psalmist that once wrote, ". . .. we spend our years as a tale told. The days of our years are threescore and ten (70); and if by reason of strength they be fourscore (80), yet is their strength labour and sorrow. . .." (Psalm 90:9-10) So what is there in labor of ninety years, or, in the case of my soldier son, sorrow in three years?

August 25, 2014 was not only the day Scott and I started our epic journey across the North America continent by Tahoe, but it was also my father's and Scott's grandfather's ninetieth birthday. So before we left Fairbanks, we decided we would call Wendell E. Blackstone to wish him a happy birthday. It was a joyous call because only a few short months before we were all sure Dad wouldn't see another day, let alone his 90th birthday. Collapsing after a Sunday evening church service, Dad was rushed to a hospital in Caribou, Maine with the news he wouldn't live another day. His heart had worn out. I had rushed up from the coast of Maine to the northern Maine town just east of my hometown with my youngest brother who had travelled home from Pennsylvania. Scott was too far away to come, but like the rest of Dad's away family, was concerned and hopeful and prayerful. God worked a miracle, even according to the doctors, and gave us back our father and grandfather for a bit more time, so that a son and a grandson could call on the day he turned ninety from Fairbanks, Alaska, like a tale that can be told!

Our conversation was short and sweet and to the point. Dad asked how our travels in Alaska had gone and to make sure we drove safely back home. He would see us when we got back. Few get to live into their 90s: "And Enos lived ninety years. . ." (Genesis 5:9) and ". . .shall Sarah, that is ninety years old. . ." (Genesis 17:17) Despite the fact that Dad was a soldier during the Second World War and an Aroostook County farm for well over half a century, he was still active enough to go fly fishing (as I write this chapter Dad is nearing his 91st birthday and would live into his 93rd year), a pastime enjoyed by three generations of Blackstones, as you have learned in this book. Scott and his grandfather have soldiering in common as well, and it was good for Scott to talk to his granddad because August 25th also holds a troubling event in Scott's memory: the third anniversary of his winning the Purple Heart on the battlefield of southern Afghanistan.

One of the things I encouraged my son to do while deployed in Afghanistan was to keep a journal: a regular recording of the events happening in the war zone and a comment or two on how he was feeling, what he thought? During our travels around Alaska, Scott talked about some of those days, as we did in our hours traveling back home. I would like for Scott to share in his own words what happened leading up to a date he and his family will never forget: August 25, 2011- the day of his grandfather's 87th birthday! Scott wrote:

## August 24, 2011

Well, it is Wednesday. I have no idea if we are leaving today. There is a rumor that when the convoy gets back here from Shauoni (a FOB-forward observation base)we are going to meet them outside the gate and then we are going to start pushing to Leatherneck (Scott's home base in Afghanistan). But, honestly, I don't think that we are going to. Yesterday was a very boring day. I didn't do anything, just hung out at my truck by myself, playing on my I Pad and listened to music. There is really not much else to do. There was one cool thing that did happen yesterday. I was eating my MRE for lunch and all of a sudden I hear something outside my door. I look and the EOD robot was right out my door picking through the trash that was out there. I guess that they were just practicing on something. I was also so bored that I shaved my head. Other than that, life is going on. I am sure if we leave today I will write again. SO till later...OUT!!

It is around 1745. The convoy made it back from Shauoni with no problems. They made it back too late for us to push back to Leatherneck tonight. Even though the Marines want us to, I guess they will just have to wait till 0500 tomorrow. I am about to have some dinner—chili mac, one of my favorite MRE's. I just got up from my nap so that is about it....back on the road tomorrow...so I am OUT!!

## August 25, 2011

Day 12 We have all the stuff we came for. We have dropped off all the loads that we had and today we are on our way back home. It is about 0423. I didn't sleep very well last night maybe because I slept all day yesterday. But I am ready to leave and get back. . . .then get back to do it again. I have no idea what is in store for today. Probably more IEDs or maybe a smooth ride home. Whatever happens it was meant to be. Well I am pretty sure I will write later with exciting stuff to tell. I have to get the truck ready to leave anyway. We roll out at 0500!

## August 28, 2011

It has been a few days since I have written in the book, and I guess I really don't know where to start. I guess I will start by saying on August 25, 2011 at around 1100 I lost 2 more of my battle buddies and friends from a road side bomb. Also in the process Mabb (Scott's driving partner) and I were hurt as well. We were just riding along. The route clearance team had just found an IED and had control detonated it. We thought all was good. We did not go more than 300 meters down the road and that is when it happened. The biggest bomb I have ever heard, and I have heard a few now! I remember the blast but after that all I remember are parts flying and flames, and black smoke. When I realized what had happened it was too late to save my friends SPC Daniels and SPC Richmond. The cab was completely in flames. Mabb and I were in shock. All we could do was sitting there crying and staring at the truck. After about 15 minutes of that I couldn't take it anymore and asked if we could go to the back of the convoy to get some air. When they got us out of the truck and to the back we just broke down. They were great guys. Daniels just had a little baby girl and Richmond was a great man. When we got to SSG truck they told us that we were getting medevac'd. I told them only if Mabb goes. I was not leaving her behind. They really didn't give us a choice. We were going. The medic on site determined that we probably had a concussion so they put us in a gun truck and took us up to the medevac site. It took a while for the bird to land because the gun ships that were flying around were getting shot at. When it was clear for them to land we got on a Blackhawk and within 10 minutes we were back at Leatherneck getting looked at. I felt really bad leaving all my friends out there to deal with that stuff but when it came right down to it I really was hurting and still am. The doctors did the entire test and determined that Mabb and I had concussions but we were not going to miss the ramp ceremony. We went back to our rooms after we were released from the Extend ward clinic. Took a long hot shower and got some real food. They came and told us late Thursday night that the ramp ceremony was not going to be until Friday so I went to sleep or I should say I tried to go to sleep. The next day, Friday, I put my friends on a plane to go home. There were about 500 people there. It was hard. They should have been going home with us but instead they were going home in a box. It was emotional. Saturday I didn't do anything except sleep and go talk to someone, which was good because all I am doing is having nightmares and can't sleep and then today the convoy got back safe and secure and we greeted them but that was it. It sucks really bad that I have to be a part of this again. I told someone the other day that I had just got over Ox and Campbell's death and was doing okay and now I have to do it again. It really sucks! But I will get through this somehow. I know I have people praying for me and I am going to get help this time and we will press on. Well, I am going to take a shower and try to get some rest. I have to be up early to do tough box inspection. Oh, and all my friends are coming back from PSB tonight so it will be great to see them. Well I guess I should say it. . .OUT!!

# Chapter Fifty-One

# Starting Our Trip Home

The official start of our journey home began at 1:00 P.M. on August 25, 2014; little did Scott and I know that it would be over in 86 ½ hours, and we would have covered 4854 miles. This part of our Alaskan adventure didn't happen as we had originally planned. As I think back on what transpired, my mind remembers this precept by Solomon recorded in Proverbs 19:21. "There are many devices in a man's heart; nevertheless the counsel of the Lord that shall stand." When will mankind understand and learn this powerful proverb. One of the finest hymns ever penned about God's divine providence is William Cowper's "God Moves in a Mysterious Way". A man who battled mental illness for most of his life, including an 18-month stay in an insane asylum; it was in that same asylum Cowper began to read the Bible and at the age of thirty-three made a profession of faith. There are some Cowper experts who believe this was William's best hymn and might have been written after an attempted suicide by drowning. There are many devices in the heart of a man including suicide, but God's will is done in the end. There are many ways to get home from Alaska, but our way and God's way often differ! These words by Cowper ought to inspire us all:

> God moves in a mysterious way, His wonders to perform;
> He plants His footsteps in the sea and rides upon the storm.
> You fearful saints, fresh courage take: the clouds you so much dread
> Are big with mercy, and shall break in blessings on your head.
> Judge not the Lord by feeble sense, but trust Him for His grace;
> Behind a frowning providence faith sees a smiling face.
> Blind unbelief is sure to err and scan His work in vain;
> God is His own interpreter, and He will make it plain!

It seems today that we are seeking counsel from just about every other source but God. We are spending too much time seeking the devices of man and spending too little time asking for the counsel of the Lord. These thoughts ought to be our motto when waiting for advice or wondering how we should travel home. I like the wording of the New International Version of the Bible on Proverbs 19:21: "Many are the plans in a man's heart, but it is the Lord's purpose that prevails!" We all make plans, and there is nothing wrong with making plans, but we must be ready to adapt when God changes those plans: "For my thoughts are not your thoughts, neither are your ways my ways, saith the Lord. For as the heavens are higher than the earth, so are my ways higher than your ways, and my thoughts than your thoughts." (Isaiah 55:8-9) How many times in your life have you seen this concept come to fulfillment in your life, as Scott and I did on our way out of Alaska? I can think of numerous times when I had planned my day down to the last detail (as I always do), and in the midst of my well-thought-out day the Lord has redirected my steps and my thoughts. As a pastor of a group of a hundred and more people, your schedule can change with a phone call and your day can be altered by a simple change in the pattern of one of your parishioners!

We know well the story of Jonah who had carefully planned a vacation to Tarshish when in the midst of his voyage his plans were changed, his direction was altered, and his focus was redirected. If you believe as I do that the plans of God have already been thought through, and the divine purpose has already been established; what could make us think that in the end it will be God's will that gets fulfilled not ours. How often has mankind tried to change the counsel of God and failed. I think of the people of the town of Babel (Genesis 11) who defied the command of God to go into the entire world. In the end they were scattered just as God ordered. A simple reading of the Bible will highlight and underline numerous situations when man planned one thing and an entirely other outcome happened. Ahab went into battle disguised thinking he could change Micaiah's prophecy concerning his fate (II Kings 22). How did that workout? Wise is the man that realized that the counsel of the Lord is the best, and besides, it will be what will happen anyway. Little did Scott and I realize as we travelled Alaska Route 2 that nothing we had planned would happen; much like my dear son's experiences in Afghanistan.

As we travelled toward Delta Junction, where we would pick up the Alaska Highway, Scott began to share more of his wartime experiences. Let me share them with you in his own words:

## October 21-24, 2010

Well I guess this was long overdue. This is the first time that I have gotten to write in my journal. That is the Army for you! Well, I told myself that I was going to start this on the day that I left. Well that has not happened. So I guess that I will have to rewind and tell you what has been going on. Thursday, October 21, 2010 I started my journey to the great country of Afghanistan where I will be a HET (heavy equipment transport) driver for the United States Army. I am excited but yet scared as well. I was deployed to Iraq in 2007-2008 for 15 months. I know this deployment is going to be way different. Well, we left Green Ramp from Pope Air Force Base at Fort Bragg in North Carolina AROUND 12:55. Before I left I had called my parents thinking that I wasn't going to be able to see them. But by the grace of God we stopped in Bangor, Maine. Mom and Dad were there waiting for me with Nana's potato doughnuts. What a treat! They got to meet some of my friends, along with some they hadn't seen in a long time. After saying goodbye, we flew 7 hours to Bulgaria. I had never been here and it is nice to say I have at least been to this country. It was a good experience! After a 3-hour layover, we headed out. I thought we were going to Afghanistan but I was wrong. We were on our way to Kyrgyzstan. I guess from what I am told it is on the China/Russia border next to the Himalaya Mountains. The mountains are beautiful. We got to Kyrgyzstan and they asked for volunteers to unload the bags from the plane and being the nice guy I am I said I would. Well, I walk off the plane and it hits me. . .the cold weather and if anyone knows me they know I hate cold weather. It was 30 degrees! So we get the bags all unloaded and got orientated to do this mission that we are here to do and they tell us that we have to be here for 2 more days. That is all good but I am ready to go get this over with, get home and start playing golf. But we will wait. . . . .So that is where I am up till this point. I plan on writing in this journal every day. I told my Dad that I would and I am going to, so I hope that the next time that I get to write I am on my way-OUT!

## October 25-26, 2010

Well, we have made the journey to Afghanistan. The last day in Kyrgyzstan was really good. It was cold there still and I never did get a good picture of the mountains. We boarded the C17 around 1700 hours their time. I thought that I was going to have a problem flying but I didn't. It was actually a very smooth ride. We made it to Camp Sebastian. It is a Marine base just south of Kandahar. It is also where Camp Leatherneck is, where I will be spending the next year of my life. When we got off the plane it was warmer than it was in Kyrgyzstan, but still colder than Iraq. I have notice that the sand here is way worse. It is nothing but moon dust which means it sticks to anything and everything. It is so messy. I don't think I am going to like that very much. We got our PCB and I am staying with some really good guys. A guy named Stanley and I are in charge of the group so we will see how that goes. I have top bunk, which is okay by me-OUT!

Our trip home from Alaska and Scott's trip to Afghanistan have now merged together.

Postscript: If you are interested in my son's Afghanistan experience, I have compiled his complete journal and his story in a pictorial book, using his own photos. I call it *Hetts in Helmand*.

*Chapter Fifty-Two*

# The Alaskan Highway and Afghanistan

THERE ARE MANY SEA routes and many air routes out of Alaska, but there is only one land route: the Alaskan Highway; also called the Alcan Highway, or the Alaskan and Canadian Highway.

I have known of the Alaskan Highway for most of my life. I think it would be true to write that it was on my bucket list for many years, but I probably never would have purposefully done it if my son had not asked. I have had friends and family members drive it, and though I am not a great roadman, I have had aspirations to experience the route myself. So at 2:30 P.M. on August 25, 2014, I started down that long road when Scott and I turned left off the Richardson Highway (Alaska Route 4) to the Alaska Highway (Alaska Route 2) to Tok. It was then I saw the largest numbered road maker of my life: 1420! We also saw our first Canadian border sign, and we knew that we were heading east and heading home.

I would learn that this famous roadway was first proposed in the 1920s and revisited in 1937, but the cost and the need were never realized until the Japanese attacked Pearl Harbor in 1941; within three months the highway was under construction (March 8, 1942). The mammoth project, the Alaska pipeline of its day, would link the Alaskan town of Delta Junction with the British Columbia town of Dawson Creek. The project was accelerated when the Japanese landed on two islands, Kiska and Attu, in the Alaskan chain of islands off its southwestern coast. Believe it or not, two crews, each starting at opposite ends, would meet at the 588 mile mark on September 24, 1942 just seven months after construction began! It was completely finished barely a month later (October 28, 1942) and in another month was dedicated

(November 20, 1942) and supplies began to pour into Alaska. It would be officially opened to the public in 1948.

Originally a dirt road, the Alaska Highway is now mostly paved. We did encounter two sections (25 miles and 17 miles) of the highway that were still dirt, but appeared to be under reconstruction and probably repaved as I write. The early miles took us by Dot Lake and through the Tanana River valley, another huge waterway that dwarfs anything you might see in Maine. Our first major goal was the village of Tok where Alaska Route 2 and Alaska Route 1 meet, an extension of the Glenn Highway we travelled earlier in our Alaska adventure. This is what they call the Tok Cutoff from Glennallen to Tok through the Copper River Valley. It took us three hours to make that journey and another three hours to reach the Yukon Border at Beaver Creek. Interestingly, the border crossing was twenty miles inside Canada, so our final mile check for Alaska stopped at mile 2613, the number of miles Scott and I had travelled by road in Alaska in just 13 days. Little did we know that we would cover that same distance in just two days!

The road was long, but scenic. There was time to reflect and contemplate about other times, and other roads. As we travelled the Alaska Highway, Afghanistan reemerged in these words from the pen of Peter: "Wherefore I will not be negligent to put you always in remembrance of these things, though ye know them. . .." (II Peter 1:12)

## October 26, 2010

Just finished day one of this 365-day deployment! I want to go home already. I hate the dust here. I woke up so stuffed up and feeling bad. We walked around the camp today looking for all the usual stuff—PC, phones and Internet and the best Defac (chow hall). We haven't found the best Defac but we have about 2 more to go. We kept telling each other we were spoiled in Kuwait because there was everything there. Tomorrow starts our first day of training—IED training. We have been talking to some guys that we are replacing. They are telling us some roads are good and some roads are bad. Guess we will see. I am tired and trying to stay on this time schedule so I am heading for bed. Peace OUT. . ..Well it has been a long time since I have written in my book but not a lot has been going on. The first mission went out yesterday to Kandahar and they have another one going out today. I haven't been doing much. We have gotten our trucks and we have been cleaning them and getting them the way that we want them. The hett we are in was in really rough shape. Most of the trucks have either been blown up or just broken down. I have been really sick the last few days but being a Blackstone I have been pressing on. Life is getting better here and getting in a routine. Today we are signing up for II MRAPS. I hope that we do gun truck security. That's all I know (Iraqi experience) and I would so love to do that here. Other than that things are great. Life here on Leatherneck is not that exciting so I will leave you for now. I am off to get some of that great Army breakfast-OUT!

## November 6, 2010

Well, another day down. It has been a long time since I wrote in the book but there really has not been much going on other than us sitting in the motor pool doing nothing other than cleaning the dirt off the trucks and watching other people going out on mission. The only thing that has happened was really cool. I got to drop off my first load with the hett! It was an Egress Trainer that is a machine that helps with a roll over and it helps you to decide which door and exit that you need to take. That was cool for me. The days are going faster and before you know it we will be coming home. We had a cook out today that had hot dogs, steaks and hamburgers. It was a little taste of home. Tomorrow is my birthday. Just another day to me! They are telling us that we might have the day off but I doubt it. Another birthday in the desert! I am off to the gym and the showers then bed. I have to try to sleep as much as I can-OUT.

## November 7-9, 2010

Since I have last written, it has been my birthday and I have found out that I am going on a mission on Monday. But let me rewind. . ...My birthday was great. We didn't do very much. We had the first day off since we have been here but I still had to work because my truck (#424) came off the road and it was leaking oil. Other than that not too bad! We have a mission and it is the first one here in Afghanistan and guess what it is going to be—the toughest and hardest mission. It is called IED Alley and as if that is not bad enough— there are no showers and defacs. There are also no toilets. If anybody knows me, they will know that I do not do well using the bathroom in the woods let alone the sand. So, we will see how that goes. I am going with a great bunch of guys and I know I have a lot of prayers going with me. I will go into more when the mission comes-OUT!

### Today is November 10.

We have officially taken over the reins from the 287th Company that we replaced. We are going to run this now and do a way better job than them. . .It is late and we are passing the time away by playing spades and rummy. It is a nightly thing in our AO but the days are flying by and soon we will be on mission and Thanksgiving will be here, then Christmas, and then leave-OUT!

### November 11, 2010

Today was a good and a bad day. The good being it was Veterans Day and they had a lot of good food. We got to get off early—well at least some of us did. I didn't because I was on some stupid detail that I volunteered for. It was major cell detail. All I did was pick up trash and clean up old mattresses and threw all the frames away. I just don't understand why we are doing stuff like that. We are here to fight a war not pick up trash but I guess it has to be done. I just think it is wrong but I have been working out a lot and getting stronger. Anyway only a couple more days till mission! I am getting excited but all the trucks are ready and good to go. Well I am going to bed after I eat my Pizza Hut. Yeah that is right. . .Pizza Hut-OUT!

### November 13, 2010

It is about 20:00. I just got back from calling the parents and e-mailing the special lady. I am now ready for this journey I am about to do. I guess it is going to be great as I walked back from the phones we are having a sand storm tonight. It looks so eerie and dark. When I got back from the phones they gave us the time line for tomorrow. Wake up is at 1 and we have to be at the motor pool at 2. We leave Camp Leatherneck at 0600 to FOB Wilson to pick up 2 88's and three breachers. I told my dad tonight what I was hauling and he was so happy. He said that he would trade places with me in a heartbeat. I have all my stuff ready to go. Now I just have to take my last shower in and get some sleep. I am really happy and scared about this one but am going to be fun to go out with 18 of my closest battle buddies-OUT!

It came to me after I read these entries in Scott's Afghanistan journal that my son approached his first Afghanistan mission much like he faced the Alaskan Highway, with one focus. This was the road he had to travel to get home.

## Chapter Fifty-Three

## The Purple Heart

SITTING ON A BOOKSHELF to the left of my desk in the study at the Emmanuel Baptist Church in Ellsworth, Maine, is a small green case with the United States of America stamped in gold letters on the front. It is simple and unimpressive until you open it up and discover its historic contents. There on a gray-felt backdrop lays a gold medal with a side portrait of George Washington highlighted by a purple background. A purple and white ribbon is attached to a clasp just above a shield with three tiny gold stars. Just above the ribbon are a small purple and white pin and a small purple and white ribbon that can be worn on a soldier's uniform. If you turn the medal over you will find stamped these three powerful words: For Military Merit. Yes, I have a Purple Heart in my office, but it is not mine. So why do I have it?

As Scott and I travelled the wilderness highway out of Alaska and into the Canadian Province of Yukon, I had plenty of time to ponder the life of the man who was now asleep in the back of the Tahoe. Scott had driven the 323 miles from Fairbanks, Alaska to Beaver Creek, Canada (1:00-7:10 P.M.), the first leg of our journey home. Our original plan was to drive through the first night with Scott doing the bulk of the nighttime driving, so I could sleep. Before Scott retook the wheel after midnight, he would catch a catnap while I drove through a late evening dusk along a winding, hilly section of the Alaska Highway. So while Scott slept, I worked our way through the Yukon section of our road trip home and thought again of the event that won my son The Purple Heart.

Like most military men, Scott talks little about his wartime experiences. For most, like my son, they are private and personal and to talk too much would seem like bragging or boasting. If anything, Scott has been too modest about his time served, and the events surrounding his winning the

Purple Heart is typical of him and so many others like him. I have known my Dad for 64 years now, and I bet in that period of time he never once brought up this wartime service for our great land. Unless asked, Dad has remained silent and so has my son. If not for his Afghanistan journal, a record I encouraged him to keep, and, if truth be known, the only reason he did it was to honor me, we would never have known what happened and how Scott felt during his deployment to Afghanistan. An experience I had craved for most of my life, it was only through my son I had a chance to know what it was like to wage war, to defend my country, to experience the horror of battle. Fascinated since boyhood with war, I never got my chance being directed away from a military experience at the height of the Vietnam War, but not so the young man sleeping behind the driver's seat of a Tahoe working its way towards Whitehorse.

An amateur military historian since the seventh grade, reading nearly 1000 books on military history, I have lived through the lives of others that have faced the foe of fear on the battlefield and have lived to write about it. The Purple Heart is not the highest military honor in the United States, but it is the oldest. What makes the Purple Heart so special is the fact that George Washington himself commissioned it. Originally it was called The Badge of Military Merit, hence the wording on the back of the medal, was first established on August 7, 1782. Only three were given out after the Revolutionary War, and over the years, until April 5, 1917, it was a rarely recognized medal. During the First World War the name was changed to the Purple Heart and was given to those wounded or killed in military action. I have learned to date just over 7,000 have been presented in the ongoing Afghanistan War, and my son has one; the last of a series of medals he would win during his eight years in the army, and like the Purple Heart, all of Scott's other medals are in a picture frame case in my study, but why?

If Scott were telling this story, he would tell you that the guys that lost their lives deserved the medal not him. I share with you now the only mention Scott makes in his journal about the day the Purple Heart was pinned on his chest:

## September 4, 2011

Well the start of the last full month here. I have not been writing because it's so crazy right now. I guess that I will have to rewind and get you all back up to speed. The last few days, I have not been feeling all that good. I am still having bad headaches from the concussion. I have been to the doctor and they think that I have done something to my neck so I will be going to physical therapy. I have also been getting help with what I saw and how I am feeling. On September 2, Mabb and I received our Purple Hearts from the 1 Star General that is in charge of all of us, General Carroll. It was a really nice ceremony. It was only the company and a few other people. My other buddies Ragan and Neauner got theirs too. When it was all over I felt okay about it even though I don't think I deserved it. With the new Army rules it says I can get one and the way that I still feel I will need what it can give me. Yesterday, I also received my Combat Action Badge. It was a long ceremony and it was really hot out. They awarded 4 Purple Heart and 87 combat action badges. We have only had one mission that has gone out since the last convoy. They had to go get some gun trucks that got in an accident that killed another soldier in our battalion and they got back this morning. All went well. It was on the hard ball (paved highway). They are preparing for a mission to leave this week but 1st Platoon is going to take this one and then we are going to take the last mission. I was just told by my platoon sergeant that I would not be going on any more missions. I am not happy about that because I wanted to go with my squad. But whatever-OUT!

As I worked my way through Kluane Wildlife Sanctuary and around the shores of Kluane Lake, one of the biggest fresh water lakes I have ever seen, I leaned back every once in a while to see how my boy was doing. Scott had learned to sleep in a truck during his many missions (nearly 40) in Iraqi and Afghanistan, so to sleep in a Tahoe in the Yukon was a piece of cake. I knew he wouldn't have to encounter any more IEDs and that he wouldn't have to witness anymore of his friends getting blown-up in front of him. As a father, it is your hope that you can take such things from your children, and as the Lord is my witness, I would have changed places with him in a heartbeat!

So to this day I am simply the keeper of the medals. It is my prayer that someday Scott will recognize the value and symbol of the colorful ribbons, shiny medals, and war pictures of him that adorn my bookshelves and study walls. They are a testimony to a brave soldier who did his duty and more and earned the recognition of a grateful nation. Scott's argument for not being deserving of the Purple Heart has always been that he came back with no scars, no wounds and yet we are discovering that some of the worst scars, the most terrible wounds can't be seen. The day Scott and Mabb received their concussions, it was a miracle of God that shrapnel from the blast didn't find them. So instead of external wounds, Scott and Mabb must live with internal scars for the rest of their lives. I am proud of a military that is starting to recognize that all wounds aren't flesh wounds and all scars aren't skin-scars. I will hold onto Scott's Purple Heart until the day he asks for it back, but each time I look at it I am reminded of the brave son I have; not only brave on the battlefield, but brave enough to go on with his life despite the battle scars. When you read this son (The final tragedy for me is that Scott never got to read this book because he died of cancer before it was finished!), remember these words from your Saviour and mine: ". . ..for the labourer is worthy of his hire." (Luke 10:7) And that includes a warrior!

## Chapter Fifty-Four

## Plan C

AFTER A THREE-HOUR NAP, Scott joined me in the front of the Tahoe. While Scott got a few winks to sustain him for the night drive ahead, I had driven us from the border of Alaska to the Yukon town of Whitehorse, 279 miles apart. In the miles just before Whitehorse, Scott and I began to talk about the route we were taking home. Originally, we had thought we would take a week to ten-days to make the journey back to Maine. Because Alaska was going to be primarily a sightseeing adventure, we decided to fish our way home, which would be a way to have another memorable adventure together.

Plan A developed in the early months of our planning for Alaska in August of 2014. Dreaming big, Scott and I thought a trip home by way of Montana would be an excellent idea to our ultimate destination of North Carolina to drop his stuff off before returning to Maine. Mike Hangge, a friend of ours, had made the trip to fish Montana with his son Mike Jr. and a friend. We had heard the stories of the tremendous rainbow trout fishery in that Western State and wanted to experience it ourselves. Our goal was to fish the Missouri River for a few days and catch brown and cutthroat trout along with the rainbow trout. Our route would take us south from Edmonton, Alberta after traveling the length of the Alaskan Highway, and stopping here and there if a good fishing hole materialized. We would pass through Calgary and recross the border back in to the good, old USA at Coutts. After fishing the Missouri, we would hit Interstate 90 heading east until Interstate 29 that would take us south. The rest would be the shortest route to Fayetteville, North Carolina we could find, and perhaps, find a few more fishing spots along the way. We would spend a day or so getting Scott settled in North Carolina before we would take the all too familiar road home to Ellsworth. When we left for Alaska in August, this was the plan in place for Scott's and my return trip to Maine, but with all plans, situations and circumstances timing often alters the original intent.

During our two weeks together in Alaska, Scott and I had plenty of time to discuss our route home. We also had gotten a chance to fish more in Alaska than we thought we would. As the miles added up and the fishing opportunities happened, the Missouri part of our return trip began to fade and a quicker route home and less time on the road seemed to be a better option, so Plan B began to fall into place. The two nights we spent on the Kasilof River were also nights reconsidering our route home. Taking a look at a map, we decided that our quickest and straightest route from Fairbanks, Alaska to Fayetteville, North Carolina was by taking a straight route to Winnipeg, Manitoba before turning southward. We would take Canadian Route 75 to the American border crossing at Emerson, which connected to US29 just north of Grand Forks, North Dakota. Our only planned stop would be at Mount Rushmore to see the four presidents carved in stone. Our hope was that we might see some interesting places along the way and maybe a fishing hole or two, but our priority was to shorten the trip, not lengthen it. From Grand Forks we would head for Minneapolis where we would pick up US35 down to Kansas City. There we would head east on US70, and from there take the routes that would get us to North Carolina in a timely fashion, hopefully cutting a few days off our original schedule. After talking and pondering a few days, we agreed that Plan B would be our new goal for getting home in five or six days. But with all secondary plans, things began to unravel when after the first day on the road home other ideas and feelings begin to emerge during a late night talk on the Alaskan Highway.

Even in my trip log I didn't make note of who brought the idea up, but I suspect it was Scott. I am the type of person that once I get a plan in my mind I pretty much stick to it. I am not one who changes his mind often. Once I determine the appropriate plan of action I see it through. In my mind Scott had already told me what his basic plans were, and I was only along for the ride, a wingman, co-pilot if you will; he was the captain and this was his trip. I wasn't thinking much as I neared the end of my first stint of driving the Alaskan Highway. As I maneuvered the Tahoe through the ups and downs, corners and curves of the twisting roadway, Scott said, "Dad, wouldn't it be shorter to head straight for Maine instead of by way of North Carolina?" I remember asking, "What do you mean, Son?" Then I added, "I thought you wanted to drop your stuff off in Fayetteville before you headed home for a month!" Scott went on to tell me that he had thought that at first, but seeing he had to go to Maine anyway what difference did it make when he took his stuff to North Carolina? It was an Army policy that when a soldier gets out, they will only pay to ship the soldier's stuff back to the state he had enlisted from. He was going to Maine at the end of September anyway. He was tired of driving, and two weeks on the road had taken its toll and really all he wanted was to get back to Maine, the sooner the better. It was then that Plan C began to materialize and before Scott took over the reins of the Tahoe at 12:30 A.M. in the early morning of August 26, 2014, a whole new goal for our journey back to Maine had been targeted.

Plan C was simple, if not radical. We would press on towards Maine only stopping for gas. We had brought along food enough for a few days, so we wouldn't even stop to eat. We would take turns driving, sleeping when we were off. Our route would be straight through the Yukon, across the Canadian provinces of Alberta and Saskatchewan until we hit the Trans-Canada highway at Winnipeg, Manitoba. We would follow the TransCanada through the provinces of Ontario and Quebec and at Quebec City we would head south to the Maine border at Jackman. It was then we realized that we could be home in three or four days versus seven to ten days. Neither of us had travelled that far that fast by car, but with Scott I was game to try. Besides, despite the opportunities to fish, I too was getting tired. This road trip had taken more out of me than I knew, and shortly after we got home, I would know why the Good Lord had changed my son's mind. After the whole affair was over I was able to think through the abrupt change in plan, and I was reminded of these precepts from the Proverbs of Solomon: "The preparations of the heart in man, and the answer of the tongue, is from the Lord. . .A man's heart deviseth his way; but the Lord directeth his steps." (Proverbs 16:1, 9) I see now that despite our well thought-through plans, A and B were not God's plans, it was Plan C! I also found this in Proverbs 20:24: "Man's goings are of the Lord; how can a man then understand his own way?"

At the time of our switch from Plan B to Plan C, I was actually happy with the switch. Would I have followed whatever Scott wanted, yes, I would, including a swing south. I was doing this not for me, but for him, to help him make the transition from Alaska to North Carolina. But now I realize that the Lord was in control of Son's thoughts and though I didn't understand it then, I do now. So here is another well-learned lesson from my Alaskan adventure. As I searched on through the Scriptures I discovered that what is true for two men traveling the Alaskan Highway, the same is true for the whole world: "This is the purpose that is purposed upon the whole earth: and this is the hand that is stretched out upon all the nations. For the Lord of hosts hath purposed, and who shall disannul it? And His hand is stretched out, and who shall turn it back?" (Isaiah 14:26-27)

## Chapter Fifty-Five

## Bison In British Columba

On our first night on the road, Scott took us from Whitehorse, Yukon to Watson Creek, British Columba, traveling from 12:30 to 5:30 in the morning: a total of 296 miles, or 898 miles from Fairbanks. I woke as Scott pulled into the only gas station in Watson Creek. It was cold, if not frosty, as we got out of the Tahoe and found that the gas pumps were not automatic; that we would have to wait until somebody came to start the pumps. It was one of the few delays we would experience during our trip across Canada.

Within the hour we were on the road again, but now it was my turn to drive and Scott's turn to sleep. I had rested really well and was ready for my next driving assignment, and what a thrilling drive I had! As Scott slept, I witnessed some of the most amazing wildlife sightings of my life in a mountainous section of the Alaskan Highway in north central British Columba. Before my driving was over I would see two herds of Bison plus seven huge individual male Bison, a mother black bear and her cub, a moose, a fox, and three Dall sheep.

Hill country, in general, is rich with a variety of wildlife. I come from hill country in Northern Maine, but if I have learned anything about wildlife in the wild they are scarce more often than they are plentiful. You will spend more time in the wilderness not seeing anything than seeing something. That is why those rare occasions like I experienced on August 26, 2014, will be remembered for a very long time. The reasons for the scarcity of wild animals are logical even for those who hardly ever travel through a wildlife sanctuary. In the winter, many animals hibernate and the rest are just trying to endure the harsh season away from open or hostile lands. In the summer, many animals are tormented by mosquitoes, flies, gnats, and a host of biting insects, so they hide themselves in the shade deep in the forest and stay away from open ground. As a result there are only a few opportunities in spring or fall with the likelihood of witnessing wildlife in significant numbers in the open. As I fought the early morning sun in my eyes driving southeast along the Alaskan Highway, I never imagined that I was about to experience something on the scale of animal sightings as we saw on our Denali adventure.

When God said, "Let the earth bring forth the living creature after his kind, cattle, and creeping thing, and beasts of the earth after his kind. . .." (Genesis 1:240) I never imagined in my childhood I would be able to personally experience seeing so many of them. Alaska had only added to the wild animals I have seen in Israel, India, and Australia. Scott had warned me that on their way to Alaska in the fall of 2012 they had seen wild Bison (Buffalo) in the section of the Alaska Highway we were travelling, but little did I dream that I would see any, and yet as I climbed through a small canyon on the top of a hill, there around a sharp corner was my first herd!

It was as if I had entered the domain of the Plains Buffalo that I had read about all my life and had seen on television throughout my life. Now here I was in the middle of a herd of over twenty. They were grazing beside the highway on a broad patch of green grass. There were males and females and smaller bison, but it was as if I wasn't even there. I slowed the Tahoe down to a crawl and eventually stopped beside the road to get a few photographs. Perhaps this is a good place to tell you that I have never had a bad experience with a wild animal, and therefore I am fearless. Yes, I got out of the car and walked toward the herd for a better picture. Crazy some would say, but as I said, no bad experiences have made me believe that wild animals are not as fierce, dangerous, or vindictive as some would have you believe. Don't get me wrong. I respect all wild animals, but I do not fear them, yet! So that has allowed me to walk up to Indian elephants, Australian kangaroos, Maine black bears, and British Columbia Bison and experience the majesty of being near some of God's greatest creations. As one moves among these wild friends of paw, hoof, trunk, and tail, a remarkable sense of respect and reverence happens. It also reminds you that these were the creatures that used to inhabit the North American continent by herds of millions, but are now just micro-herds of a couple of dozen.

I enjoyed my first herd of Bison a few extra minutes before returning to the Tahoe; Scott slept through the whole experience! I moved on down the road with a new urgency to keep my eyes open, and sure enough my diligence was rewarded within a few miles to come across a lone male Bison feeding beside the road. What impressed me most were his two massive horns, but like the others he showed me no concern as I slowly drove by him. Over the next few hours, I witnessed again and again that brief interlude one gets with one of God's wild creatures. Ten miles from the first herd of Bison I came across a second herd, about the same size but spread out along the grassy side lanes of the Alaskan Highway. Like the first herd, this herd seemed to care little for the slowing Tahoe drifting by and the staring driver. A few more pictures and I was off again, but as before, a few miles down the road I began to encounter single male Bison. Scott would tell me later that he was told those were the dominant males who loved their solitude except during mating season. All I know is I was able to see nearly fifty buffalo in my travels through British Columba, what an honor!

Despite the fact that was the first time I had seen buffalo in the wild, it was my next animal encounter that was the most special to me. I have always loved seeing black bear in the wild, a rare sight indeed. Over my years in Maine, I have only had enough encounters to count on one hand, so as I came around another one of the thousands of corners on the Alaskan Highway there she was beside the road and her little bundle of black beside her. Because I was going so fast I was by her in a flash. I still have a mental picture of the pair in my mind. Not the most powerful creature in the world, but in my opinion, one of the most noble. Not the most recognized animals in the world, but in my opinion, one of the most fantastic. Not the friendliest beasts in the world, but in my opinion, one of the most grand. The black bear is an emblem of that untamed part of the animal kingdom, and as I drove on through the early morning light I was in her realm not mine. I flew by the mother and her cub so quickly they didn't even move, and by the time I slowed down and looked back they were gone, just like a dream. Over a four-hour period of time I would see nearly 60 wild animals in just two hundred miles. We still had 3500 miles to go and in those 3500 miles we wouldn't see another wild animal!

When God made the animals, He also made caretakers for those animals, "So God created man in His own image, in the image of God created He him; male and female created he them. And God blessed them, and God said unto them. . . have dominion. . .over every living thing that moveth upon the earth." (Genesis 1:27-28) I felt for a short few hours that I was driving through my own wild animal reserve. I meet no car, and no car passed me. It was as if I had the road to myself and I was venturing through a mountain sanctuary of wildlife there for my viewing and my viewing alone. It has always amazed me that when you have such wildlife encounters alone (Scott was still sleeping) the world seems to stop and it is just you and them—creature and caretaker.

## Chapter Fifty-Six

## Slim Jims, Twinkie's, And Cheetos

By the time we finished our first day (one o'clock on August 25 to one o'clock on August 26, 2014) of travelling from Alaska to Maine, we had journeyed from Fairbanks, Alaska to just beyond Fort Nelson, British Columba, a total of 1354 miles in just four gas stops. At Fort Nelson we put in $126 worth of gas! Our change of plans before Watson Creek and Fort Nelson (340 miles between) had refocused us, putting blinders on us, to the point all we now saw was the finish line: the parsonage of the Emmanuel Baptist Church in Ellsworth, Maine. Nothing else matter but making it to Maine and fast!

As I have always done on road trips, I began to keep track of the mileage, places we stopped, and the average times. For example: it took us 17 hours to cover the first 1000 miles of the trip and another 17 ½ hours to do the second thousand miles. During those second thousand miles we crossed into Alberta, Canada and finished the Alaskan Highway. It was 300 miles from Fort Nelson to Dawson Creek, located on the border between British Columba and Alberta where the grand highway ends. Our next leg took us from Dawson Creek to Whitecourt, Alberta, just outside Edmonton, a distance of 272 miles. We had come out of the mountains and into the foothills, and we began to see before us the great open spaces of the plains. As with the Plan C's directives, Scott and I would switch off with each gas-up, and while the one rested the other drove. By the middle of our second day on the road, we had a pretty good routine going, little realizing the toll it was taking on our bodies let alone our mental attitude.

Periodically we would snack on the food we had bought in Fairbanks and put in the Tahoe. So what does one eat on a marathon road trip across the North America continent? Scott had his soda, and I had my water. Scott and I had our favorite candy and crackers, but for our main meal, we pretty much ate Slim Jims and Cheetos and Twinkies for dessert! This might not seem like much to you, but we now had no time to stop for a sit-down meal. In the first 48-hours of our journey, we drove 46 of them. Now you are beginning to understand how we could have made it as fast as we did. Something had to be sacrificed and eating healthy was one of many. In our second day we covered 1350 (2704 miles from Fairbanks, Alaska to Minnabor, Manitoba), including a 481-mile stretch between Whitecourt, Alberta to Saskatoon, Saskatchewan. By the time we reached Saskatchewan, the open terrain of the Great Plains engulfed us. I have never before experienced such distances between places, where you could see from one horizon to another. We passed massive fields of grain as harvest season was upon the plains with huge grain elevators and trains pulling miles of cars full of grain and oil. I thought Alaska was big, but I experienced a new bigness driving across the Canada provinces of Alberta, Saskatchewan, and Manitoba. It was also along that leg of our road trip we finally reached Coleen in California and told her of our change of plans. We were going to beat her to Maine! We would pick her up at the airport that Sunday.

Our third day on the road started just outside Winnipeg, Manitoba and took us into Ontario. Before this day was done we would cover another 1223 miles through some of the most beautiful country I have ever witnessed, the hilly, scenic drive from Thunder Bay around the north shore of Lake Superior. We did it in five legs: Winnipeg, Manitoba to Dryden, Ontario (219 miles), Dryden, Ontario to Thunder Bay, Ontario (304 miles), Thunder Bay, Ontario to White River, Ontario (180 miles), White River, Ontario to Blind River, Ontario (283 miles) and Blind River, Ontario to Dead River, Ontario (319 miles). By the end of our third day on the road, we had covered 4027 miles. It was in Dead River we did stop not only to get gas but our first real food of the trip: cheeseburgers and onion rings at a Burger King. It had taken us 16 ½ hours to travel our third 1000 miles and 17 ½ hours to get to 4000 miles. We had just over 800 more miles to go! One of the postscripts to our travel across Ontario was the fact that that section of our trip was longer than the Alaska Highway at 1434 miles!

Up to this point, we had no difficulties with the Tahoe or the terrain over which we were traveling. Our final leg of the trip was taking me into familiar territory having been along the Saint Lawrence and Quebec City. I told Scott if he could get us to the TransCanada on the other side of the Saint Lawrence, I could get us home from there. What I didn't figure on was Ottawa and Montreal. I am terrible driving in big cities. If I would be honest, I despise cities, especially mega-cities. Sure enough we had travelled nearly 4500 miles without missing a turn, but at our first important turn in Ottawa, we missed the road to Montreal. It only took Scott fifteen minutes to turn us around, but by that time our relationship was tense. Three plus days in a car will do that to you. We only got back on track when Montreal threw us another curve. Under construction, at night, and poor signs will prove disastrous every time. Sure enough, instead of crossing the Saint Lawrence at Montreal we were on the wrong side of the river, and I didn't know where we were. It was then we decided to dig our Scott's GPS unit and let it direct us back home. While gassing up outside Montreal, we got the GPS going, knowing that we could reach home on this one tank of gas if the GPS unit would guide the way. We were 421 miles from home. The last leg would prove to be a piece of cake through Quebec City and Jackman.

In the end, we would drive 83 hours in the 86 ½ that it took us to travel from Fairbanks, Alaska to Ellsworth, Maine, a total of 4854 miles. All totaled, Scott drove 45 hours and I drove 38 hours, taking us 15 hours to travel the last 854 miles, the slowest part of the trip, and why not? This is how bad it was. After we got to the Maine border, we crossed at 4:30 A.M. on August 29, 2014 in Jackman, I got in the back of the Tahoe letting Scott drive us the rest of the way home. I woke as we passed the Eastern Maine Medical Center on the banks of the Penobscot River in Bangor. I asked Scott why he had come this way, certainly out of our way, and he told me that when he hit 95, the main highway that cuts through the center of Maine, at Waterville the next thing he remembered he was north of Bangor. Ellsworth is southeast of Bangor. Despite the detour we arrived home safely at 7:30 A.M.

In the final total, it cost Scott just over $1600 in gas to make this trip, including the 15 gallons we carried all the way from Fairbanks to Ellsworth. We never were close to using our reserves. When Scott poured that gas in his tank, a full tank to a full tank, we had to gas up nineteen times. In my seventeen days away from home, I travelled 5588 miles by plane and 7467 miles by car, 2613 in Alaska and 4854 miles across Canada, for a total of 12,492 miles. Both Scott and I collapsed into bed when we got home and didn't wake up until late afternoon. It was an adventure I will never forget, but do not wish to repeat. All I could think about were these words by the Psalmist when he wrote, "Except the Lord build the house. . . except the Lord keep the city, the watchman waketh but in vain (and could I add, except the Lord direct the trip the driver driveth in vain—read the next chapter and you will understand why I write this)!" (Psalm 127:1) But the best is what the Psalmist writes next, ". . .for so He giveth His beloved sleep." (Psalms 127:2) Rest at the end of a long road trip is one of the sweetest rewards of any journey!

## Conclusion

## Kidney Stone Miracle

My memorable trip to Alaska and back might have been over, but the story wasn't finished. Just 30-hours after I landed back in Ellsworth, Maine I had a serious kidney stone attack and the events that follow are the real miracle of this amazing adventure.

When the pain began to grow on a late Saturday afternoon I thought it was a blood clot moving into my leg. I never thought of a kidney stone because the pain and the area of discomfort were different than the other three during the 1980s and 1990s. Why did I think a clot? I had just travelled over 12,000 miles in cars and planes and four-wheelers in just 17 days; in Scott's car alone I had driven over 2600 miles touring Alaska and over 4800 miles traveling from Fairbanks, Alaska to Ellsworth, Maine in just three and a half days! Surely it was a clot from all that sitting? But it didn't take the doctor or nurse at Maine Coast Memorial Hospital very long to discover that I was indeed having another kidney stone attack. I had even driven myself to the hospital because my wife was still in California visiting our daughter. Remember Coleen decided that driving back to Maine from Alaska wouldn't be as much fun as checking out where her daughter and new son-in-law were living, and my son was off visiting some Maine friends. Scott had just finished his eighth year in the United States Army and was home for a month before beginning his career in the Army Reserves in North Carolina. Needless to say, Scott was surprised when he came home to find a note on the kitchen counter stating that I had gone to the hospital in great pain. The miracle was clear. I could have had the kidney stone attack at anytime and anywhere, and to have had the attack in Alaska or Canada wouldn't have been fun at all. I have come to believe it was the Lord changing our minds. Our original plan was to take a week to ten days to drive home and our first planned path home was by way of Montana (fishing) and North Carolina (golfing) before returning to Maine. Our plan C was to go directly home, straight across Canada. "The steps of a good man are ordered by the Lord: and he delighteth in his way." (Psalms 37:23) God knew and was gracious to get me home before He took away my health and started me into a series of events that would take months to finish.

At the writing of this conclusion to my Alaskan trip, I have just passed the four-month mark in this health ordeal of 2014. X-rays revealed that I had three kidney stones, two in my right kidney and one in my left kidney. Over the last third of a year, I have had three procedures to get rid of the stones. The first two, Esther and Ezra—I have named all of my stones because they are like delivering children. I love to tell the story that took place after my first kidney stone when I told my wife the pain was worse than childbirth pain, and my proof was a lady in my church at the time that had just had her first kidney stone. She had an interesting perspective on the subject because she had also delivered seven children. I asked her on my first visit which was worse and she said she would have seven more children before she had another kidney stone, except they are the ugliest children you would ever want. For those interested, the first four stones were Adam, Bernice, Caesar, and Dan! Doctor Curlick, my urologist, even took pictures of the twins from my right side. They came out easily with a method of actually going in and removing them with a cystoscopy; I had never had that done before. The last (Festus) was the size of a quarter and had to be blasted in a procedure called lithotripsy; I had had that procedure before without any problems. It was the first lithotripsy (yes, the stone was so large it took two attempts to mash it up into small enough pieces so that I could pass them on my own) that got me in trouble. Unknown to me or the medical personnel at Maine Coast, I got a hospital staph infection while having that procedure done and later in the hospital picked up pneumonia. Ten days later I experienced the worst chills and hot flashes I had ever endured and a fever over 103. Again I found myself in the emergency room at Maine Coast Memorial Hospital, and this time I wasn't leaving with a few pain pills and an appointment to see an urologist!

I was shocked when the attending physician told me she was moving me up into intensive care. I had visited plenty of patients in the ICU, but this was going to be my first visit as a patient and little did I know that visit would last six days! I tell people all the time that I visit people in the hospital in the hopes my visits will be enough and that I won't have to stay very long in a hospital; there is a big difference between going in and coming out to going in and staying awhile. I was a very sick boy; the worst of my life! It was eventually revealed that I had a kidney infection and it was bad, very closing to going septic (getting into my blood). Not only did the infection affect my kidney and bladder, but also my blood pressure went haywire (70 over 40) and my sugar spiked (199) and then to top it off my heart went out of rhythm. This affected areas of my body I had never had a problem with before. To make a long illness short, I would spent a total of ten days in the hospital; the only longer time was when I got the chicken pox at nineteen while a freshman at Bob Jones University where I spent nearly two weeks in isolation. Then I was only really sick for a couple of days, just contagious. Then there was the pain in passing all that gravel after the last lithotripsy, including another trip to the emergency room for the 'good-stuff'. My drug of choice is now toradol. I would miss thirty days of work in September and October and November, and for about as many days I was on half-days; I have never had a stretch like this in my life of not working, including another bout with pneumonia on Thanksgiving which laid me up for another week.

To say that I have been a healthy individual for most of my life would be an understatement. Other than three bouts with kidney stones, an injury or two, and the rare struggle with the flu, I have been blessed throughout my sixty-four year old life with good, if not excellent health. Few have been the days that I have been laid up for very long with an illness or sickness, and as for accidents, very few. Perhaps, up until the autumn of 2014, the longest I had been laid aside was a back injury I sustained while working at a chicken company in New Hampshire in the 70s during my first pastorate in Pembroke, New Hampshire. Even then it took only a few weeks to get back into the swing of my life. A young body heals quickly. Then a second attack with a blown-out disk in my spine during my third pastorate in Eastport, Maine in the 1980s laid me up for a few days, but I was quickly back in the Lord's work. I have lived most of my life with the philosophy "that I can get as much done on a sick day as a health day"! Even when I felt bad I always seemed to have the strength and drive to press-on. So to say I have experienced a true physical shortcoming would be a falsehood. In all this, I came face to face with this Biblical truth. God not only gives us our health (". . . . .God. . . . .who is the health of my countenance. . . . ." (Psalms 42:11 and 43:5), but He can also take it away (Job 2:6) in His divine purpose for our lives.

But praise be to the Father! When the Good Lord decided to take away my health He was gracious enough to get me back home. I believe my physical Waterloo is behind me, and I am only engaged in mopping-up operations now.

# POSTLUDE

# . . . . . . AND BACK

I HAVE DECIDED TO end this Alaska adventure in the same manner I began, with the words to a song. Over the years I have taken many (over 150 to date) familiar tunes and put new words with them, simply to change the message. Granted, I have done this to "psalms and hymns and spiritual songs" (Colossians 3:16) and this will be my first and probably my only secular song, but I thought it fitting to end my Alaskan book this way. If you recall, I started my reminiscing by explaining why I chose the title I did for this Alaska memoir. Taken from an old 60s song by Johnny Horton called "North to Alaska". I would have you remember the tune to that country classic and sing a summary of my Alaskan adventure. Each time I attempt this practice of making something new out of something old I remember these world by the Psalmist David, "And he hath put a new song in my mouth. . ." (Psalm 40:3) So here is my "North to Alaska and Back" song:

> The Blackstones left Maine in the summer of twenty-fourteen,
> Their hope was to see Alaska while the foliage was still green.
> They crossed the continent wide to the land of the midnight sun,
> In hopes two weeks with their firstborn would be lots of fun.
> From Fairbanks to Fox they travelled to Alaska's old pipeline,
> And then back into the city with friends and King Crab to dine.
> A bit of fishing at the North Pole and a visit with Santa Claus,
> For others this was lots of fun, but from me, little applause!
> We travelled south in a light rain across the majestic wilderness,
> In hopes that at Denali National Park we might gain access.
> To see the wandering caribou, the Dall sheep, and the grizzly bear,
> But we found that to travel far inland we had to pay a fare.

Our trip through the heart of Denali was full of creatures wild,
But at a far distance each animal seemed to be timid and mild.
The twin peaks of Mount McKinley awash in a brilliant noon light,
Was more than we expected from our journey to that site!
Our travel back was filled with more caribou, sheep and bear,
And six hours into the trip from the bus rose a wondrous cheer.
There before us on a corner, atop a hill, an unbelievable sight,
A mother grizzly with her two frolicking cubs in full daylight.
We journeyed on southward with a stop at Montana Creek,
Then just north of Wasilla we failed to see McKinley's peak.
So onward we travelled through Anchorage and Cook's Inlet,
With Scott our driver, our faithful guide, and former Army Vet!
The Kenai came next with a wonderful rustic lodge to rest,
And to fish a world-class rainbow river was about the best.
But the water was high and the fishing was slow is all I'll say,
About the day and a half we spent north of Kachemak Bay.
To visit our friends the Kings was next on our Alaska trip,
And this was a part of our northern adventure we would not skip.
Four-wheeler rides and moose stew were only part of the thrill,
As we explored the Matanuska Valley both uphill and downhill.
Two days we spent with the Kings in their town of Chickaloon,
But the best was a flight we took over a glacier one afternoon.
In a calm wind, under a brilliant sun, we looked a glacier in the eye,
And floated over a snow-white valley in an ocean blue sky.
Then it was off to Valdez by the Glenn and Richardson highways,
Through a series of valleys and mountain passes that felt like a maze.
But the Bridal Vail Falls and Horse Tail Falls we stopped to see,
And like every fall I ever saw, they were playing their water synonymy.
We passed in awe the mighty bald eagle in his perch on the river Lowe,
Then we drove into Valdez village in search of our overnight bungalow.
Our reservations at the Best Western had been mixed up somehow,
So we travelled across the bay to where the salmon were running, and wow!
I spent my day in Valdez fishing for a 'silver' fish that never came near,
But I got to wade in a sea of pinks and watch the otters and seals from a pier.
The morning broke full of fog as we departed Valdez Sound,
Our destination for the day was back to Fairbanks town.
Through miles of hills and miles of plains we traveled north to see,

Broad, grayish waterways and snow-capped mountains three.
And in a small pond my wife would fly fish for a trout called 'bow',
To which her husband and her son could only shout "Bravo!"
And in a gold mining claim north of Fox, behind a concrete hedge,
We discovered an ancient mining monster, called Number Eight dredge.
And from the gravel of a bag panned through a bit of water,
We found gold enough to make a necklace for Opal's daughter.
Then on a plane we put Coleen, so Scott and I could roam,
And she could visit the Legaspi's in their new Californian home.
The Chena River was next in search of some big arctic grayling,
But only a few were found and handled, so let us stop singing.
Hailey and Brandon joined us for some fishing at 45.5 Mile Pond,
But we only found stocked fish in the fishing hole in that great beyond.
We packed our bags and prepared the Tahoe and U-Haul for their journey,
Calling home for Dad's 90th birthday, and remembering Scott on a gurney.
Three year before when he was caught up in a battlefield explosion,
That killed two of his friends, and resulted in his and Mabb's extraction.
A difficult event that has stayed in his mind to this day and will not depart,
A bitter anniversary, a tragic happening that earned Scott the Purple Heart!
Our road trip across a continent started on the famous Alaskan Highway,
And included a Yukon road, an Alberta lane, and a Saskatchewan byway.
For it was in a Canadian province we decided to alter our destination,
And turned the Tahoe eastward away from our southern migration.
Instead of traveling on to North Carolina we headed back to Maine,
Unbeknownst to Coleen who was coming home by plane.
Instead of a week on the road we did it in just three days and a half,
And I know you are thinking impossible and some of you will laugh.
But my record it true and accurate, Scott will verify this amazing story,
Of our unbelievable trip across Canada we seek and require no glory.

Barry Blackstone

Postscript: Little did we know then that our son Scott would only have less than three years to live at the end of this adventure. On the two year anniversary of our epic trip to Alaska and back, Scott was diagnosed with stage four liver cancer and would die within six months at the age of 39. I have written of that journey in a book I call "Twoscore: Beyond the Bend". Hopefully the next book I will get published!

www.ingramcontent.com/pod-product-compliance
Lightning Source LLC
Chambersburg PA
CBHW051926160426
43198CB00012B/2061